US v. THEM

US
V.
THEM

THE AGE OF INDIE MUSIC
AND A DECADE IN NEW YORK
(2004-2014)

RONEN GIVONY

ABRAMS PRESS, NEW YORK

A Library of Congress Control Number has been applied for.

ISBN: 978-1-4197-7526-0
eISBN: 979-8-88707-336-1

Printed and bound in the United States
10 9 8 7 6 5 4 3 2 1

Abrams books are available at special discounts when purchased in quantity for premiums and promotions as well as fundraising or educational use. Special editions can also be created to specification. For details, contact sales@abramsbooks.com or the address below.

Abrams Press® is a registered trademark of Harry N. Abrams, Inc.

ABRAMS is represented in the UK and Europe by Abrams & Chronicle Books, 22–24 Ely Place, London EC1N 6TE and Média-Participations, 57 rue Gaston Tessier, 75166 Paris, France.
abramsandchronicle.co.uk and media-participations.com
info@abramsandchronicle.co.uk

ABRAMS The Art of Books
195 Broadway, New York, NY 10007
abramsbooks.com

Also by the Author

24 Hour Revenge Therapy
(or, The Strange Death of Selling Out)

Not for You: Pearl Jam and the Present Tense

Dedicated to the Memory of

Scott Hutchison
Sam Jayne
Jóhann Jóhannsson
Billy Jones
Trish Keenan
Brian McBride

In every age in every successful country, it has been important that at least a small part of the cityscape is not dominated by bankers, developers, chain stores, generic restaurants, and railway terminals. This little quarter should instead be the preserve of—in no special order—insomniacs and restaurants and bars that never close; bibliophiles and the little stores and stalls that cater to them; alcoholics and addicts and deviants and the proprietors who understand them; aspirant painters and musicians and the modest studios that can accommodate them . . . Those who don't live in such threatened districts nonetheless have a stake in this quarrel and some skin in this game, because on the day when everywhere looks like everywhere else we shall all be very much impoverished, and not only that but—more impoverishingly still—we will be unable to express or even understand or depict what we have lost.

—Christopher Hitchens, "Last Call, Bohemia"

It has been a long time now, and not many remember how it was in the old days; not really. Not even those who were there to see and hear as it happened, who were pressed in the crowds beneath the dim rosy lights of the bar in the smoke-veiled room, and who shared, night after night, the mysterious spell created by the talk, the laughter, grease paint, powder, perfume, sweat, alcohol and food—all blended and simmering, like a stew on the restaurant range, and brought to a sustained moment of elusive meaning by the timbres and accents of musical instruments locked in passionate recitative. It has been too long now, some seventeen years.

—Ralph Ellison, "The Golden Age, Time Past"

Music historians exalt being in the right place at the right time, those critical moments and locations where revolutions and movements are spawned. This is tough on those of us stuck in suburbia or the provinces. This book is for, and about, the people who weren't there at the right time and place . . . but who nonetheless refused to believe it was all over and done with before they joined in.

—Simon Reynolds, *Rip It Up and Start Again*

Contents

Prologue: 2010

The invitation came by email, in December, on a Thursday, at 1:42 P.M. The sender was a friend who owned a record label, with whom I had produced a few shows. The subject line was "Saturday night." It read as follows:

> Do you have plans? Because there's something you'll definitely want to go to . . .

As it happens, I did have plans; in those days, in that place, you always did. I knew the person writing wasn't one for idle chitchat, so I asked him what was up. Four minutes later, he replied:

> This is top-secret, so tell no one . . . Jeff Mangum is doing a loft show for a small gathering of people. Want to come? It would be around 9 P.M. or so . . .

From any other source, it would have been an inside joke, an early April Fools' gag—like an RSVP for Thomas Pynchon's birthday party. But coming from Ben Goldberg, it was weirdly plausible. He was an industry veteran who had worked with Jeff's band, Neutral Milk Hotel, as the publicist for Chapel Hill's Merge Records. They stayed in touch after Ben left the job to run his own record label, Ba Da Bing (founded 1994), where he would sign artists such as Beirut and Sharon Van Etten. A few months earlier, I had helped Ben organize a benefit for Chris Knox—a singer-songwriter from New Zealand—where Jeff had made his first public appearance in almost ten years, having been something of a recluse following the feverish reception of his album *In the Aeroplane Over the Sea* (1998). His set was only five songs, but it occasioned instant headlines in *The New York Times*, NPR, *Rolling Stone*, and *Pitchfork*; since then, there was only silence. For anyone who cared about a certain school of songwriting, lo-fi, literary, enigmatic—indie, to use a now-generic term—he was our Salinger, our own white whale.

Off the top of your head: who is your favorite singer? The one you always dreamed of seeing in concert? What is your favorite album? The one you reach for when you're up, or down; the one you never seem to tire of; the one you can't remember life without? For me—for much of my twenties, and thirties, and forties—the singer was Jeff Mangum; the album was *In the Aeroplane Over the Sea*.

I couldn't sleep that night. I spent the next two days perspiring, punch-drunk. Before I canceled my existing plans, I double-checked with Ben's assistant, who reassured me that the gathering was, in fact, a go. On Friday afternoon, a follow-up arrived. The subject line was "Loft Show Tomorrow Night." It read as follows:

> **Time:** Please do not be later than 8:30 P.M. Not only would lateness require someone to continue standing in the cold outside waiting for people to show up, it also would mean them potentially missing the start of the show, which is not fair . . . not fair at all!
>
> If you are going to be late, please text me, as that will be the only way you will be able to get in. This is an apartment building, not a typical venue, so I will need to meet you downstairs (probably annoyed).

Lineup: Playing first will be Forma, a great local group who are kind of the house band of this loft space. The main attraction will perform afterwards. We expect the show to likely be finished by 11 P.M.

Address: 330 Ellery Street, Brooklyn. The closest subway stop appears to be the Flushing Avenue stop on the G train.

Admission: five bucks. The only reason we're charging admission is because we have to rent a PA. Everyone has to pay to get in. Ian MacKaye would even be cool with how much this is costing.

We are kindly requesting that you do not take photos nor videos of the performances. Let's enjoy the moment and let it live on in our memories!

For once, I was early. It was an open, spacious room, with high ceilings, three flights up—a former elementary school that now served as a residence and performance space dubbed The Schoolhouse. I brought a six-pack and added it to a communal table near the kitchen. There must have been a dozen people hanging out when I arrived, and maybe fifty when the show began. There was a tiny, makeshift stage, a folding chair, a music stand, a microphone, and a modest pair of speakers. Forma, the opener, were set up in front, behind a battery of analog synths. We sat down on the floor, cross-legged, or found a place to stand toward the back. There was a long line for the bathroom, and someone smoking by the window. I parked myself in the middle, resolved to hold my spot.

At half past nine, Jeff came onstage and took a seat. He wore red flannel and a pageboy cap; he seemed a bit nervous. He opened with a song called "Oh Comely," and for the next nine minutes, the audience was stone-still. He started "In the Aeroplane Over the Sea," and most of us were overwhelmed, but slowly found a way to sing. He switched between a pair of acoustic guitars. He didn't speak until mid-show, when he invited us to sing along to "Ghost," a song he said he'd never played solo—a song that seemed to prophesize: "And one day in New York City, baby, a girl fell from the sky." By then, the crowd was on its feet; I thought I was the luckiest person on the planet. He played for almost ninety minutes—ten songs total—and ended with my personal favorite: "Two-Headed Boy, Part Two." I felt a lump in my throat as he sang the bridge, which could have been about that very night: "God is a place where some holy spectacle lies." Endearingly, he thanked us half a dozen times for listening, between repeated apologies for his woeful stage banter.

For anyone who cared about a certain school of songwriting, it was a once-in-a-lifetime event. But for those who lived in Brooklyn in the aughts, this was a regular occurrence. It happened nearly every night, for years on end, at DIY establishments in Williamsburg, Greenpoint, Bushwick, and Gowanus, but also in Red Hook, Fort Greene, Bed-Stuy, and Clinton Hill, to give a partial list. Like every music scene, it's a story that can be told only in part. That's what this book attempts to do.

Introduction

The experts all agreed: New York was past its prime. The lively, restless, multiethnic tapestry that once attracted poets, painters, and immigrants was unaffordable, a fortress for the one percent. "If New York City is a business, it isn't Wal-Mart," Michael Bloomberg said in 2003. "It isn't trying to be the lowest-priced product in the market. It's a high-end product, maybe even a luxury product." Embodying the mayor's outlook was the new Time Warner Center, a $1.8 billion eyesore that dwarfed Columbus Circle, opened in 2004. Encased in walls of glass, fifty-three stories high, the monumental complex offered an oligarch's view of Central Park, a four-story mall, a five-star hotel—already booked two years in advance for weddings and bar mitzvahs—a 60,000-square-foot Whole Foods, a concert hall for Jazz at Lincoln Center, and apartments that ran to the high eight figures. Its early tenants included Masa and Per Se, where a three-hour meal was $400 a person (or $700 in today's dollars)—"before tax, tip, and sip of saké or bottled water," the *Times* would write—and a meal for two could easily exceed $1,000.

"I arrived at the tail end of an era when New York had remained basically unchanged for thirty years—a real city," wrote Gary Indiana of the '80s. "The ersatz, provincial, 'post-9/11' New York is a holiday camp for university students and a pied-à-terre for Chinese billionaires, a place any young painter, writer, or musician would be wise to avoid, since it's no longer possible to live there on slender means." It was a commonplace of the Bloomberg era. The famously profane, intractable metropolis had been defanged. "Is New York too safe?" asked *New York* magazine in 2005. "New York is safer and richer but less like itself, an old lover who has gone for a face-lift and come out looking like no one in particular," Adam Gopnik opined in *The New Yorker*. "What once were streets filled with people who actually spoke to each other, now replaced by androids," went a letter to the *Times*.

The mythical nights at Max's Kansas City, CBGB, the Mudd Club, and the Paradise Garage had been consigned to history. "It's not the exciting place it used to be," Madonna said in 2008. "It still has great energy; I still put my finger in the socket. But it doesn't feel alive, cracking with that synergy between the art world and music world and fashion world that was happening in the '80s." The humorist David Rakoff described a "metropolis of streets once thriving with local businesses and services now consisting of nothing but Marc Jacobs store after Marc Jacobs store and cupcake purveyors."

The cost of living, the income gap, suburban chain stores, and luxury development had made New York a shadow of its former self. "I wouldn't move here now," said Fran Lebowitz. "The kids who come here are either rich or are moving here to make money in business, which is a dull kind of kid anyway." In 2010, the city's unofficial poet laureate, Patti Smith, suggested young people should look elsewhere:

> New York has closed itself off to the young and the struggling. But there's always other cities. I don't know—Detroit, Poughkeepsie, Newark. You have to find the new place because New York City has been taken away from you. It's still a great city, but it has closed itself off from the poor and creative burgeoning society. So my advice is: find a new city.

Even the lead of *Sex and the City* bemoaned: "There's just so much money now, and the city is so affluent, and all the colors, all the shops . . . All of that stuff that made it possible to live in New York is gone," Sarah Jessica Parker would say. "I guess there are places in Queens that are affordable."

* * *

Investigate the music of New York in the early aughts, and you'll encounter some version of the following. In the years before and after the millennium, a circle of Manhattan-based bands—The Strokes, the Yeah Yeah Yeahs, and Interpol, to name a few—revived the legacy of rock music downtown, inherited from Television, the Ramones, Patti Smith, and The Velvet Underground.

In a nutshell, this is the argument of Lizzy Goodman's captivating oral history, *Meet Me in the Bathroom*, and of the memoir by her late partner, Marc Spitz, entitled *Poseur: A Memoir of Downtown New York City in the '90s*. It's a delicious tale—with larger-than-life characters, unchecked debauchery, extensive talking shit—and one I wish I had experienced in person. But it's not the New York that I lived in, or could really claim to know.

I never did cocaine with Courtney Love at Don Hill's or 2A. I never saw The Strokes play at the Mercury Lounge or anywhere else for that matter. I caught the Yeah Yeah Yeahs for the first time in 2013, at Coachella. I never cut a rug at any of the cool dance parties like Motherfucker or the Misshapes; I never made it to Luna Lounge or Brownies. I did get to see Interpol on their first tour—in Orlando, Florida, a five-hour drive from where I lived, each way.

I moved to Brooklyn in July 2004. That same week, the Democrats had nominated Massachusetts senator John Kerry for president at their convention in Boston. A young, obscure state senator from Illinois, Barack Obama, had electrified the crowd. "There is not a liberal America and a conservative America," Obama claimed. "There's the United States of America." The speakers similarly emphasized patriotism and national unity. One week later, a series of ads impugning Kerry's service in Vietnam began to air. In late August, the GOP convened at Madison Square Garden, along with 500,000 protesters and 12,000 police. It was the year of "Jesus Walks," "99 Problems," and "Since U Been Gone." *Napoleon Dynamite, Fahrenheit 9/11*, and *Garden State* were in theaters. That spring, Massachusetts became the first state to legalize gay marriage. The occupation of Iraq was in its sixteenth month; the photographs from Abu Ghraib had surfaced in April. The president's approval rating was under fifty percent. It seemed increasingly possible America was ready for change.

And something else was in the air, something unfamiliar, alternately auspicious or adverse. In January, Apple introduced GarageBand, its free home-recording software, and *The Apprentice*, Donald Trump's reality show, premiered on NBC. After 148 years in business, the Domino Sugar refinery in Williamsburg ceased production. In February, the earliest incarnation of Facebook was launched, and Tower Records filed for bankruptcy. Modest Mouse attracted outrage from fans for licensing a song in a commercial for Nissan. In the spring, BMG and Sony Music announced a merger, along with over 2,000 layoffs; EMI and Warner Music also laid off thousands of employees. In Minneapolis, the Pixies played their first show in over a decade, initiating a wave of lucrative reunion tours. In August, a blog named *Brooklyn Vegan* went up. The Bowery Presents hosted their first event with Sonic Youth at Webster Hall. Google had its initial public offering; Gmail, Flickr, and Firefox were born; "FOMO," "podcast," "paywall," and "sharing economy" were all coined. And in *The New York Times*, in October, the critic Kelefa Sanneh wrote "The Rap Against Rockism," a prophetic case for the merits of pop and the pretensions of rock and roll.

* * *

The early aughts were an age of radical uncertainty, disorder, and dread. Americans awakened from a decade of prosperity and peace to find themselves enmeshed in endless war—in Iraq, in Afghanistan, and on the home front. The enemy was everywhere: letters laced with spores of anthrax, snipers on the Beltway, and sneakers packed with explosives. In Jakarta, Bali, London, and Madrid, hundreds died in attacks on nightclubs, hotels, and trains. In Baghdad, Mosul, Basra, and Kabul, civilians were massacred every day. There was a new vocabulary: "enhanced" interrogation, stress positions, black sites, enemy combatants, and extraordinary rendition. There was a color-coded terrorism advisory from Homeland Security; there was a coalition of the willing and an axis of evil.

In politics, it was an era of deceitfulness, complacency, consensus, and the flag. The country singer Toby Keith urged an old-fashioned ass-whoopin' "Courtesy of the Red, White and Blue." It symbolized the nation's mood. Annie Leibovitz photographed Bush's war cabinet for *Vanity Fair*. The Dixie Chicks were blacklisted for criticizing the president. The Capitol cafeteria was serving freedom fries. A White House official told Americans to watch what they say. For offering that 9/11 was not "a 'cowardly' attack on 'civilization'" but "an attack on the world's self-proclaimed superpower, undertaken as a consequence of specific American alliances and actions," Susan Sontag was denounced. The president himself had said, "Either you are with us or you are with the terrorists," and most Americans agreed. Republicans and Democrats alike had voted to authorize the invasion of Iraq. In under eighteen months, the world had gone from "We are all Americans" to shock and awe, regime change, and preemptive war.

A sense of turbulence was only aggravated by technology. Our brains were being rewired. In the space of just a few years, we went from flip phone to iPhone, Friendster to Facebook, disk drives to the cloud. Entire industries were overturned and conceived overnight. The Internet was an extinction-level event for newspapers, entertainment, and many more. At the turn of the century, cameras, classifieds, travel agents, record stores, and CD-ROMs were part of daily life; soon, they were obsolete. As Marx and Engels wrote, all that was solid would melt into air. Nowhere was this more true than in the music industry.

* * *

By late 2004, the widely hyped rebirth of rock downtown had proved ephemeral. It seemed like an eternity since the emergence of a scene on the Lower East Side—but in reality, it was barely three years. The Strokes and Interpol were treading water after underwhelming follow-ups; the Yeah Yeah Yeahs had gone quiet. The Walkmen made a visceral, beguiling record, *Bows + Arrows*, to little effect. The early promise and enthusiasm generated by *Is This It*, *Fever to Tell*, and *Turn on the Bright Lights* had reaped a harvest of pretenders, one worse than the next.

The clearest sign that change was underway came in 2005, with the eviction of CBGB—the launching pad of punk—and its replacement by a store selling $800 pants. (Still to come was DBGB, the upscale Bowery bistro.) To some, it was proof that old New York had lost a piece of its soul, but not to everyone. "CBGB: End of an Era, or Good Riddance?" asked *Time Out New York*. Some pointed out that the venue had been little more than a tourist trap for years. Some saw the boutique as preferable to another CVS or Starbucks. And some knew that the New York music scene had merely migrated, in search of kindred souls, new directions in music, and less exorbitant environments to live, play, and work. "As the whirlwind of New York hype continues to sweep up anything with tussled hair, ill-fitting denim, and fashion shootability," Andy Beta wrote, "the city's bands are overcome by a desire to press forward and experiment with less conventional sounds." There was a new circle of groups that would define the coming decade, and few of them had the means to live in Manhattan.

"One of the things the scene struggled with [around 2005] was that for the first time it didn't have a geographical base," said the composer Taylor Ho Bynum. "It was very dispersed. Some musicians lived in Red Hook, and we did sessions there. Some lived in Greenpoint or Williamsburg. Some were farther away . . . But no one lived in Manhattan proper because no one in our generation could afford to live there." The cultural supremacy of downtown Manhattan was yielding to an insurgency in Brooklyn.

* * *

The last place I'd expected to find a counterculture was Michael Bloomberg's cronut-crazed New York. But that's exactly what I found onstage and in the crowd at Union Pool, Galapagos, Southpaw, Northsix, Zebulon, Monkey Town, Secret Project Robot, Tonic, Roulette, Goodbye Blue Monday, Studio B, Cake Shop, Pianos, Glasslands, Barbès, Death by Audio, Market Hotel, and 285 Kent; in the unlicensed venues of Williamsburg, Greenpoint, and Ridgewood; at lofts in Gowanus, studios in Bushwick, discos in Bed-Stuy, and temples in Fort Greene; at Empire Fulton Ferry Park, among seventy-seven drummers, on 7/7/07; at the Mermaid Parade, the block parties, the pool parties, the Northside Festival, the Siren Festival, and the night Daft Punk brought a pyramid to Coney Island. The only limitation was your own stamina.

On a Tuesday night in Williamsburg, you could choose from six or seven shows within a quarter-mile radius. It never took long to find someone you knew because no matter where they lived, you always ended up along that singular strip of Kent Avenue, where it was both a party and an experiment in self-governance, every single night. The rooms were muggy and constantly congested; the sound could be dicey; the bathrooms were unspeakable; and everyone stood, or found a seat where they could. We were not there for the amenities—we were there for the bands, the company, the alcohol, a chance to meet an interesting stranger. The atmosphere was part of the allure. Beer was from a can and booze a plastic bottle. Compared to Manhattan, the scene in Brooklyn felt more unsupervised and lawless, like the adults had left the kids and gone on vacation. The floor was usually sticky; the bouncers were blasé; the smoking ban, loosely enforced. When the musicians were onstage, the sound would rumble through the walls, out the front door, and off the adjacent buildings.

This is not to say that life was perfect; in ways, it was inherently problematic. For all of its avowed inclusiveness, the Brooklyn scene was overwhelmingly white, male, and privileged, at every level. The bands were just assumed to be four white guys that met in college. Women making music were either overlooked or the object of innuendo, hostility, and condescension. People of color were the exception. Queer people might have felt the same. The rooms were booked primarily by men; the same was true of the booking agents, artist managers, and record labels. And yet: for all its faults, it was an example of the right time, in the right place, and everyone—artists and audience alike—was equally involved.

It was an era of immense anticipation, possibility, adventure, and naïveté: when screens had yet to be ubiquitous; when blogs could launch an artist based on enthusiasm; when bands created venues out of sheer necessity; when life online was more ramshackle, freewheeling, and democratic than today. But it was also an environment of acceptance, entrepreneurialism, and curiosity—one that was ultimately powerless before the forces of development, technology, and capital. Some of these artists found a measure of mainstream success; some were important to no one but each other. Many others came and went, reminders of a uniquely fertile moment—the age of indie—that now means little more than a term of marketing.

"You had the feeling that out of their collective talents would emerge something central to our culture," wrote Joe Boyd in *White Bicycles: Making Music in the 1960s*. "There was a feeling that nothing was nailed down, that an assumption held was one worth challenging." It was a decade when you eagerly observed the output of your peers, in which it felt both natural and overdue to start a blog, upload a song, or produce your own show. There was no such thing as a spectator.

* * *

Today, Brooklyn is a brand, a destination, and a world capital. But for most of its four-hundred-year history, it was overshadowed by the behemoth across the river—a view that would persist until the new millennium. "Often a week passes without my 'going to town,' or 'crossing the bridge,' as neighbors call a trip to Manhattan," Truman Capote wrote in 1958. "Mystified friends, suspecting provincial stagnation, inquire, 'But what do you *do* over there?'" In *Low Life* (1991), Lucy Sante would write,

"New York is incarnated by Manhattan (the other boroughs, noble, useful, and significant though they may be, are merely adjuncts)." Bohemians had been coming to Brooklyn since the days of Walt Whitman: writers such as Thomas Wolfe, Hart Crane, Carson McCullers, and Richard Wright made it their home. Locals such as Spike Lee, Biggie Smalls, and Jay-Z brought the borough to global consciousness. But it was only in the Bloomberg years that it achieved a critical mass of artists, infrastructure, audiences, and ideas—emerging as a credible alternative to Manhattan, a counterculture all its own.

The atmosphere in which the scene would flourish had everything to do with economics. The rents were more affordable—that is, for some. It may have been impossible to live in Manhattan, but in Brooklyn, you could make it work on something less than a full-time job. In the late 2000s, an apartment in Williamsburg, Red Hook, or Clinton Hill was still somewhat reasonable. Affordable rents enticed aspiring musicians— composers, producers, instrumentalists, improvisers, songwriters, and DJs—along with an adventurous, enthusiastic audience. In those years, much of Brooklyn felt like an intimate, implausible, unmonitored, unmapped, and self-sustaining ecosystem of clubs, collectives, DIY spaces, and amateurs booking shows, starting venues, and throwing parties. Omnivorous, artistic-minded people were moving to the city in historic numbers, and Brooklyn was the catalyst: the source of their vitality, ambition, and desire to participate in something new. "There's still this acceptance and understanding in Brooklyn," said Bobby Matador of the band Oneida in 2006. "Do whatever you do with passion, and I'll give you a chance."

The scene was organized without division by genre. A show would open with an instrumental group, an electronic set, a singer-songwriter, then a DJ, or a rock band, or some variation thereof. Guitars and violins accompanied laptops, pedals, and drum machines. Krautrock, freak folk, post-punk, lo-fi, shoegaze, free jazz, musique concrète, and other subgenres could all be found in dialogue. Listeners encountered sound worlds that were unfamiliar—and this, in turn, inspired a great deal of hybridity, experiment, and fusion. The Brooklyn bands incorporated elements from both pop and the avant-garde, combining psychedelia, minimalism, noise, dub, doo-wop, disco, found sound, R&B, Eastern Europe, and African guitar music. An all-embracing synthesis of styles: that was the spirit of the aughts in Brooklyn.

* * *

Artistically and philosophically, the Brooklyn scene understood itself as "indie": a word that was already vague, if more or less discernible by sound. To rework a critic's definition of the novel: an indie band was one that fundamentally had something wrong with it—too weird, too sad, too willfully opaque—and undermined itself with dissonance, irony, or affect. In many ways, by the mid-2000s, the term was an antique. The MP3 had done away with the constraint of scarcity, rendering once-rigid dichotomies (majors and indies, commercial or underground) practically obsolete. The quintessential indie bands—Death Cab for Cutie, Built to Spill, Modest Mouse—were all on major labels. But in the absence of a term with which to group musicians as dissimilar as Joanna Newsom, Death Grips, and Blood Orange, indie seemed as good a word as any. It was a grab-bag term, a big, broad tent, allowing one to speak of bands that paved a middle road between obscurity and popular appeal.

More important than its acoustical properties were indie's outlook, ethos, and ideology. For more than three decades, "indie" was a synonym for self-reliant, enterprising, and amateur, in the old sense: pursuits done out of love. The thinking was: there is nothing complicated about making music; anyone can do it, and everybody should. In the mid-'70s, a wave of labels would emerge in the U.K. who saw independence of mind as an adjunct of the indie model. "If you only have WH Smith selling books, then you only get a certain kind of book," said Geoff Travis of Rough Trade. "If you set up a viable system that sells other kinds of literature, then you give people a chance to decide for themselves." In the U.S., the labels SST, Touch and Go, Dischord, Sub Pop, and

Homestead were among the first to enshrine independence as a point of pride, a vocal stance, a form of protest. In hindsight, this well-meaning conviction would lead to something gained and something lost. From here on out, the indie world was less about democratizing music than a rejection of mass culture. By the early '90s, the term was understood effectively in a negative sense, as the antithesis of the mainstream. The videos on *TRL* were glorifying girls gone wild, factory-made boy bands, and Neanderthals like Kid Rock, so indie made a virtue of intelligence and authenticity. The radio and the charts were celebrating Bentleys, bottles, and bling, so indie artists made art for art's sake—itself a form of middle-class privilege. "The community that I come out of is just interested in doing your own weird art project," said Dave Longstreth of Dirty Projectors, "not making something sellable. You probably couldn't sell something with this music." (He would learn otherwise.) The implication was: another world is possible, and it could start right now.

For thirty years, the indie world defined itself in terms of its distance from the mainstream. But by the mid-to-late aughts, it seemed that indie music had *become* the mainstream: in movies such as *Garden State, Juno*, and *Little Miss Sunshine*, teen soap operas like *The O.C.*, late-night talk shows, car commercials, *SNL*, and even Super Bowl ads. The National would hit the campaign trail with Barack Obama. Albums by Modest Mouse, Arcade Fire, and Vampire Weekend all debuted at number one. The word itself had taken on a new if not entirely opposite meaning: now it described almost everything. From day one, "indie" was synonymous with opposition or antithesis: us and them. But opposition to what, exactly? In the '80s, it meant the major-label world and MTV. In the '90s, it meant materialism and machismo. By the mid-aughts, in a country that had reelected George W. Bush by a decisive margin, it was unclear what role, if any, a counterculture would play.

* * *

Around the continent, it was the same story. In reaction, perhaps, to the rap-rock and boy-band music of the late '90s, local scenes were emerging that revived the spirit of the '70s downtown. The most bountiful were in Providence, Los Angeles, Baltimore, Montreal, Toronto, Memphis, Atlanta, and San Francisco, where artists collaborated, shared bills, booked tours, ran labels, and pooled resources. They were encouraged by inveterate and lifelong listeners, for whom the Internet would be a means of finding kindred souls from silos of common interest. These scenes had been decades in the making. So when a confluence of art, technology, and commerce elevated indie to the masses in the second half of the decade, the parts were all in place.

The nucleus for indie in the aughts would be the place that *New York* magazine once called "the sane alternative to Manhattan." The bands who moved to Brooklyn were as original and eccentric as their adopted home, and equally impossible to define. TV on the Radio, The Fiery Furnaces, Dirty Projectors, and Animal Collective were writing deranged pop songs for a fervent, growing audience. Black Dice, Oneida, Liars, Sightings, Parts & Labor, Gang Gang Dance, and Battles were melding noise, psych, punk, and math rock. White Magic, Okkervil River, Phosphorescent, Sharon Van Etten, and the Woodsist label were producing gothic Americana. The National, Sufjan Stevens, and LCD Soundsystem would soon have their breakthrough. Oxford Collapse, The Hold Steady, Ambulance Ltd., and Grizzly Bear would all make their debut. It was a fortuitous time and place to be young and besotted with music.

* * *

Unlike its predecessors from the '70s, the Brooklyn scene was recognized from the outset as a unique creative conduit. "It's gotten to the point where I had to stop constantly writing about Brooklyn because every week there seemed to be another five bands that were really interesting," wrote Alex Miller, an editor of England's *NME*. "All Hail Brooklyn: Alt-Rock Thrives in Alt-Borough," went a headline in the *Times*. "Is there a 23-year-old alive in northern Brooklyn who's not making music right now?" asked

New York in 2009. "It may be a good deal harder to get rich in the music business than it was a generation ago, but that doesn't seem to have deterred anyone. What are they all after?" That same year, the Brooklyn scene was encapsulated on *Dark Was the Night*, a compilation organized by Bryce and Aaron Dessner of The National. "On this record, we tried to capture this musical renaissance, which may not have the cultural impact of grunge or punk, but is equally significant from a cultural and creative standpoint," said John Carlin, its executive producer. "It's an assertion of Aaron and Bryce's generation. These artists are not fringe or marginal."

At its apex, the scene comprised a galaxy of independent clubs, promoters, festivals, free offerings, and unlicensed establishments from Williamsburg to Sheepshead Bay. Its leading lights were firmly in the vanguard of American music. All of this led up to 2009, a year in which the Brooklyn scene achieved a kind of critical hegemony: from *Rolling Stone* to the *Los Angeles Times*, NPR, *The Guardian*, and even *Time* magazine. In *The Village Voice*, eight of the top twenty albums in the annual critics' list were by Brooklyn-bred talent. For some, it was irrefutable that the best new music in the world was being made in this community, by our friends and neighbors. And now the word was getting out.

* * *

On an exquisite Sunday in August of 2009, Jay-Z and Beyoncé went to Williamsburg. Along with over 6,000 fans who had waited two hours in line—"a sea of plaid, straw hats, flow-y dresses and V-necks," according to *Gothamist*—they watched an hour-long performance on the waterfront by Grizzly Bear, who had just released their landmark album, *Veckatimest*. It was the season-end finale of a series once held at the long-empty McCarren Pool. The Pool Parties came to life in the summer of 2006, with free performances by local indie acts. Besides the music, there were Slip 'N Slides, Hula Hoops, and constant people-watching: a catwalk, theme park, and pickup scene, all at once. The parties instantly became a staple of summer in the city—so much so that, in 2008, the mayor announced a $50 million renovation of the pool, ending its life as a concert venue. The series moved a few blocks south, to East River State Park, a once-bustling railyard where boats off-loaded cargo for more than a century. The band was introduced before a cloudless skyline by an unlikely emcee: New York's senior senator Chuck Schumer.

The king and queen had been busy. In 2008, Beyoncé released *I Am . . . Sasha Fierce*, her third consecutive number one album, and the epochal "Single Ladies (Put a Ring on It)." Jay-Z announced that he was parting ways with his label, Def Jam, where he had served as president and CEO, and signing a $150 million deal with Live Nation, inclusive of recordings, touring, and merchandise. In the coming weeks, *The Blueprint 3* became his eleventh straight album to hit number one, led by the world-conquering "Empire State of Mind," in which the pride of Marcy Projects grabbed the crown: "Statue of Liberty, long live the World Trade / Long live the king, yo—I'm from the Empire State."

That afternoon, however, Bey and Jay were in civilian mode. They'd been invited by Beyoncé's younger sister, Solange, herself a longtime friend, fan, and future collaborator of Dirty Projectors, Chairlift, and Vampire Weekend. They watched the show from the soundboard and introduced themselves afterward to the band. "They're very lovely, down-to-earth people," said Chris Bear, the group's drummer. "We're big fans of their music as well." Long before the concert was over, they were the subject of countless tweets, texts, and blog posts. "Jay-Z, Beyoncé Hang with Hipsters, Catch Grizzly Bear Show," went one headline. Short of a visit from the first family—whose inauguration Beyoncé had performed at, in January—it was hard to imagine a more illustrious endorsement.

The following day, Jay-Z gave an interview to MTV. "I don't understand why people are always surprised to see me at shows," he shrugged. "I've always said that I believe in good music and bad music, so I'm always at those type of events. I like music." He continued:

[Grizzly Bear is] an incredible band . . . what the indie rock movement is doing right now is very inspiring. It felt like us in the
beginning. These concerts, they're not on the radio, no one hears
about them, and there's 12,000 people in attendance. And the
music that they're making and the connection they're making to
people is really inspiring. So I hope that they have a run where
they push hip hop back a little bit, so it will force hip hop to fight
to make better music. Because it can happen. Because that's what
rap did to rock.

No one knew it then, but late 2009 was both the pinnacle and the
precipice of the indie age in Brooklyn. It was a year in which the optimism of the new administration was evident in music, popular ("I Gotta
Feeling," "Party in the U.S.A.") and otherwise. For some, it was the year
of *Merriweather Post Pavilion, Bitte Orca,* and *Veckatimest,* the trinity
of early Obama indie; for some, the year of Phoenix, The xx, or Passion
Pit. But it was more than that. An archipelago of DIY establishments in
California, New England, and points between was in its prime. An ethos
of artistic self-reliance was the norm.

It also represented a turning point in modern music. For a very brief
window, all it took to be the buzziest band in America was an impossibly
compelling hook, a pleasing vocal, above-average lyrics, a strong arrangement, an interesting backstory, a few hundred fans, and an email address
or two. You didn't need a publicist; you didn't need a record label; you
didn't even need CDs. It was an inexact and time-intensive process for
the listener; there were far more duds than gems. But when it worked, it
felt miraculous. In retrospect, it signified the end of "indie" as an underground phenomenon, and the onset of a certain obsolescence. From here
on out, it was diminishing returns.

Today—when the supremacy of pop is absolute; when Williamsburg is
better known for its rooftop bars than for bands; when men with guitars
seem like a relic of a more blinkered time—Jay-Z's esteem for indie rock

might seem peculiar. The multimillionaire, executive, and icon, applauding the aspirations of indie? The lyricist who once explained, "My bills through the roof—can't do numbers like The Roots," sermonizing for Grizzly Bear? It sounds far-fetched: an indie group imparting anything to hip hop, the world's most popular art form. (Imagine Jay endorsing "the indie rock movement" in 2026.) In those days, though, the notion that there might be something honest, useful, decent, or inspirational in indie rock was not as unlikely as it seemed.

It's hardly a coincidence that the age of indie transpired when the recorded-music business was in free fall: when the conventional authorities, assumptions, and obstacles were being displaced. Since 1999—the year the record industry was at its all-time peak, and Napster went online—tens of billions had been lost to digital piracy, along with nearly all the jobs related to career development. Radio had been absorbed by a nationwide conglomerate; retail, decimated. With the adoption of Myspace, YouTube, and GarageBand, the barriers had never been lower. At South by Southwest, David Byrne gave a talk entitled "Record Companies: Who Needs Them?" By 2010, industry-wide revenue had fallen by more than half in the preceding decade. The fantasy of gold or platinum could no longer be entertained; aside from licensing, the only way to earn a living was onstage. The audience rewarded bands who excelled in a live setting, and word got around fast.

With major labels on life support, some musicians went the way of self-release: Brian Eno, Radiohead, and Nine Inch Nails. As record companies slashed their publicity budgets, other corporations were happy to step in. Joni Mitchell, Paul McCartney, and even Sonic Youth released their albums through Starbucks. Red Bull allotted tens of millions to its eponymous academy and festival over twenty years. Intel would collaborate with Vice for The Creators Project, underwriting artists like M.I.A. and Interpol. Amid the vacuum caused by illegal file-sharing, a new form of patronage would take shape: in 2009, the crowdfunding platform Kickstarter launched in a tenement building on the Lower East Side, and soon outpaced The National Endowment for the Arts in terms of annual funding.

The age of indie overlapped with the decline of print and music journalism as a profession. On any given week in the early aughts, *The New York Times*, *The Village Voice*, *Time Out New York*, and *The New Yorker* offered comprehensive listings, online and in print—a priceless public service for musicians, the public, and posterity alike. For much of the decade, it was common to find a half-dozen concert reviews and profiles in the arts section of the *Times*; by 2014, it was rare to see more than one. The emphasis had shifted to celebrity interviews, podcasts, and TV. In the early aughts, an all-star team of music critics was fanning out nightly across New York: Kelefa Sanneh, Ann Powers, Ben Ratliff, Maura Johnston, Steve Smith, Allan Kozinn, Jon Pareles, Anne Midgette, Melena Ryzik, Christopher Weingarten, Tom Breihan, and Alex Ross. A decade later, only Pareles and Ross were covering live music, and Ross had moved to L.A. The new authority were Internet natives such as *Pitchfork*, where, for a decade or two, a rave review could propel an artist from obscurity to festivals and late-night TV almost overnight.

* * *

By 2014, the city I had lived in for ten years looked much different. In Williamsburg, along the waterfront, three beloved DIY establishments, all in the same complex—285 Kent, Death by Audio, and Glasslands—announced a nearly simultaneous closing. According to a trade publication, the properties were not fulfilling their "post-gentrification potential," given the lack of office space in the area. It soon emerged that Vice, the countercultural media colossus, was moving in. After three terms and twelve years in office, Mayor Mike had been succeeded by Brooklyn's Bill de Blasio, who had compared New York under Bloomberg to "a tale of two cities." De Blasio would rapidly accomplish the impossible by making the city nostalgic for his precursor.

"Here's the thing," Spike Lee told an audience in Brooklyn:

> I grew up here in New York. It's changed. Why does it take an influx
> of white New Yorkers in the south Bronx, in Harlem, in Bed-Stuy,
> in Crown Heights, for the facilities to get better? . . . People want to

live in Fort Greene. People want to live in Clinton Hill . . . they move
to Williamsburg, they can't even afford Williamsburg now because
of motherfuckin' hipsters. What do they call Bushwick now? What's
the word? East Williamsburg?

On Staten Island in July, Eric Garner, a forty-three-year-old father of
six, was fatally asphyxiated by Daniel Pantaleo, a New York City police
officer. He'd been approached for selling cigarettes on the street—two for
a dollar. "I can't breathe," Garner said, eleven different times, face down
on the pavement. In Ferguson, Missouri, the following month, a white
policeman fired a dozen shots at Michael Brown, age eighteen, hitting him
six times. His body was left out in the street for four hours, and helped
to ignite a global movement: Black Lives Matter. The Obama-era rhe-
toric about a postracial society seemed like a fiction—or worse, a fantasy.

In the Brooklyn of 2014, you looked around and wondered where it all
went wrong. The free outdoor concerts at East River State Park had been
disbanded years ago. In their place was Smorgasburg, where you could
find kombucha Popsicles, cucumber lemonade, and the world-famous
ramen burger. TV on the Radio, Grizzly Bear, Dirty Projectors, and
Animal Collective had all released new music in the past two years; reac-
tions ranged from incomprehension to indifference. The Walkmen were
on indefinite hiatus. The founders of Grizzly Bear and Dirty Projectors,
Ed Droste and Dave Longstreth, had moved to L.A.; the former was writing for *Vogue* about executive frequent-flier status; the latter was writing
songs for Solange, Rihanna, and Kanye.

The age of indie had gone stale. Vanilla outfits like The Lumineers,
Mumford & Sons, and Of Monsters and Men commercialized the sound
of middlebrow indie, offering an ersatz, derivative, and insipid product.
While sheer inertia fed the festival circuit, the *Billboard* charts were telling a different story. Around the country, everyone was listening to the
same thing, and it wasn't bands from Brooklyn. It was a time of blockbuster releases from Taylor Swift, Adele, Beyoncé, Drake, and Lady Gaga.

A generation of black auteurs—Frank Ocean, The Weeknd, Miguel, and Janelle Monáe—had all made notable debuts. In Ferguson, and around the world, Kendrick Lamar's "Alright" became a protest anthem. "The Rap Against Rockism" was the new orthodoxy; the Brooklyn scene was more or less an afterthought.

Jay-Z and Beyoncé were still keeping up with the kids, if under tonier circumstances. In March—along with Kim Kardashian, Madonna, and Björk—they made a brief appearance at the Park Avenue Armory, where The xx performed before an exclusive crowd of only forty. In 2014, *Bloomberg Business* reported that Brooklyn, "where a resident would need to devote 98 percent of the median income to afford the payment on a median-priced home of $615,000," was the least-affordable place to buy a home in the entire country. It was a new decade, and things had changed.

* * *

Needless to say, the decade from 2004 to 2014 was more than just a watershed for indie rock. It hinged on three decisive world events, all intertwined: the Bush reelection, in which America would double down on the war in Iraq; the economic crisis of the late 2000s, in which millions lost their jobs and homes; and the high hopes engendered by the first black president, along with populist revolts on the right (the Tea Party) and the left (Occupy Wall Street). In the twenty-first century, the great unwinding caused by a meaningless war, an environment of jingoism, and the effects of the recession all were felt in contemporary music.

There was a current of implicit protest, politics, and even patriotism in the indie world, whether it was The National's "Mr. November," "Start a War," and "Fake Empire"; TV on the Radio's "Red Dress" and "I Was a Lover"; Animal Collective's "You don't need to go to college"; Parts & Labor's *Mapmaker*; The Walkmen's "In the New Year"; or Sufjan Stevens releasing *Illinois* on the Fourth of July. That said, it's telling that there wasn't a lot more.

These artists were confronting a distinctly new and disillusioning landscape. A post-9/11 world, in which the nation's mood had turned from grief and soul-searching to bellicosity, know-nothingness, and paranoia; a misbegotten, self-defeating invasion; and a bitterly divided electorate, red states and blue. They were part of a generation that was uninsured, unemployed, or in debt, and watched Wall Street being handed billions. Our grief derived from growing up in one version of the country and then finding yourself in another, from the awareness of an ugly truth: in mounting a calamitous occupation, America had not prevailed in the war on terror, but lost. For anyone who felt ashamed, isolated, or angry at the direction their country was taking, these songs were a way to connect with something larger than yourself.

It wasn't just the music: its magnitude derived from the audience. The age of indie brought together overachievers, college dropouts, trust-fund babies, nine-to-fivers, unknown greats, opinionated weirdos, and socially inept savants. It always felt like something big could manifest at any time; it felt like you were looking toward the future, not the past. "Every hour of the day, somewhere in greater New York," Jonathan Franzen wrote in *Freedom* (2010), "some energetic young person was working on a song that would sound, at least for a few listenings—maybe for as many as twenty or thirty listenings—as fresh as the morning of Creation." What was inspiring about the time was the belief that there were still new trails to blaze; that anybody could take part; and that there were thousands who felt the same. Concert-giving and -going were more than mere diversion; they were a part of everyday existence. The Brooklyn scene revived a sense that the most invigorating art form at the moment in New York was music, much like the golden age of jazz, folk, punk, and hip hop before it.

"Young people have a biological right to be excited about the times they're living through," Simon Reynolds wrote in *Rip It Up and Start Again*. "If you are very lucky, that hormonal urgency is matched by the insurgency of the era, and your built-in adolescent need for amazement and belief coincides with a period of objective abundance." In

Williamsburg, Bushwick, Gowanus, and elsewhere, the decade from 2004 to 2014 was precisely that: an embarrassment of musical riches. Part of it was the sense that blogs and social media were democratizing the music industry. Part of it was the excitement of having access to almost anything with the Internet. And part of it was a moment of unmistakable artistic abundance. There was no need to romanticize the old New York; there was too much happening right now.

* * *

Who gets to tell the story of a scene?

Is it the people who were there at the outset, who saw it in its infancy, when it was completely unknown? Is it the people who came after them, and saw it at its height? Is it the supposed experts—journalists, historians, critics—or the people who served the drinks, and worked the door, and mopped the floors? It's everyone, or at least it should be.

This is a book about a dozen or so individuals and bands with a curious claim to fame. By all the rules of musical biography, they would be considered nonentities: they earned no gold or platinum records, headlined no major festivals, performed in zero Super Bowls, and sold modestly, if at all. A few of them achieved a degree of renown; a few would nearly make it big, only to self-destruct; as of this writing, though, none is a household name. Yet what they did was more decisive for the culture of New York than billionaire philanthropists whose names were carved in concert halls, more enduring than bands with fifty times their sales. It was this: they were part of a scene that changed people's lives.

* * *

Us v. Them—from an LCD Soundsystem song—is at once a social history and a first-person account of ten years in New York. It examines the overlapping lives and careers of some bands and individuals who helped to shape the Brooklyn scene, creating a sum that was greater than its parts. It brings together a variety of voices—from artists, impresarios, and industry professionals to the reporters and bloggers who covered it in real time. As a corrective to the tendency among certain journalists and critics to overlook the work of people such as The Twisted Ones and Mighty Robot crew, Noémie Lafrance, Brooke Baxter, Rolyn Hu, and the Shinkoyo collective—and to reorient the story from the usual suspects—I tried whenever possible to tell the story using their own words.

The book is organized in three parts. It starts with the Republican National Convention in 2004; it comes to a crest with the improbable success of Grizzly Bear, Animal Collective, and Dirty Projectors in 2009; and it ends with the eviction of 285 Kent, Death by Audio, and Glasslands in 2014. Part one explores how the creative community of the aughts came together. Part two charts some of the changes in the music business, technology, journalism, and patronage that those artists would exploit and be exploited by. And in part three, the Brooklyn scene confronts the forces of development—the fruit of its success. As a work of narrative history, *Us v. Them* is an attempt to chronicle how this community of artists, listeners, and amateurs came to be, and to explore how that scene would end up unraveling.

For all my zeal, a thread of doubt runs through this book, as it does for a few of its subjects. "Sometimes I feel like Grizzly Bear, in particular, has come to represent an idea of Williamsburg and consumerism," said Daniel Rossen, of his group's legacy:

> Elitist, white hipster consumerism or something. It's almost shameful now, in a way. I feel strange about it, because on one hand I feel really proud about what we did. We really cared about what we were making, especially in the early days, and it sort of breaks my heart that Grizzly Bear just came to be a symbol of that time. But it is what it is. Life goes on, you move on. [*Laughs.*]

Was the age of indie a sandbox for college-educated yuppies, or does the ethos and idealism it implied still have meaning? Isn't the one dependable part of life in New York—well, change? Was there really

anything unusual about those years in Brooklyn, or did they just feel
that way because I happened to be living there in my late twenties? Isn't
every period more or less the same? But here I am doing precisely that—
trying to work out why a moment twenty years ago meant so much to
me, and everyone I know.

This book does not pretend to be a comprehensive history of music
made in Brooklyn from 2004 to 2014. It pays particular attention to a
handful of artists, labels, and venues, but they were by no means the
only ones who made it happen; another writer might have chosen an
entirely different sample. (A book that's even wordier than this would
have discussed venues such as Zebulon and Market Hotel; labels such as
Daptone, Woodsist, and Northern Spy; platforms such as late-night TV,
Soundcloud, Bandcamp, and Kickstarter; or artists such as Black Dice,
White Magic, Aa ["big A, little a"], Das Racist, Helado Negro, Matana
Roberts, Oneohtrix Point Never, and Laurel Halo.) Research involved
more than a hundred hours of interviews over eighteen months. I chose
to write about the lives of lesser-known musicians, as I think that their
experience was more representative of the scene, and more useful in
terms of understanding the era. The bigger personalities of New York in
the aughts have been covered elsewhere, and the absence of their names
bears no relation to their import. In *The Other Paris* (2015), Lucy Sante
remarked, "This book is not intended as a polemic, for which it's much
too late anyway." This book might be intended as an elegy—or a blueprint,
because I'd like to think it will happen again. I mostly mean it as an act
of tribute to an era when celebrities and senators embraced cerebral
indie rock, the underground was international news, and Brooklyn was
the epicenter.

2004

"*Shake it like a Polaroid picture . . .* " "You think video games are addicting? Try Apple's new music-composition program, GarageBand . . ." After Furor, Janet Jackson Is to Be Cut from Grammy Awards . . . Officer Avoids Indictment in Killing on Brooklyn Rooftop . . . Howard Dean withdraws from U.S. presidential race . . . Bush calls for ban on same-sex marriages . . . "What happened to the antiwar movement?" Americans burned and mutilated by Iraq mob . . . Bush Expresses "Deep Disgust" Over Abuse of Iraqi Prisoners . . . *"And we'll all float on anyway, well . . ."* Donald Trump is hotter than ever as star of the hit *The Apprentice . . .* April was the deadliest month for U.S. soldiers in Iraq . . . Veterans Group Criticizes Kerry on His Record in Vietnam . . . Iraq Videotape Shows the Decapitation of an American . . . Same-sex couples exchange vows in Massachusetts: President reissues "urgent" call for ban . . . *Fahrenheit 9/11* Wins Top Prize at Cannes . . . Thousands Protest in Rome Against Bush Visit and Iraq War . . . RONALD REAGAN DIES AT 93; FOSTERED COLD-WAR MIGHT AND CURBS ON GOVERNMENT . . . "Islam, more than any other religion human beings have devised, has all the makings of a thoroughgoing cult of death . . ." "The latest niche networking site is TheFacebook.com. Founded earlier this year by Harvard undergrad Mark Zuckerberg . . ." Bush's Rating Falls to Its Lowest Point, New Survey Finds . . . Bin Laden Is Said to Be Organizing for a U.S. Attack . . . New Jersey Governor Resigns

After Admitting Gay Affair . . . "Republican Tom Tancredo warned that immigrants are 'coming here to kill you and to kill me and our families . . .'" As It Goes Public, Google Says It Is Worth Up to $36 Billion . . . Vast Anti-Bush Rally Greets Republicans in New York . . . At Least 900 Arrested in City as Protesters Clash with Police . . . "The thesis of *The Plot Against America* is paranoid, too—a fascistic U.S. government suspending civil liberties and persecuting minorities deemed a threat to security . . ." U.S. DEATH TOLL IN IRAQ NEARS 1,000 . . . Is John Kerry fit for command? . . . *"Heroes and villains, just see what you've done . . ."* Conditions in Ohio Point to Kerry, but Bush Runs Strong . . . "The latest Pew Research Center survey of 1,307 registered voters, conducted October 15–19, finds President George W. Bush and Senator John Kerry tied at 45%–45% among registered voters, and 47%–47% among likely voters . . ." In Video Message, Bin Laden Issues Warning to U.S. . . . In Final Days Before Vote, Divided Electorate Expresses Anxiety and Concern . . . Bush wins second term by a solid margin; Kerry failed to connect on economy . . . Bush to Push a Big Agenda—Vows to Spend "Political Capital" on War, Tax Law . . . Rebels Routed in Fallujah; Fighting Spreads Elsewhere in Iraq . . . November 2nd-deadliest month for U.S. troops . . . Former Pantera guitarist among four killed at club . . . Thousands Die as Quake-Spawned Waves Crash onto Coastlines Across Southern Asia . . . *"Every time you close your eyes, lies, lies . . ."*

Shock and Awe

They came on bicycles, by subway, and on foot: people of every age, ethnicity, and class; with little kids and loved ones, all in ninety-degree sun. They hoisted handwritten signs that said "Regime Change Begins at Home," "BUSH LIES, WHO DIES?," and "Eradicate Mad Cowboy Disease." They represented antiwar groups, veterans, religious organizations, gay and women's rights, labor unions, environmentalists, and immigrants— anyone, in short, who couldn't countenance another year of butchery, ineptitude, and deceit. Borne by pallbearers, draped in the flag, a thousand cardboard coffins symbolized the dead in Iraq. There were banners, shirts, and buttons calling the president a criminal, a warmonger, a fraud. The multitudes were packed as densely as a train at rush hour; the streets were baking in relentless heat; the mood was spirited and orderly. At Madison Square Garden, the site of that week's Republican National Convention, a buffer zone had been established with blockades and emergency vehicles. They walked from Chelsea up to midtown, then to Union Square. It was among the largest demonstrations in U.S. history, and the biggest ever at a political convention: from West Fourteenth to Herald Square, the crowd was estimated at 500,000 protesters. Outside a theater near Broadway, they met a group of visiting Republicans.

"Four more years," said the delegates.

"Four more months," the response.

The demonstrators were flanked by helmeted police in riot gear and camouflaged National Guardsmen. Blimps and helicopters watched from the sky. Between the city and the federal government, $65 million were spent on security for the convention, with fighter jets enforcing a no-fly zone over Manhattan, the Coast Guard patrolling waterways, and a deployment of 12,000 police officers and supervisors a day. The NYPD had been preparing for the past eighteen months, intent on averting the disturbance that engulfed the WTO meetings in Seattle five years earlier. On August 30, 2004, the GOP converged on Madison Square Garden to endorse a second term for George W. Bush.

NYPD Commissioner Ray Kelly praised the organizers for keeping the march peaceful. Then he rounded up approximately 1,800 protesters in orange netting over the next few days, busing them to a makeshift detention center at Pier 57, which lawyers called Guantanamo-on-the-Hudson. A sign revealing the presence of asbestos hung in plain view; oil and gas pooled in puddles. Some were held for more than twenty-four hours. A journalist wrote, "We had nowhere to sit, to sleep. If we begged for food, we were given an apple. Our belongings were confiscated; we hadn't been charged with a crime." The city would eventually be made to pay $30 million in settlements and litigation, with the NYPD admitting no liability.

In a brazen act of scheduling, the very first Republican convention in New York was only days before the anniversary of 9/11. A seven-minute video showed the president after the attacks: his bullhorn moment at Ground Zero; greeting the wounded at Walter Reed; and his ceremonial pitch during the 2001 World Series at Yankee Stadium. Lead-off speakers included the triumphant former mayor, Rudolph Giuliani, and Arizona's John McCain, who hailed the president's agenda in the Middle East. "From the first Republican president, Abraham Lincoln, to President George W. Bush," Giuliani said, "our party's great contribution is to expand freedom in our own land and all over the world." But it was California's governor, Arnold Schwarzenegger, who stole the show: "And to those critics who are so pessimistic about our economy, I say: don't be economic girlie-men."

On Thursday, September 2, the president accepted formally his party's nomination. "If America shows uncertainty and weakness in this decade, the world will drift toward tragedy. This will not happen on my watch," said Bush. The president allowed himself a few moments of levity. "Some folks look at me and see a certain swagger, which in Texas is called 'walking.'" Bush concluded by invoking God's will. "Like generations before us, we have a calling from beyond the stars to stand for freedom. This is the everlasting dream of America—and tonight, in this place, that dream is renewed." The delegates were on their feet.

* * *

In retrospect, it was all a dress rehearsal for 2016.

The Democratic candidate had an impeccable CV, but also a perception of being opportunist and elitist. He liked to go windsurfing off the coast of Nantucket; his wife was worth an estimated $500 million; they owned a minimum of five houses. Like most Democrats, his record was in lockstep with the White House: he had voted in favor of the Patriot Act, the use of force in Iraq, and Bush's education policies. In three separate debates with Bush, he never said "Abu Ghraib," "torture," or "detainee." He started his acceptance speech with a salute and a feeble "I'm John Kerry, and I'm reporting for duty." Then again: a shameful and duplicitous case for war, the occupation and insurgency, the wasted lives, Guantanamo and Abu Ghraib were what Americans were being asked to ratify. For all the shortcomings of Kerry as a candidate, the thought of four more years under Bush, Cheney, and Rumsfeld should have made you queasy.

The eighteen months before Election Day had been a blooper reel of arrogance, propaganda, and magical thinking. When U.S. troops captured Baghdad on April 10, 2003, conservatives and liberals rejoiced. Writing in *The Weekly Standard*, David Brooks quoted Orwell: "Now that the war in Iraq is over, we'll find out how many people around the world are capable of facing unpleasant facts." In early May, on the deck of an aircraft carrier, below a banner reading "Mission Accomplished," the president declared that we would soon bring democracy to Iraq. By late summer, it was dawning on some that the war had only begun. American troops were being killed by roadside bombs, booby traps, and IEDs. Insurgents were attacking symbols of the occupation, exploding a massive bomb at the United Nations headquarters in Baghdad, killing twenty-three.

In January of 2004, at the State of the Union, the president announced his opposition to gay marriage. Regarding the war in Iraq, he said, "We're seeking all the facts. Already, the Kay Report identified dozens of weapons-of-mass-destruction-related program activities." At the White House Correspondents' Dinner in March, Bush made light of the invasion. At one point he showed a picture of himself in the Oval Office, searching for something. "Those weapons of mass destruction have got to be somewhere," he said, referring to the case for war. There was a shot of Bush peering under a couch. "Nope. No weapons over there." Then another photo of Bush looking below his desk. "Maybe under here?" Laughter filled the room.

On April 28, CBS's *60 Minutes II* broke the story of Iraqi prisoners being tortured at Abu Ghraib. The graphic pictures showed American soldiers demonically giving thumbs-up signs while detainees were forced to simulate sex acts, wear leashes, cower before dogs, pile into human pyramids, and—in the most horrific image—stand arms outstretched, hooded, on a box, and attached to wires. Reporters obtained a memo from the Justice Department that offered legal justification for everything short of homicide.

In the summer of 2004, the number of insurgent bombings and attacks grew to a hundred a day. What started as a war between a handful of religious factions morphed into an army of jihadists who had sworn to drive the U.S. from Iraq. By the fall, the violence was ten times greater than when Bush declared "Mission Accomplished." In late October, insurgents dressed as police executed forty-nine Iraqi soldiers, and a satire of American militarism, *Team America: World Police*, came out in theaters. A senior adviser to the White House told *The New York Times*: "We're an empire now, and when we act, we create our own reality." The final Gallup poll showed Bush and Kerry in a dead heat, with each attracting forty-nine percent of voters.

* * *

My college class had graduated in the unsuspecting days between the bursting of the dot-com bubble and 9/11, in the maw of a recession, in the spring of 2001; history was waiting. An alumnus himself, the president had spoken at our commencement. "To those of you who received honors, awards, and distinctions," he said, "well done. And to the C students, I say: 'You, too, can be president of the United States.'" My friends were starting jobs in corporate America, on Wall Street, in finance and consulting. They had six-figure salaries, signing bonuses, and eighty-hour weeks at McKinsey, Goldman Sachs, and Credit Suisse. I didn't have the corporate gene—that much I knew from my encounters with authority—but I had trouble seeing how to make ends meet. As an English major, with a focus in postmodern literature, my skills were limited, at best. I moved to Austin, Texas, then my childhood room in South Florida. I tried applying for jobs in publishing, journalism, education, and advertising. I left my résumé at restaurants, bookstores, and bars. I picked up some part-time work in copyediting and graphic design. After eighteen months of interviews and economic ruin, I was hired by an environmental nonprofit in Boston, as a grant writer. I lived in Central Square, in Cambridge, with roommates. I took the Red Line to an office job five days a week. I couldn't say it was the life that I'd imagined for myself. But then, how many people had a job that they enjoyed?

I learned that grant writing was easy: less writing than cutting and pasting paragraphs and spreadsheets. It only took a few hours to assemble a proposal or report from what you had on file, and there were only so many places you could apply. Once it was in the mail, I was free to do as I pleased. I was lucky: there weren't forty hours' worth of work to do, or even ten. To some extent, it was like this for lots of us who had low-power office jobs. Some passed the time by sending emails or instant messages on the clock; some worked on passion projects, rabbit holes, or side hustles. I spent my days reading music blogs and message boards, toggling between tabs and browsers. We were the young and bored at work. Our numbers were legion.

In the spring of 2004, I saw a listing for a grant-writing position in New York. I had misgivings: the job was with a vast nonprofit, with thousands of employees nationwide. Its mission was ambiguous ("empowering communities"); the work involved applying to a byzantine bureaucracy of city, state, and federal government agencies. Nevertheless, it was a ticket to New York. I bought a twenty-dollar seat on the Chinatown bus and interviewed in early June. I found a place in Carroll Gardens, Brooklyn, that July, just four weeks before the GOP's convention.

* * *

The morning after the election was overcast in New York. It was November 3rd, a Wednesday, which meant you had to go into work, or call in sick—a more appropriate response. The president had won decisively. It was my first experience of overwhelming shame as an American. It would soon be second nature.

I had spent the night before at a party that turned from merriment and cautious hope to all-consuming despair. I remembered the president's speech in August. "This is the everlasting dream of America—and tonight, in this place, that dream is renewed." Confounded, I took the subway back to Brooklyn. A man at Fifty-Seventh Street was openly weeping. It was hard to comprehend that over sixty million adults had voted for a second term, recommitting to the quagmire in Iraq. Even after countless dead, even after Abu Ghraib, America had stayed the course. Were we living in the same universe?

To those of us who had voted for change—who were embarrassed by the ignorance, mendacity, and incompetence of the Bush White House, who told themselves the electorate might be fooled once, but not twice, it was a disenchanting wake-up call. To vote for Bush in 2000 was one thing, when the alternative was the anemic Al Gore; to grant him four more years of mayhem was another thing entirely. For those who had believed in the essential decency of the American people, it felt as though we were exiles in our own country, as though the masks were coming off. Was this the nation we had lived in all along?

A month after the second inaugural address, in February, an article appeared in *The Sunday Times* of London. "I was visiting New York last week and noticed something I'd never thought I'd say about the city," the columnist Andrew Sullivan began. "It was quieter."

> There were little white wires hanging down from their ears, or tucked into pockets, purses or jackets. The eyes were a little vacant. Each was in his or her own musical world, walking to their soundtrack, stars in their own music video, almost oblivious to the world around them. These are the iPod people.

Around the end of 2004, I saw a listing for a dream position: a grant-writing job at Lincoln Center. I sent a résumé and got an interview. I took the train to Fifty-Ninth Street and walked up Broadway. I saw the Metropolitan Opera House, the fountain, and the Juilliard School. I rode the escalator up to the second level of Lincoln Center, overlooking the plaza. The opening was with the Chamber Music Society, a term I had to Google before the interview. When I was offered the job, and gave my notice at the large nonprofit, my supervisor didn't seem surprised.

He said, "I wondered when you'd come to your senses." I started work
in January of 2005.

* * *

On a good day, it was forty-five minutes, door to door, and double that
on shitty days. It wasn't long before you memorized the entrances and
where to board the train. You came to recognize the people on your
route. There were the assistants in their twenties reading novels, the
older couples sharing the *Times*, the men in Yankees caps, studying
the *Post*. There were the parents and the kids with lunch boxes. There
were receptionists, executives, and middle managers in tennis shoes.
There were a lot of iPods and BlackBerries. The smell of coffee, nico-
tine, and perfume filled your nose. There was a tacit choreography and
protocol. The trains were always full.

The Chamber Music Society was on the tenth floor of a building at
Sixty-Fifth and Amsterdam; the top thirteen stories were Juilliard student housing. You shared the elevator with aspiring musicians, actors,
and ballerinas in their tutus. From the street, it wasn't all that clear how
you were supposed to enter—up a hidden stairwell, to the mezzanine,
through security—a fitting metaphor for the castle-like complex, prior
to its Bloomberg-era makeover. With its arresting scale, its gray façade,
its travertine marble plaza, it was a set from European cinema, a citadel,
a monument to music and the arts.

I felt preposterously blessed. I didn't know that I was eating lunch
where there was once a neighborhood called San Juan Hill. I didn't
know that 7,000 families had been displaced by Robert Moses in the
'50s—mostly black and Puerto Rican—under the banner of "urban
renewal." I didn't know that the place I so proudly worked in was a mau-
soleum of sorts, and one that meant the erasure of a neighborhood; I
saw what I wanted to see. We were across the street from the New York
Philharmonic and the New York City Ballet. We were a minute from the
Library for the Performing Arts, close to Central Park, and up the block

from Carnegie Hall. It was easy getting out of bed every day; it was hard to be cynical about a place like that.

By raising money for an arts nonprofit—for chamber music (small ensembles), and art in schools—I thought I had escaped the fate of friends who had jobs in finance. While they were calculating assets, earnings, and return on investment, I was writing grants for string quartets; while they were serving corporate America, my shareholders were Bach, Beethoven, and Brahms. I thought I had a job where I could do a tiny bit of good, if only for the length of a concert—or at least do no harm. I thought I had a job where I could have a clear conscience. I had a lot to learn.

The calendar was bracketed by two major events—the season kick-off in the fall, and a big spring gala—from which a third of our budget derived. The rest of the time we spent soliciting rich people. There were the cultivation nights in galleries, auction houses, and mansions on Fifth Avenue. There were the monthly board meetings, where catering was served on fine china. There was a toast at intermission in the patrons' lounge with warm white wine and finger food. There was a multimillion-dollar capital campaign.

It was a time of almost feudal regard for the affluent. The best and brightest flocked to private equity, consulting, and hedge funds. The mayor was one of forty billionaires in town. Names like Sackler, Koch, Bass, Weill, Perelman, Kravis, Langone, Lauder, and Tisch adorned the walls of hospitals, concert halls, museums, and universities—an elevated form of money laundering. Nonprofits vied for tax-deductible contributions from the brass of Goldman Sachs, Bear Stearns, and Lehman Brothers. An estimated $900 million were raised for phase one alone of Lincoln Center's renovation. Silent auctions, charity galas, and high society had its own page in the *Times*. On Central Park West, apartments were on sale for $80 million. The *Michelin Guide* came to New York, listing 500 restaurants in Manhattan, and two in Brooklyn. The cultural phenomenon of the moment was *The Apprentice*, starring Donald Trump, whose season-end finale was broadcast live from Lincoln Center.

The overall artistic heads at the Chamber Music Society were a married couple. She was a pianist and a pedagogue; he was the cellist of a leading string quartet. As a duo, they played the major concert halls of Asia, Europe, and everywhere else. With help from wealthy friends in tech, they had started a festival in Silicon Valley. They lived among his many Grammys in a classic six on the Upper West Side. *The New York Times* called them chamber music's power couple. They always walked in pulling suitcases; their office would sit empty for weeks at a time.

Reporting to the husband and wife was Norma, the executive director, a tall and elegant woman in her fifties, who had trained as a pianist. Her bookshelf had biographies of Beethoven; her desk had piles of promotional CDs; her office had an upright and a view of the Hudson. She oversaw a staff of twenty—marketing, fundraising, education, production, artistic—and the personalities involved. She stroked the egos of the husband and wife, and the patrons, and the board; she answered for the budget and projected earnings, expenses, and deficits. Her face was kind, and pale, and serious; her hair was silver-gray. My first week at work, she offered me her ticket to a piano recital at Carnegie Hall.

The people in the office were either in their fifties, with children, or a lot like me: recent graduates and transplants, who lived in studios and walk-ups in Brooklyn or Queens. They had roommates, landlords, and student debt; we all had moved from somewhere else. Desmond was from Alabama and a gentle giant; Jihyun was a cellist from Korea who had studied at Juilliard; Jara was from Ohio and arranged the kids' concerts. For most of us, it was our first or second taste of postcollegiate office life, our first or second glimpse of gainful employment, in all of its anticlimax.

Bizarrely, however, there was little in the way of actual work, at least as far as grant writing. There were twenty institutions giving us up to $350,000 a year; once you had a foot in the door, the grants were practically assured. Each day I spent an hour or two assembling annual requests to foundations (Rockefeller), corporations (MetLife), and government (NEA). This left me with at least thirty hours a week to fill. As long as I met my deadlines, my supervisor's leash was long. I frequented the library; I sat in on rehearsals; I went for long walks in the park. The offices were deserted in the summer; the season ran from October to May.

I made a few good friends. Maureen and Drew were both my age, and both of Irish Catholic stock. They were the Sid and Nancy of chamber music. Maureen was from New Jersey; she always had a knowing grin, as if she had just heard something saucy, possibly about yourself. Drew was from L.A. He lived in Brooklyn with his girlfriend, TJ, a chef; he passed away when he was forty-three. My other friend was Valerie— Drew's boss—a forty-something former flutist and native of Illinois. She was intense and taciturn, meticulous and Zen. She had a leather jacket, owned a motorcycle, smoked Parliament Lights, and hipped me to her weed dealer.

The days were long and leisurely. You had to be at work by nine and there until five, but no one kept track or monitored time off. You went to lunch however long you pleased. You were on the honor system. We gossiped by the copier. We stared into computer screens and sat beneath fluorescent bulbs. The dress was casual. The stakes were small. Unless it was a special circumstance, you weren't even expected at the concerts; after all, they started late. By 5:05, the office was silent. Most of my coworkers dashed for the train, their kids, and families, but I was in no rush. I went to everything from Sunday matinees to school concerts, from baroque to modern. To my surprise, I learned I like chamber music—the nerdier, the better—Beethoven quartets, Mozart sonatas, Haydn trios, Bach on the piano. Who knew? I'd always just assumed they were for old ladies. At times, it sounded like the ambient and instrumental side of Sigur Rós, a band I'd followed since college. I started wondering why almost everyone at Alice Tully Hall had silver hair and hearing aids, and how the people that I saw at Sigur Rós's shows could be enticed.

It wasn't just a mental exercise. The crisis was acute: the audience—if not the art itself—was dying out. In cities large and small, orchestras were filing for bankruptcy. Subscriptions and attendance were both on the wane; the average ticket buyer was over sixty. Where exhibits at the Metropolitan Museum drew record crowds, Americans, at best, were cool to classical music: a genre beloved by eggheads, elites, and serial killers. The days of Leonard Bernstein's concerts on CBS were as remote as Mozart. In Washington, D.C., as an experiment, the violinist Joshua Bell played in a subway station at rush hour. A reporter counted: seven people stopped to listen. In public schools, the arts were underfunded if they existed at all. Where donors and philanthropists had long supported local orchestras, they now were shifting their priorities to conservation, social services, and public health. The ones that did support the arts were sometimes controversial: a member of the Metropolitan Opera board had pledged $25 million, only to be arrested for money laundering and fraud. We weren't asking if our work was subsidized by plutocrats; we simply wanted a piece of the pie.

One evening at work, I knocked on Valerie's door. She waved me in. I was writing a proposal for a new grant fund, set up by the state attorney general, Eliot Spitzer, funded through settlements with the record industry over bribes to radio programmers, or payola. Her desk was piled with CDs, spreadsheets, and scores. She walked me through the numbers for the proposal. It was close to quitting time. Before I stood to go, I asked her something I'd been mulling over since I saw Do Make Say Think—an eight-piece group from Toronto with bass, guitar, and drums, but also violin, saxophone, and trumpet.

"Dumb question," I said. "What does 'chamber music' mean?"

She narrowed her eyes in mock suspicion.

I said, "I know the dictionary definition: music played by smaller ensembles, for a small audience."

"That's right," she said.

"So if a string quartet played at a club, is that chamber music?"

"Of course it is," she said. "Matt Haimovitz did that."

"But what about a smaller group that has guitars?" I asked. "Isn't Radiohead kind of a chamber-music group?"

She said, "Radiohead?"

"Or, you know, John Coltrane," I said. "Why isn't he chamber music? Or is he?"

She paused to think.

"Is it because they're playing in a club?" I asked. "Or does it have more to do with the audience?"

* * *

In 2006, I pitched a series where musicians from the worlds of indie rock and electronic music shared a stage with piano trios, string quartets, percussionists and so on. Using my grant-writing skills—and my abundant free time—I drafted a proposal. I argued that the Lincoln Centers of the world had overlooked an audience of young and highly motivated listeners. I said that there were people in their twenties who were devotees of instrumental music, ambient, and post-rock—chamber music by another name. I said that there were concerts at Bowery Ballroom where people stood in reverent silence, quieter than Carnegie Hall. I made a list of names from Andrew Bird to Yo La Tengo, and paired them with composers from Bach to Arvo Pärt. I knew to have a budget and marketing plan. Norma helped me get a meeting with the husband and wife.

The cellist said, "What is *Brooklyn Vegan*?"

The pianist said, "How much time did you spend on this?"

The cellist said, "You're telling me that somebody who listens to [he checked the page] the Radioheads will suddenly have the capacity for Bartók?"

The pianist said, "Who asked you to do this?"

"Sorry," I said. "Capacity?"

* * *

In late 2006, with lots of help, I organized a concert at a church on Sixty-Sixth and Amsterdam, which I had learned about from Valerie—and then a second show, and then a third. I wasn't motivated by the thought of a career: I just needed to break even.

The concerts were didactic in nature. There was an arrangement of *The Rite of Spring* before Deerhoof; The Mountain Goats requested Schubert; The Books had the composer Timo Andres playing Ives. I was led by the belief that anyone who liked Stereolab would also like Stravinsky, that there were connections to be revealed between seemingly dissimilar sounds. Whatever kind of music I was into at the time— polyphony, post-rock, ambient, minimalism—I offered it in concert, trusting the audience to make the inference. There were no lectures, no formality: only music. The word "impresario" had yet to enter my vocabulary, but that's what I became. I called the series Wordless Music: a name intended to suggest a continuity between contemporary and classical. Lots of people got confused and called it Worldless; they still do.

In the ensuing months, it won a following, limited but loyal. What surprised me was the makeup of the audience. I had expected a few musicians, some students, people who read *Pitchfork*, or anyone who went out in Brooklyn—the usual suspects. But out of nowhere, it seemed, there were a few older people in the crowd; thank-you emails from a sixty-something accountant, a retiree, a widower; and simply curious New Yorkers who had seen a listing in *Time Out* and figured what the hell. There was an article by Alex Ross in *The New Yorker* where the shows received outrageously high praise. In turn, this led to my working with musicians I had long admired from afar. In the first two years, we did shows with Explosions in the Sky, Stars of the Lid, Do Make Say Think, Andrew Bird, Colleen, Amiina, Nico Muhly, Glenn Kotche, Nels Cline, Eluvium, Hauschka, Polmo Polpo, Múm, and Sigur Rós. I did the first headlining shows in New York for Flying Lotus, Max Richter, Julia Holter, and Jóhann Jóhannsson. A show I booked with Grizzly Bear in 2007 (where Paul Simon introduced himself backstage, and the band encored with "Graceland") was named the year's best by *Stereogum*, whatever that's worth. Of all the work in which I have ever been engaged, it was the concert series that meant the most. In due time, it would bring me to Carnegie Hall, Madison Square Garden, the Sydney Opera House, and—yes—Lincoln Center; to work with Terrence Malick, Jonny Greenwood, and Paul Thomas Anderson; and shows with Neutral Milk Hotel, Broadcast, and Spiritualized; but that's a different book. I spent my days behind a desk on Sixty-Fifth and Amsterdam—but more and more, I was going out at night in Brooklyn.

Oneida (*The Wedding*)

In his second year at Yale, in 1833, American theologian John Humphrey Noyes had a startling insight. From his readings on the second coming of Christ, Noyes became convinced it had already occurred: to be precise, in 70 AD. This meant that humankind could find salvation in this world and not the afterlife. He spent the next few years developing his ideas on religion, economics, marriage, and communal living. In 1847, Noyes was indicted for "adulterous fornication" and fled with several followers to upstate New York. The Oneida community, as it came to be known, was a utopian experiment. The members lived together, practiced mutual criticism, and were expected to contribute according to their ability. A hundred fifty years later, a group of young musicians took those same principles—salvation, community, experiment, utopia—and formed a band called Oneida.

* * *

Oneida is an easy band to take for granted. They started in 1997, when *Titanic* was in theaters, and they're still going strong thirty years later. If Interpol was the archetypal Manhattan band, aloof and debonair, Oneida was the avatar of Brooklyn DIY, naïve, industrious, and self-sabotaging.

Their songs could stretch the better part of an hour. Their shows bore little resemblance to the records. They specialized in marathon performances that went as long as twelve hours. They liked to open with a piece that had a single note and a duration of fourteen minutes. Their gigs were rituals of psychedelic light, endurance, and states of transport; no two sets were alike.

You always saw the same people at an Oneida show: musicians, more often than not. Onstage, the band was nondescript, in faded shirts, shorts, and glasses; if they looked like they taught middle school, it's because one of them did. They made an album every year, or just about: ten alone by 2009, and, as of this writing, twenty-plus LPs, EPs, and live recordings. But most of all, Oneida and their friends established a community—the one that history would come to know as Brooklyn DIY.

* * *

When John Colpitts moved to Brooklyn, in 1996, there was little in the way of a scene, at least as far as indie rock. "It was the typical Manhattan patronizing attitude," he said. "This will be hard for people to accept today, but Brooklyn rock music was considered a joke." If you weren't born there, you didn't say you lived in Brooklyn; you said you lived in New York. When Oneida called themselves a Brooklyn band in 1997, they were being contrarian, like repping Delaware. "And it got laughs. People found it absurd. That doesn't mean it was right, but that was the perspective: Brooklyn did not really exist culturally." In a borough that had already produced myriad musical legends—The Notorious B.I.G., Jay-Z, Black Star—it was an arrogant myopia that would pervade the scene to come, if one with a degree of truth for bands. The eyes and ears of critics were planted in Manhattan; outside the East Village, venues were few and far between. As late as 2001 in Brooklyn, John says, "there was nowhere to play. If you played there it was DIY or the terrible bar in Williamsburg called The Charleston," an ancient dive with little charm and a cantankerous bartender; it's still around.

Not that Manhattan was much better. While the '90s had brought a
wealth of house, jazz, and hip hop luminaries, New York's rock scene was
"largely incoherent and nationally insignificant," in the words of writer Jesse
Rifkin. "Nobody was thinking New York was going to be the next Seattle,"
said LCD Soundsystem's James Murphy. The biggest bands were Girls
Against Boys, Skeleton Key, and Jonathan Fire*Eater. The hottest trend
in town was "illbient," the briefly faddish fusion of ambient and hip hop,
adored by galleries and arts institutions, where listeners sat and nodded
gravely. Downtown, Tonic, Roulette, and the Knitting Factory were known
for their adventurous programming, but open slots were at a premium.
In Montreal, Bristol, and Chicago, cerebral outfits such as Godspeed You!
Black Emperor, Portishead, and Tortoise were fusing chamber music, electronics, dub, jazz, and found sound. More broadly, "intelligent" dance music
and underground hip hop were ascendant; guitars were all but obsolete.
It's not that there weren't venues in the city for rock music, but that they
were demeaning, cynical, and crass. "Back then, in Manhattan, you could
play these terrible showcases at somewhere like CBGB, or find yourself
on an eight-band bill at someplace like The Spiral, which was pointless,"
John said. Or you could buy a keg of beer and fill an empty warehouse,
factory, parking lot, or alleyway in Williamsburg with other transplants,
amateurs, and eccentrics, charging two bucks at the door.

"We were definitely out of step," John recalled. "We were into glam
rock . . . We dressed up before every show in the earliest days." To empha-
size the fundamental cheesiness of playing rock music—and the disparity
between their on- and offstage lives—they gave themselves codenames.
Behind the kit, John Colpitts became Kid Millions; singer and guitarist
Pat Sullivan, Papa Crazee. On keys was Bobby Matador, a.k.a. Fat Bobby,
known to his family as Robertson Thacher. And multi-instrumentalist
Frank Wells was Hanoi Jane. The lineup would record four full-length
albums in their first five years.

From a dire necessity—because no one else would book them—Oneida
and their circle forged a scene in Williamsburg. John would later write:
"We wanted to play shows in front of people, so we had to will something

to happen." They met the owners of a basement space called Rubulad, on South Fifth Street, which hosted rent parties. They met the founders of the pirate radio station and performance space free103point9. They met the Good/Bad Art Collective, a group of Dadaists from Denton, Texas. Their most significant relationship, though, was with the holy fools behind Mighty Robot (a multipurpose art space on Wythe) and The Twisted Ones (a DIY promoter): John Fitzgerald ("Fitz"), Artur Arbit, Etain Fitzpatrick, and Erik Zajaceskowski. The Twisted Ones had produced a show with Acid Mothers Temple, Sightings, and Oneida just a few days after 9/11. They had booked the Yeah Yeah Yeahs, Oneida, and the Liars in a parking lot in 2002. "It was powered by a cable that we ran from Mighty Robot, down the stairs, across the street that cars were driving up and down, and we put the carpet from the living room on top of it and taped the carpet to the road, and there were 2,000 people in the carpark, and about 1,000 people watching from the Williamsburg Bridge," Fitz says. "We built this community of people through these amazingly random connections. Meeting a band. Going to see them. There's some DJ playing. Talking to the DJ. He happens to be on WFMU. And then they start to talk about the shows that we were putting on in Brooklyn on the radio. There was a lot of that, I'd say, between '97 and 2002."

The Twisted Ones were instrumental in the growth of nontraditional venues: foundries, lofts, and Polish meeting halls. "It was someone who was like, 'Dude, I've got this space. Come by,'" says Hanoi Jane. "We're like, 'This is insane. We're gonna do a show here.' This is what was happening in pockets all over. We'd seen this in Winston-Salem. We'd seen this in Denton. 'There's a place in New York that we're gonna pull off having shows?' That's how that whole scene was like. There's more music than there is space for it. People that had the keys to venues didn't necessarily want to host you. But there were people that want to see you play, so you had to find the spaces to give them a chance."

"I think Fitz saw all this empty space, and he was always hustling in that way—finding a new place and finding bands," says John. "I mean, he knew stuff before anyone. This is the thing: The Twisted Ones—they were *psyched*. They were partiers, you know? It was a party scene." "They were like us," Bobby Matador says. "They were weirdos who were like, 'Let's do what we want in these spaces,' because nobody cared. We were making unholy noise, and we were having parties, and people were like, 'Oh, you can do this here.' It became a kinship."

What many came to know as indie rock in Williamsburg was shaped by Fitz, Oneida, and their peers, but it was slow at first. "They ended up the big-brother band to a lot of us that came to Brooklyn in 1999 or so," says Parts & Labor's Dan Friel. "It felt like they were there two years before all these other bands that got really big, and showed the way for playing warehouse spaces in Brooklyn, building your own community, and generally not giving a fuck."

* * *

Their first apartment and rehearsal space was a nightclub in Clinton Hill. The club had closed its doors a few years earlier, after "some kind of shootout or robbery," and was left in a state of ruin. They shared it with a fundamentalist Christian who planned to open a community center; he had painted "Remember the Blood" in the entryway. For 1,700 square feet, the rent was $300 a month. They asked themselves: "Shit, can we afford this?" The building was a couple blocks from where Biggie Smalls had grown up. He had just been shot and killed, at the age of twenty-four. "People talked about him a lot," says John. Five abandoned homes sat on their street alone. At the time, people were dumping crates of unused vinyl. John took them home, and that was how they learned about Afrika Bambaataa. The person cleaning out the club called it El Shaddai's, where Kid and Crazee wrote much of their debut. Released by Turnbuckle, an indie label in New York, *A Place Called El Shaddai's* (1997) only hinted at the albums to come. Oneida started getting good once Jane and Bobby joined later that year.

In the fall of 1997, they toured the U.S. for almost three months. It was a different epoch in the music business. Times were flush: the album leak, the MP3, and the effects of peer-to-peer were still to come; the sale of compact discs was at an apogee; the record industry had capital to burn. Oneida's label paid them salaries to tour, engaged a European publicist, and even fronted them a van. The only thing it didn't do was help them find an audience. In Bloomington, Indiana, they played for seven people in a basement; battling boredom or frustration, Crazee played completely naked. Despite the publicist on payroll, the tour yielded one review: a single paragraph in a free alt-weekly. It was far from a rave. Nevertheless, it felt like a triumph.

For their second album, *Enemy Hogs* (1999), Turnbuckle paid for multiple photographers and critics from the U.K. to visit New York. It was a tactic used a decade earlier by Seattle's flagship indie, Sub Pop, when they had wined and dined the writer Everett True, resulting in a priceless cover story on the label for *Melody Maker*. Much like Sub Pop—who impishly invented the idea of the "Seattle scene" as a publicity stunt—Oneida spun a loosely truthful tale of an emerging circuit in Brooklyn. "The journalists were pretty cynical," says John. "But we made sure they left convinced. We crafted a narrative for them." If anything, they jumped the gun: it took until 2001 before the music press discovered Brooklyn—at which point, Oneida was on their fifth album.

In many ways, their biggest sin was one of unlucky timing. In 1999, with little warning, Turnbuckle folded. The band would have a long relationship with Bloomington's Jagjaguwar—the future home of Bon Iver, but then a fledgling start-up. "Every record was a mess," John said. "They would release it, and there would be some mistake. You know, with Jagjaguwar—I mean, God bless them, but—in the beginning, it would be like, 'There was a mix-up with the distributor. So that EP you guys put out, I'm not sure it's gonna be available anywhere.' At the time, we were just cranking. So we were like, 'Well, we'll get the next one.'"

Their follow-up needed little explanation: *Come on Everybody Let's Rock* (2000), a tongue-in-cheek salute to the guitar, and one that would just barely miss the coming resurgence of rock on the Lower East Side. Released on September 17, 2001, *Anthem of the Moon* was overshadowed by events small and big: the Liars' near-concurrent *They Threw Us All in a Trench and Stuck a Monument on Top*, which won an instant following, and the departure of Crazee, the band's guitarist, cofounder, and front man. His last recording with the band, *Each One Teach One* (2002), came out via Doug Mosurock's Version City label as an elaborate double gatefold LP, a full five years before the rebirth of vinyl. Propelled by the fourteen-minute "Sheets of Easter"—a masterpiece of minimalism—it was at once the band's artistic peak and critical breakthrough.

Depending, that is, on whom you asked. To say they weren't for everyone would be an understatement. To scuttle any hint of moderation, they opened every show with "Sheets of Easter"—whose lyrics went, "You've got to look into the light light light light light light light," ad infinitum—equal parts Philip Glass and My Bloody Valentine. To some, it was a mystical experience, akin to altered states, ecstatic chant and reverie; to some, it was a quarter hour of punishment. In Chattanooga, Jane recalled, they played for twenty scary dudes with a wild look in their eyes. "I remember them stomping around the room thinking we were saying 'die, die, die.' These crazy old hillbilly men going 'die, die.'" In Baltimore, they played an emo matinee. "It was a packed room, so no one could get away from the stage," Bobby said. "It was amazing for us to have this single thing that we were doing, and some people are reacting as if this is the most antagonistic, perverse thing imaginable that a band could do."

Each One Teach One was euphorically received. "A fully formed, mostly instrumental psych masterpiece by a quartet at the peak of its game," said *Magnet*. "Some of the most inspired psychedelic mayhem this side of Acid Mothers Temple or Butthole Surfers," said *Mojo*. Along with albums by Bruce Springsteen, Wilco, and Beth Orton, it had been named among the year's top ten by *The New York Times*. In Italy, the band was on the cover of a music magazine, *Blow Up*. "People recognized me on the street in Naples," John wrote, "and if you've ever been to Naples, you know that might not be a great thing. But it was a great thing for us. We got a taste of adoration, and it was really fun." Former tour manager and Jagjaguwar co-owner Jonathan Cargill says, "I think it was in Rome, opening for Cat Power. So maybe not the right crowd to do a twenty-four-minute 'Sheets of Easter.' I thought it was incredible. I'm like, 'This is what it's all about. This is an event. This is an aesthetic happening that people are witnessing.'"

Meanwhile, the scene Oneida had predicted half in jest was now a reality—and the local press was taking note. It was the year of *Beaches & Canyons*, by Black Dice; *Citizens of the Universe*, by USAISAMONSTER; and Sightings' self-titled debut. "Unlike in years past, the center of this perfect-storm convergence of New York acts is Brooklyn," wrote *New York*'s Ethan Brown in April 2002. "In the last year, a musical beachhead has established itself in Williamsburg and other Brooklyn neighborhoods," the *Times* wrote in August: "New clubs like Northsix, Club Luxx, Warsaw and Southpaw are starting to supplant those in Lower Manhattan as rock hothouses." And in September, the Liars were on the cover of *New York* magazine. For all the critical acclaim of *Each One Teach One*, compared to their contemporaries, Oneida was an afterthought.

"It felt like this ravenous spotlight had shone down on this scene and missed us," John says. "You have all these fantasies about what you're doing. You think there's some goal of success, or of making a living, but you don't know what that looks like. It was hard to be in that moment and feel like we were battling indifference. Then to be like, 'Wait a minute. We've been here this whole time. This is our fifth record.' The only thing to do was just keep slogging away, which is what we did."

With Crazee departing for the band Oakley Hall, Oneida's future was suddenly in question. "It was gut-wrenching," Jane recalls. "I took it personally. I was heartbroken and furious. We had been working toward collectively financing our first new van. We were so sick of blowing out transmissions and having the bottom fall out of vans and worrying if we're going to get over the Rockies for the thirtieth time, if the van will handle it. This was our first grown-up choice. This was like marriage. Because we are not wealthy people. We were going to have car payments, and we were weighing that with how much it made sense to tour. Stepping up our touring. Doubling down. Like, 'It's Oneida time. Let's lean into this.' I'd only taken jobs that agreed they would give me the time off to tour, and if they wouldn't, I would decline. We were about to say yes, and start customizing the van, and Crazee was like, 'I need to talk to you guys.'"

"It's like we were back to square one," John says. "It was a shock for all of us, because he's, like—I don't want to diminish anyone in the band, because they're all brilliant—but Crazee had something else. He's got a great voice. He's a great performer, great songwriter. So when he quit, it felt like, 'I wasted the last five years.' Jane went back to school. Bobby started considering other careers."

"The first instinct was to fill the space that Pat left behind," Bobby says. And then they wondered what their music would sound like if they didn't. "I started to realize that the less I played, the more I leaned into the minimalism and repetition—if I actually go the other direction and minimize, it creates space. So there's this moment of real aesthetic change where we had to figure out that we didn't need to fill the space. In fact, we could do something really different."

* * *

By 2004, Mighty Robot's neighbors on Wythe Avenue were filing noise complaints. The Twisted Ones had relocated to Berlin. Their mantle was inherited by a young and entrepreneurial promoter named Todd Patrick— known as Todd P—who had arrived from Texas (by way of Portland, Oregon) in 2001. He rapidly became synonymous with economical, out-of-the-way, all-ages shows, but on a scale that dwarfed The Twisted Ones, for better and for worse. He had a gift for finding artists long before they rose to fame; he could have been a highly paid A&R man. He booked some of the earliest appearances by Animal Collective, TV on the Radio, Dirty Projectors, Matt and Kim, Dan Deacon, Deerhunter, and Real Estate. He had more than a few critics—for his undisguised ambition, but also for the treatment of his staff, who often would be underpaid, if they were paid at all. At the same time, he mentored countless young promoters such as Ric Leichtung (285 Kent), Joe Ahearn (Silent Barn), and Edan Wilber (Death by Audio). "There was a need for what he did," says John. "He filled the need."

Also in 2004, Erik Zajaceskowski and his friend Karl LaRocca signed a lease for a two-story, 15,000-square-foot factory at 270 Kent Avenue. They named it Monster Island. It housed a screenprinter (Kayrock), a gallery (Live With Animals), an all-purpose art space (Secret Project Robot), and a music venue (Monster Island Basement). Along with Erik's partner, Rachel Nelson, they organized installations, group shows, and annual acoustic block parties, in every part of the building and on the sidewalk. It was also where Oneida and their friends in Pterodactyl, Company, and Ex-Models were invited to create a rehearsal space and studio they called the Ocropolis. "It was Erik, Rachel, and Kayrock's way of helping us be part of the Monster Island community," says Jane. John says, "People chipped in labor for free studio time. It took months, but was kind of like a community barn raising."

In May 2005, Oneida put out their finest album yet: *The Wedding*, a virtuosic set of chamber pop, comprising thirteen tracks of tape delays ("High Life"), exotic instruments ("Run Through My Hair"), Sabbath-style stoner rock ("Did I Die"), forlorn ballads ("Know"), and rousing string arrangements ("You're Drifting," "The Eiger"). It was far and away their most accessible LP, foreshadowing a time where it was unremarkable to see an indie band performing with a chamber orchestra, as Oneida did for *The Wedding* at The Kitchen in Chelsea. Not that many noticed. "Another year passes, and another brilliant Oneida album fails to make its mark on history," went a review. It was a year of several major albums for Jagjaguwar and its sister company Secretly Canadian—Anohni and the Johnsons' *I Am a Bird Now*, Okkervil River's *Black Sheep Boy*, and Black Mountain's self-titled debut—all of which eclipsed Oneida, once again.

"I thought it would blow everyone's minds when it was released," says John. "It never did. But that's okay. Rough Trade didn't like it.

Jagjaguwar probably didn't do much with it . . . We were listening to
The Left Banke, The Zombies. We wanted to make a chamber rock/pop
album. That was the concept. My childhood friend Brian Coughlin did the
string arrangements. I cried singing 'Know' in the studio. It was a really
devastating, lonely time for me." They made the album with producers
Barry London (who would later join the band) and Nicolas Vernhes (who
would record with Animal Collective, Dirty Projectors, and Spoon). "We
worked with people before they became famous," says John. "That's the
story of Oneida."

* * *

Oneida never quit. They marked their ten-year anniversary at MoMA
PS1 with their pals in Dirty Faces, Sightings, and Ex-Models. They
made their *Moby-Dick*—a trilogy entitled *Thank Your Parents: Preteen
Weaponry* (2008), *Rated O* (2009), and *Absolute II* (2011). They shared
a stage with Portishead, The Flaming Lips, and Yo La Tengo. "We arrived
in the middle of the opening band, Oneida," one reviewer wrote. "Dear
God, my ears . . . that is all I was thinking. I was not alone as I noticed
around me, similar scrunched faces of those with confused and hurting
ears . . . Who picks these bands?"

In 2011, Monster Island's lease was up; Oneida played the grand farewell. Erik Zajaceskowski and Rachel Nelson found a space in Bushwick,
where they spent the next five years before their rent was raised by half.
"It's mundane and it's easy to get exhausted by it all," John wrote. "Rachel
and Erik have been martyrs to the cause of DIY for most of their lives
in New York . . . They got no respect. They made no money. Their every
non-working hour was spent making these spaces work. They did it all
for the scene. Everything! It's wild what they accomplished."

"Erik and Rachel are saints," says Bobby. "Because they were doing
something that they know is not going to be recognized, and is not
going to be monetizable on a big scale: spending your life to create not
a counterculture, but a subculture. Counterculture has incredible value,

because of how it shapes what comes next, and shapes the overarching culture right when the forces are in opposition. Subculture can have a much longer arc, and much more inherent value. The ambition is purely about community and culture. And the sacrifice of energy is extraordinary." The same could be said for Oneida, who persevere despite their ages and the odds, thirty years on.

"We were able to weather it," says John. "There were these really key moments. We were playing at a venue in Memphis. Nobody was there. The promoter was like, 'You guys don't have to play,' and it was like, 'We're gonna play. We always play.' At one point, Bobby was upset because we'd be talking about how we weren't that good. Bobby was like, 'No. We are *the best band in the world*. We are *the best*.' And I was like, 'Wow. He believes that we are.' I mean, this guy, who, like—he knows so much about music. I'm in awe, and I'm just lucky. I'm just so lucky that he's in my life."

"I've always likened Oneida to the Seattle grunge scene," observes Jonathan Cargill of Jagjaguwar. "They were kind of the Mudhoney. They're the grandfathers. They were the linchpin. Both for us the record label, but also for that whole Brooklyn scene. They were the cornerstone— the difference being that Mudhoney became a much more popular band than Oneida ever did. To me, a testament to their success is that they're still a band. All the other bands that were blowing up back then are no longer around. I think that it's its own form of success. And they're still really good friends, and just really good people, and making really good art. Maybe time will tell. But that catalog just keeps getting bigger and bigger. And how many bands can say that?"

Noémie Lafrance

A spiral staircase in a criminal courthouse; a five-story municipal garage; a fort on Governors Island; a mound of salt by the Manhattan Bridge; an undulating roof by Frank Gehry; and an abandoned swimming pool in Williamsburg. For much of her career as a choreographer, Noémie Lafrance made every inch of her adopted city a performance space. Where most saw merely infrastructure—unloved and mundane—she saw the makings of a stage, a dance, a place to congregate. Where most saw only roadblocks and red tape, she was unwavering, resourceful, and possessed: in other words, a New Yorker.

Born in Rivière-du-Loup, two hours north of Quebec, she went to school in Ottawa and Montreal. She showed an early skill for making things. "I always liked sewing," Noémie says. "Since I was seven years old, I used to sew clothes for my dolls, and for myself." She studied dance and visual art as a teenager. "I wanted to be like Madonna," she said, "and I discovered dance was something I really loved." She had an influential instructor at an art school. "He was doing what he called 'environmental dances.' It was using different aspects of the architecture of the school . . . I think the site-specific vision came from that experience." She learned the history of modern dance: Yvonne Rainer, Trisha Brown, Martha Graham. She moved from Montreal to the Lower East Side in 1994, the year that Giuliani took the oath of office as mayor of New York, and squatters in Tompkins Square Park hurled bottles at police.

"I left when I was twenty years old to study at the [Martha] Graham School," Noémie says, "and I just stayed." She moved into a squat in Alphabet City called Serenity House. "We didn't pay any rent. All we paid was the phone, twenty bucks a month. There was a whole community. We had free electricity. Someone would go into a manhole and connect the power . . . I only stayed about six months, but it felt a lot longer in my life history." She found herself a massive loft among the former factories of Williamsburg. "I told my friend at the Graham School: 'You know what? We're going to move to a place in Williamsburg, and we're going to have our own dance studio.' We found a space and fixed it up. And I was twenty, twenty-one."

The Graham technique was physically demanding, formal, and conceptual. Noémie says, "Martha Graham's work is very heroic and inspired by Greek mythology, very dramatic, and very intense." Noémie started making her own dancewear for her classes at the school. "You need a special machine to work with stretchy fabric. I kind of taught myself. I had this machine and I started making unitards. And then people in the dressing room were like, 'Would you make me one?' I would go to the fabric store and bring in different samples, and people were like, 'I want this one, I want that one.' And so at some point, I ended up putting flyers in all the schools, and people were sending me checks in the mail, and I was making unitards and leotards at home. My friend went to [the manufacturer] Capezio and got a $3,000 order. I had a few people sewing. I got a few machines. This was the time where all the factories were going to Asia, and Williamsburg was filled with mostly knitting, but a lot of sewing, too. A lot of factories were getting emptied out, and they were throwing all this stuff away. We had about ten employees sewing."

They launched a storefront in Greenwich Village; they went to trade shows in Atlanta and Vegas. "So we started selling all over the country."

The business grew to $500,000 a year in sales—a massive learning curve. "We were always reinvesting, 'cause you have to buy more fabric, you have to do the marketing. We were working twelve-hour days and not paying ourselves. What was also problematic: I wanted to dance, and have a dance company. My whole idea was, we'll have the business, and start a dance company with the profits." She wound the business down and founded an experimental dance troupe, Sens Production, in 2001. She self-produced her New York debut that August with *Descent*, a piece choreographed for a twelve-story staircase in Tribeca. The audience started at the top of the stairs and followed the dancers all the way down to the ground level. It was a hit: the show would win the prestigious Bessie Award for achievement in choreography, and was soon restaged. She formed a nonprofit, built a board of directors, and wrote the grant proposals herself.

In 2004, she staged the piece *Noir* in a municipal parking garage on Essex and Delancey as part of the Whitney Biennial. She dressed her dancers in trench coats, fedoras, and dresses from film noir. The audience watched from inside parked cars; the lighting came from a generator; the score was piped through the car radios. She got approval from the Department of Transportation. She raided thrift stores and sewed costumes. She even sourced the cars from strangers in exchange for free parking at the garage. "I have dreams all the time about the cars," she told *Time Out New York*. "I'm *going* to get the cars. There's no question about that. There are certain things that I will compromise on. We might have four costume changes instead of six, but we *will* have the cars." It was all a prelude to her largest work yet.

* * *

August 1, 1936. "Some 75,000 Greenpointers hailed the opening of the eighth of the city's eleven new swimming pools at McCarren Park," *The Brooklyn Daily Eagle* wrote. "Amplifiers carried [Mayor La Guardia's] address to the milling thousands in the streets and the crowded rooftops surrounding the park." With a capacity of 6,800, the pool had a design inspired by the massive Karl-Marx-Hof housing complex in Vienna and the baths of Caracalla in Rome. Financed by the Works Progress Administration, the project was an effort to provide expansive recreation and alleviate conditions for the poor amid the Depression. It instantly became a hub of the community, a place for families who couldn't afford vacations—a relic from when public works were tied to principle and equity.

March 6, 1989. "Larger than a football field and graced with majestic architecture, the McCarren Park swimming pool was considered a wondrous place when it opened in Brooklyn in 1936," wrote *The New York Times*. "Now it sits crumbling . . . devastated by neglect, vandals and drug addicts who regularly breach its walls since the pool was closed." In 1984, officials closed all eleven of the city's pools and planned a major renovation. But residents who lived around McCarren Park said that its pool should close for good, contending that the place was overrun by drug dealers and sex workers. "There appears to be community consensus in favor of its demolition and replacement by a modern gym," said Henry J. Stern, the head of Parks and Recreation. "If [Robert] Moses were commissioner today, the bathhouse would have been long gone and replaced by something more useful."

* * *

She paid the rent by fixing up dilapidated lofts in Williamsburg. "Our place was all messed up when we moved. So we're sanding the floors, putting up sheetrock, and little by little, you know: 'How do you do tiles? How do you do plumbing?' I'd work on a show for six months, and then we'd renovate a space. It was pretty extreme, 'cause we were sort of broke . . . Meanwhile, the landlords were super happy, 'cause these spaces were zoned as commercial. We were converting them into residential on their behalf. They didn't have to deal with all the Building Department red tape."

At the time, "you'd walk down the street in Williamsburg, and you'd see people with paint on their pants. It was common. Everyone was fixing up spaces and renting them out. This whole Airbnb thing started out from what we were doing. We were all taking these spaces and renting out rooms, and not having to pay rent ourselves. This is the problem, right? In New York, rent is so expensive—you can't afford to work as an artist and do these shows if you're not stable. There are people in New York just constantly moving and looking for jobs. You can't live that way. You can't get anything done. This is the reality."

She started scouting out the neighborhood. "I used to snoop around all the time in Williamsburg. I'd go to the waterfront. I was curious about abandoned spaces and buildings. I would just explore." The place she kept returning to was the long-abandoned McCarren Pool. "It was a space you'd do your walking meditation. People would skate there. There was a 'no trespassing' sign, but you could still get in. There were always holes in the fence. So I had my eye on that spot for a long time." She decided it would be the perfect place to mount a dance performance.

She called the Brooklyn parks commissioner, Julius Spiegel. "He was a very nice man. Mr. Spiegel. His office was in Prospect Park. Very classical, circular office. I enjoy that kind of thing. It was an adventure, right? I'm this little girl, like, 'I want to do a show in the pool.' They're looking at me, laughing a little bit. And they say, 'No, you can't.' This is the thing you have to understand: when I go to a site and deal with the Department of Transportation or the Department of Buildings and they look at you, like, 'You can't do this,' I'd say, 'You don't understand. I want to do this.' There's this conversation that starts to occur. The pushy me is saying, 'What's the problem? How can we resolve this?' This was really my skill. My negotiating skills are what made these things possible. They said in *The New York Times* that I wouldn't take no for an answer, which is true, but it was also this kind of flexibility I had. 'Okay, so what's the problem?' I would ask. And they'd say, 'Well, the space is in derelict condition. It's gonna need a lot to fix it up. We think this is going to cost half a million dollars.' They were looking at me, thinking, 'And you don't have half a million dollars.' I explained that we were going to raise money, and I needed to know: 'What exactly needs to be done?

Give me the list.' They actually drew up a list of all the things that needed to be fixed. I didn't think it added up to a half a million dollars." Eventually, they arrived at a sum of $250,000. And that was how she ended up collaborating with Clear Channel, the world's biggest event promoter and radio conglomerate, soon to be rebranded as Live Nation.

* * *

The Parks Department had gotten calls about the pool from Clear Channel in the past. Noémie says, "The woman who was in fundraising at the Parks Department wanted to get a sponsorship opportunity. She wanted me and Clear Channel to go fifty-fifty on the money. I thought, 'Wow. You gotta be kidding me.' You know how much money they have; we're a small nonprofit dance company. She had me meet with them. She organized a meeting at the Parks Department. In their minds, this was going to be a more long-term-type thing. We were going to use the pool for a five-year period. They were calling it 'interim use' until they found the money to actually renovate the pool. I was selling the project like, 'If I do a show there, you'll get attention to the pool, and you'll get money to renovate it.' The artist's spiel. 'Artists will bring attention to this space.' But you see how the whole dynamic works: people using other people. Because in the end, I was the one who really moved the big pieces. I managed the renovation. They needed me because I was the nonprofit aspect of this, which was the only way that Clear Channel could get in there. They couldn't do it on a commercial basis. It would be like launching a commercial venture on public property."

The laundry list of overdue repairs was substantial. "There were some cement cracks that people could trip on. There was a flagpole that needed to be removed. They wanted to secure the roof on the pumphouse so that the shingles wouldn't fly out, and they wanted us to put a banister around the pool, which was upsetting, because I wanted people to sit on the edge of the pool . . . Then there was some cement work to do around the entrance. There's a little ticket booth that was falling apart, and we fixed it, which was nice. There was some stucco to do around the edge so it wouldn't fall on people's heads. Yeah, that was mostly it . . ."

Noémie told the world she was doing a show in the pool before she had any permits, and before she had negotiated anything with the Parks Department. "Because of timing with grants, which are over a year out, I had to fundraise for the show before I got permission. I had all these grants coming in, and I would insinuate that I had permission, even though I had only had a few conversations with Mr. Spiegel. We got along. I could feel that he was a great guy, willing, and that we would work this out somehow. You can feel that kind of openness when it comes your way. I was going hurdle by hurdle, as you have to do with difficult projects. That's kind of my technique, too: you're putting these things out in the world, and you're showing the world that it's gonna happen. And then the world sees that it will or must happen. There's an energetic potential there. And part of why I moved to New York is for that reason: because I wanted to do things."

After several rounds of negotiations with the Parks Department, Clear Channel put in $200,000, and Noémie, $50,000. "We were raising money through art funding and grants. It's not a lot of money there. Most of it went to the renovation. This is the difference: Clear Channel didn't have to do a thing. I was the one negotiating with the Parks Department, making sure things were progressing, hiring a contractor, overseeing the work." At first, Clear Channel hoped to do their shows on alternating days with Noémie. Then they postponed things for a year.

"I could have managed the construction job myself, and probably for less money, but Clear Channel didn't want that. They wanted to manage the contractor. I had a contract with the Parks Department that said they could cancel my show at any time, for any reason, even if they caused the delay. And we're investing not just the $50,000. We invested lots of time and money between the dancers, the technicians, costumes, props, lighting, and all the expenses. Some of my staff were so worried. They would say, 'Why don't we just have it in [McCarren] park?' In my mind, we were gonna do it in the pool, or we're not doing it at all. My board members were nervous, too. I might be a high-risk/high-reward type, but the risk element with the pool was out of control."

* * *

May 3, 2005. "City officials agreed yesterday to let developers turn the decaying north Brooklyn waterfront, with its relics of Brooklyn's industrial past, into a neighborhood of residential towers with a park-like esplanade along the East River," wrote *The New York Times*. "The rezoning, which was approved unanimously by a key City Council committee, would transform the long-crumbling waterfront into a residential neighborhood complete with 40-story luxury apartment buildings, shops and manicured recreation areas." In an open letter to the city council, the activist Jane Jacobs wrote, "If you follow the proposal before you today, you will maybe enrich a few heedless and ignorant developers, but at the cost of an ugly and intractable mistake." Within the next few months, condominiums such as The Edge ("Hardcore Luxury"), North8 ("Williamsburg. All grown up."), 184 Kent ("A Loft Well-Lived"), and Northside Piers ("Manhattan is so five minutes ago") would all start going up.

* * *

On July 26, 2005, Noémie stood beside a representative from Clear Channel, members of the city council, and the parks commissioner, Adrian Benepe, at a press conference in McCarren Park. Benepe announced that starting in the fall, the pool would be reopened on an interim basis as a public events venue. "I think it's fair to say that we would not be here today without the almost impulsively creative energy of Noémie Lafrance and Sens Productions," said the commissioner. "She had this crazy idea." For the first time in twenty-one years, the public would have access to the pool in mid-September with *Agora*—a word in ancient Greek that means a place to congregate. Performed by thirty dancers in the basin of the pool, five days a week, the piece was soon extended to October 1, and caused a tsunami of press, as Noémie had predicted. "Ms. Lafrance did everything she could to make a match between human bodies and an arena this big," wrote John Rockwell in the *Times*. "Men splashing in a rubber pool. Another man wheeling his armchair, television set (functioning) and living-room lamp about the pool. People kicking soccer balls and beach balls. Others on roller skates and bicycles. A flamenco group. Another ensemble in white . . . Geometric movement patterns to define the space." In December, the live-promotion side of Clear Channel was spun off as Live Nation.

"It's interesting," says Noémie. "In New York City, if you want to do a show or an event, and you put flyers and posters in all the restaurants, bars, and theaters, people will come. I used to walk around and put up posters by myself. I would put flyers everywhere. People would run into me and laugh, but, hey: if no one else is putting up the posters, I will. I would always have a certain enjoyment in talking about the show and getting people excited to come. Inviting them. It's a beautiful sharing. You're making this for people. You want them to be able to enjoy it. There's some love in that kind of sharing. It wasn't just a commercial thing where you're trying to get people to buy the tickets.

"The turnout was amazing—more than I expected. Some nights, it was 2,000 to 2,500 people. Some of the other shows I did sat maybe a hundred. Clear Channel came to one of our shows, on a Wednesday night, and they were blown away 'cause there were 2,000 people. This was going to work for them. If there's 2,000 people to go see a dance show in the middle of nowhere in Williamsburg—back then, this was considered off the beaten path. That's how the commercial world is. They only want sure things. They don't really go into uncharted territories.

"There were times where I thought I was the only person who really cared enough to see this through and make it happen, no matter what . . . I mean, this pool project really took a lot out of me, on all levels: emotional, relational. My board quit. We ended up going under at the end of *Agora*. Because, you know, you're a nonprofit—you need to keep some cash to keep moving—but we spent everything. I had to let some people go. It was hard to come back after that. You burn some bridges. It's unfortunate . . . I tried to say that to the board. 'We made it happen. Aren't you happy?' And they weren't. They were pissed at me because we were in debt. I did feel at the time like it was life-or-death. The beauty of being naïve." Despite it all, she presented *Agora II* twelve months later with a crew of over a hundred dancers, singers, and musicians at McCarren Pool.

*   *   *

The following year, on July 9, 2006, a promoter who had been invited through Noémie, JellyNYC, produced the first of nine free concerts at the pool. The bill was stacked with acts from Brooklyn: Dragons of Zynth, Les Savy Fav, Beans, and Holy Fuck. It was a gorgeous afternoon, but hardly anyone was coming in: the bars on Bedford Avenue were jammed with hipsters watching Italy play France in the World Cup. By four P.M., the pool was frighteningly empty—and then the game concluded. A procession of 3,000 wide-eyed young people entered the gates. The organizers remembered, "They got right into it: dodgeball, Slip 'N Slide, crowd-surfing. And then Les Savy Fav blew them away . . . It was an amazing moment. All these people waving their country flags, taking photos of the venue, just so excited to be there. In an instant, I went from utter panic about the biggest mistake of my life to euphoria. I was overcome."

Also in July, the first of six concerts booked by Live Nation took place. Over the next three summers, at least 300,000 people saw free and paid events with TV on the Radio, MGMT, Beach House, Wilco, M.I.A., and—in their Brooklyn debut—the Beastie Boys. Red Bull, Scion, Myspace, Topshop, Hoegaarden, and Sixpoint offered freebies. The *Times* reported in 2008: "No other stage has so definitively established itself as the pre-ferred strolling grounds for the latest and most bizarre hipster plumage."

Not everyone in Williamsburg was so enthused. In tandem with the interchangeable glass towers rising by the day along the waterfront, the Pool Parties were an unmistakable if well-intended harbinger of gentrification. "The basic need of that pool is as a pool and recreation center for all the peoples of North Brooklyn, which includes a lot of black people and a lot of Latino people," a resident told the *Times*. "Its basic needs are not for the fashionistas of Williamsburg." In 2008, the mayor announced a $50 million renovation that required the pool to close for four years. The final Pool Party at McCarren Park was held on August 24 of that year, with Yo La Tengo, Ebony Bones, and Titus Andronicus.

McCarren Pool reopened with a ribbon-cutting in 2012. Mayor Bloomberg was joined by Adrian Benepe, the parks commissioner, who took a dip in the pool; local dignitaries; and borough president Marty Markowitz, who said, "I don't want to go off the 'deep end' here, but we all know that Brooklyn 'swims laps' around everyone else . . . Kudos to Mayor Bloomberg, Parks Commissioner Adrian Benepe, Brooklyn Parks Commissioner Kevin Jeffrey and former Commissioner Julius Spiegel, Community Board 1, Open Space Alliance Executive Director Stephanie Thayer and Chair Steve Hindy, and everyone involved with renovating McCarren Pool." A press release circulated after the ceremony. The pool, it said, "closed in 1984 and sat unused until the summer of 2005, when the empty pool basin opened as a venue for concerts, dance, and movies." Conspicuously unmentioned—uninvited, even—was Noémie Lafrance.

* * *

January 29, 2024. "For those who remember the Williamsburg of long ago, or even a decade ago, walking its streets can be disorienting, like running into an old friend who has had extensive plastic surgery," wrote the *Times*. "In a dramatic transformation, more than 500 condominium buildings have sprung up there since 2005, and much of the north side has become an upscale shopping district." In "Williamsburg: What Happened?," an illustrated timeline charted forty years of "total transformation." Under 2005, it read, "The concert promoter Ron Delsener Presents donates money to clean up McCarren Park Pool, the long-neglected, 55,400-square-foot swimming pool, so that an experimental dance performance can be staged there, with plans for ten more events the next summer." A picture is captioned mistakenly: "Company [*sic*], a dance troupe, rehearses *Agora* at the McCarren Pool."

In 2008, Noémie staged *Rapture*, a site-specific work for the roof of the Fisher Center at Bard College, designed by Frank Gehry. She did the choreography for Feist's classic video, "1234." In 2009, in her loft, she staged a piece called *Home*, where members of the audience were seated at a table with Noémie herself, eight months pregnant, as the main course. Three weeks later, she had a boy and named him Ulysses.

She left New York and moved to Montreal in 2018. "I lived there twenty years," says Noémie, "so kind of a long time. But I go back, and there's a couple of things that feel reminiscent of that era. I feel like there are leftovers of that moment. You know—when you go to a party at four in the morning, and everybody's gone, and there's all these leftovers everywhere. 'There *was* a party here. We know that.'

"At the end of [*Agora*], I felt proud that we did it. And then there's this weird feeling. People think that you're so great because you did this and that, but it's not really you alone who did it, so you can't take all the credit. But you know what it is? It's that you're the only person who did believe it totally, or to the end, through all the hurdles, the letdowns, and naysayers, and that's why it happened. All you need is someone else to believe. If you believe in it, you believe it's gonna happen, and you tell yourself, 'This is gonna happen. We're gonna make this happen.'"

Adam Shore (I)

At age fifteen, in 1987, Adam Shore applied to work at Spec's Music, a chain of record stores in Florida. The manager told him employees had to be sixteen, by law, and to apply again in a few months.

Adam thought it over. He told the manager, "If you're not going to hire me, I'm just going to come in here every day for a year and help out the customers." And that was what he did. For several months, when school let out, he walked the aisles and asked if he could be of any assistance—all pro bono.

He was a product of the '80s, raised on MTV, *Rolling Stone*, divorce, and the Top 40. A middle child, born in Toronto, his family settled in suburban Boca Raton when he was eight. His mother was a model and location scout; his father was a salesman, from real estate to brassieres; neither finished high school. He was an awkward kid who went to private school and had to wear a tie. His new classmates made fun of his Canadian-isms. When Adam was twelve, his parents separated. He and his brothers saw their father once a week.

When he was feeling down, he cheered himself up with music. He tuned in to a station that only played The Beatles every Tuesday. He had a television in his room and watched the videos on MTV from when he first got home until he fell asleep. He had a knack for memorizing the chyrons lower-left: artist, title, album, and label. For years, he made his own Top 40 charts with typewriter and Wite-Out, and swore they were superior to *Billboard*. He studied *Rolling Stone*'s "100 Greatest Albums of All Time" like a religious text.

In the Florida of the '80s, major tours were infrequent, at best, but Adam made the most of it. At age twelve, he saw Cheap Trick at Florida Atlantic University, his first show. At the Hollywood Sportatorium—in local parlance, the Snortatorium—he saw Bryan Adams and INXS. He saw the Jacksons at the Orange Bowl, where also he saw U2, touring *The Joshua Tree*. He kept a mental log of headliners and openers. He was the kind of music fanatic who would tell you that he caught the tour when the Beastie Boys opened for Madonna—and then confess that he was stuck in traffic when the Beastie Boys were on.

He worked in record stores all through high school and college. It was a time of healthy competition. Besides the mom-and-pops, there was Virgin, Tower, Camelot, Sam Goody, Peaches, Coconuts, and Strawberries, among the national chains. CDs outsold vinyl for the first time in 1988, cassettes in 1989. Between ubiquitous releases by Whitney Houston, Michael Jackson, Guns N' Roses, Def Leppard, George Michael, and Bon Jovi, the music industry was printing cash: in Florida, Spec's had eighty stores alone.

In 1989, he went to college at Columbia. The week of freshman orientation, he got a job at Boomer's, a chain of record shops around Manhattan. He worked there all four years in school, at the store on Fifty-Fifth and Broadway, by the Ed Sullivan Theater. When he lived in London for a semester during his junior year, he found a job at the enormous Tower Records in Piccadilly Circus. He was working on the day that Freddie Mercury died, in 1991, and hundreds of grief-stricken fans showed up at the store.

Back at Columbia, he helped to start a student radio station at Barnard, WBAR. He wrote record reviews for the college newspaper.

He did an internship for *Night Music*, a short-lived and unlikely offshoot of *Saturday Night Live*, whose bookings ranged from Sonic Youth and Miles Davis to The Residents and Sun Ra. He worked unpaid in the video department at Columbia Records; in college-radio promotion, at Virgin; and eventually, at MTV, where he could be a fly on the wall during programming meetings. He could hardly comprehend his good luck.

All of which made it surprising how hard it was to find a job after graduation. He sent a résumé to a couple dozen radio stations, record labels, promoters, and publicists in the *Recording Industry Sourcebook*. He got three responses. The first was from a company that managed children performers. The second was from Michael Dorf—the owner of a club on Houston Street, the Knitting Factory—who was hiring someone to book tours. The salary was $15,000. Adam figured he needed $18,000 to live in New York, and asked for twenty-four hours to arrange a loan from his parents. Dorf said okay. One day later, when Adam called him back, Dorf said that he had hired someone else.

The last reply was from TVT, a label started by the wily and litigious entrepreneur Steve Gottlieb, a graduate of Yale and Harvard Law School. As he would readily admit, Gottlieb had little interest in music. What he had was an unfailing intuition for what the public in the Reagan era wanted, and that was the good old days. In 1984, he raised a quarter-million dollars to license dozens of TV theme songs from *I Love Lucy*, *Leave It to Beaver*, and other favorites of the '50s and '60s for the first of many compilations. He called the label TeeVee Toons. Bolstered by a savvy ad campaign, *Television's Greatest Hits* sold 300,000 copies in its first year. Working out of his apartment on Central Park South, he hand-delivered cassettes and LPs to local stores; they couldn't keep it in stock. He was interviewed by Jane Pauley on the *Today* show and Garry Shandling on *The Tonight Show*. "People like to deny how much of our culture is centered around television," he told *Time*. Tapping a bottomless market for baby-boom ephemera, *Television's Greatest Hits* would go platinum, spawning seven different sequels. He soon branched out: in 1986, TeeVee Toons became TVT Records.

In 1988, a demo tape arrived at TVT, postmarked from Cleveland, Ohio. Entitled *Purest Feeling*, the self-recorded songs were written by a handyman, janitor, and engineer named Trent Reznor. The music was suffused with dejection, torment, and self-loathing; the songs were undeniable. Despite the label's reputation for novelties and schlock, Reznor signed with TVT. By 1992, the first Nine Inch Nails album, *Pretty Hate Machine*, had sold over 500,000 copies, on its way to triple platinum. It would also lead to an ugly, protracted, and personal dispute between Reznor and Gottlieb, dramatized in a song from the *Broken* EP: "Happiness in Slavery."

By the time Adam was hired at the label, in 1993, Nine Inch Nails had left for Interscope, amid much litigation and resentment, but TVT was flourishing. The year before, they had acquired Wax Trax!, the scene-defining industrial label from Chicago, whose catalog included Ministry and KMFDM. They'd also signed a distribution deal with Warp, the rising electronic label based in England, home to Nightmares on Wax, LFO, and a young Aphex Twin. It was a bull market for experimental music: in the post-Nirvana feeding frenzy, the major labels offered deals to acid-drenched auteurs and oddballs like The Flaming Lips, Boredoms, and Butthole Surfers.

As TVT's publicist, Adam wrote press announcements, label copy, and artist bios for twenty new releases a year. He got to work with figures he had only dreamed of meeting: Gil Scott-Heron, the musician, poet, and activist; Juan Atkins, a founding father of techno; and Underworld, the mighty electronic duo. He oversaw the U.S. rollout of the first four-teen Warp albums, including *Artificial Intelligence* (the formative IDM compilations) and the earliest releases by Autechre, Richie Hawtin, and Aphex Twin. For every album, EP, soundtrack, and compilation TVT put out, he had to stuff hundreds of CDs in bubble-wrap mailers, then follow up by phone, as such:

"Bob Christgau? Adam from TVT. Have you had a chance to listen to the Sister Machine Gun record?"

"I'm eating dinner."

The label was expanding its footprint. In the mid-'90s, TVT had success with techno, post-grunge, and hip hop, as well as movie scores and compilations. In 1995, they had a string of hits with the *Bad Boys* and *Mortal Kombat* soundtracks, which both were certified platinum; but then, even the *Grumpier Old Men* soundtrack (another TVT release) was guaranteed to sell substantially. They signed nu-metal and industrial bands such as Sevendust and Gravity Kills, who sold millions. They inked a worldwide distribution deal with Warner Bros; they opened offices in London and Toronto. Adjusted for inflation, the record business was grossing $25 billion a year.

Still, a man can only stuff so many envelopes, and after three and a half years, Adam had grown tired of publicity. He hated calling people on the phone. He hated pestering them by fax and email. Most of all, he hated how difficult it was to get press coverage. With signings such as Boards of Canada, Squarepusher, and Broadcast, Warp could take credit for some of the decade's most distinctive music—not that you would have known it from *Rolling Stone*. Between the worlds of pop-punk, Britpop, and rap-rock, it was a decade of guitar saturation. With few exceptions— Simon Reynolds, David Keenan—critics didn't have the tools to write about electronic music. Adam asked about a reassignment.

Steve Gottlieb was reluctant to find a new publicist. He interviewed some people, but never seemed to pull the trigger. "You're doing a better job, anyway," he said to Adam, who suspected he was being strung along. It was one of several unsavory aspects of the workplace. Payments to vendors happened once a week, and only for an hour. Employees lined up outside Gottlieb's office with a list of overdue accounts; like an emperor, he would decide who was deserving of pay. One afternoon, Adam knocked on the door.

"Steve," he said, "I love this company. I want to keep working here. But I can't be a publicist anymore. So I'm going to leave now. If you hire a publicist, I'd really like to come back as a product manager." He packed up his desk and went home. One week later, a publicist had been hired.

He worked at TVT for almost five more years in marketing and A&R. He went on tour with Underworld. He served as a liaison for imprints with Ice Cube and Snoop Dogg. He signed two wildly prolific bands, Guided by Voices and The Brian Jonestown Massacre, with underwhelming sales. He had a part in the production of thirty records, and a role in an award-winning documentary at Sundance, *Dig!*—about the rivalry between The Brian Jonestown Massacre and The Dandy Warhols, and the world of indie rock.

Most of all, he got an education—in marketing, publicity, and overseas distribution, as well as in some of the more distasteful sides of the business. By the end of the '90s, Steve Gottlieb was more interested in suing people than signing them. The label was entangled in dozens of lawsuits with publishers, producers, and unpaid manufacturers, distributors, and musicians. When Adam got the chance to run his own label, TVT would be a model for what not to do. He put in his notice in early 2000.

He spent the next few years on new pursuits. He tried his hand at artist management with a psychedelic band from New Jersey and a female hip hop trio. With some friends, he launched an email list for music obsessives called the Mishpucha ("family" in Yiddish). They threw events at The Pyramid, on Avenue A, and The Frying Pan, in Chelsea; Ann Powers wrote a story for the *Times*. A start-up gave them $17,000 for a party. The bubble was about to burst.

He went to India and Thailand for six months. On the flight from JFK, he took a stack of *VICE* magazines. It was a recent discovery of his and many of his friends, men and women alike. Founded in 1994, *VICE* got its start in Montreal. In 1999, the company moved to New York. Like the contemporaneous lad mags in the U.K. (*Maxim, Loaded, FHM*), *VICE* was an unfiltered cesspool of testosterone and lechery; unlike them, it trafficked in casual racism and homophobia. It was misogynistic, malignant, and lewd, if not without a certain gonzo quality, like Eddie Murphy's old routines; it also had decent music writing. On his travels in Southeast Asia, Adam thought about proposing a column on metal and electronic music.

Right around this time, the magazine was meeting with Atlantic Records about collaborating on a new imprint: Vice Records. When Adam got back to New York, a friend connected him with the cofounders of *VICE*, Shane Smith and Suroosh Alvi. He interviewed and then accepted the position of general manager and head of A&R for Vice Records in the fall of 2002. He shared an office in Williamsburg with Alvi, Smith, and their partner, Gavin McInnes. Adam was employee number thirteen.

Henry Havemeyer

In *Candide* (1759), Voltaire's eponymous naïf arrives in Suriname, the Dutch colony, where he meets an enslaved man, "stretched out on the ground, with no more than half of his clothes left . . . the poor man had no left leg and no right hand."

"Good God!" said Candide. "What are you doing there, my friend, in such a deplorable state?"

"I am waiting for my master," says the unnamed man. "When we work in the sugar mills and get a finger caught in the machinery, they cut off the hand; but if we try to run away, they cut off a leg . . . It is the price we pay for the sugar you eat in Europe."

Voltaire's contemporary, Montesquieu, had written of the link between the sugar trade and slavery: "It is well known that not a barrel of sugar arrives in Europe but is stained with human blood." By the mid-eighteenth century, at least 100,000 enslaved Africans were taken every year to the Americas. In New York, the sugar industry attracted families like the Roosevelts, the Rhinelanders, and the Van Cortlandts, but by far the most successful were the Havemeyers.

They had emigrated from Germany (by way of London) in 1798, and opened a refinery six years later in the Village, on Vandam Street. They prospered from a worldwide craze for tea and a continuous supply of sugarcane from the Caribbean, Brazil, and Louisiana, where it was harvested by slaves. In 1855, they moved the plant to Williamsburg, where undeveloped land, a deep-water harbor, and cheap, abundant immigrant laborers were attracting their competitors. When the plantations of the South were destroyed in the Civil War, sugar became New York's most profitable manufacturing industry, up through World War I. By 1870, the Havemeyers were processing more than half the sugar in the United States.

In 1882, their main refinery was destroyed in a fire, and hastily rebuilt. It underwent a vast expansion that would increase capacity to 1.2 million pounds a day, and dominate the waterfront for more than a century. The plant employed tens of thousands of immigrants, mostly Polish—hired so they couldn't report the misery the job entailed. They worked around the clock, in twelve-hour shifts, in sauna-like conditions, in temperatures above one hundred degrees. To help the laborers rehydrate, the company arranged to have beer brought in several times a day, and sold at cost. In 1886, the workers of the plants in Williamsburg went on strike for better pay and recognition of a union. They asked for a reduction to a ten-hour shift and wages of $1.75 a day. The owners locked them out and brought in the police, which led to rioting; a strike in 1910 was similarly crushed. "A life of perpetual torture," wrote the *New York Tribune*: "not infrequently death comes quickly to [the sugar laborer's] relief."

The Havemeyer plant's capacity gave the family a significant advantage, and, in 1887—in his biggest coup—Henry Havemeyer persuaded his competitors to form a monopoly that was known as the Sugar Trust. According to historians Matthew Postal and Paul Raphaelson, the trust controlled as many as seventeen refineries, and leveraged its position "to outmaneuver competitors, manipulate suppliers, bribe government officials, perpetuate inhumane working conditions, preserve indentured servitude on plantations, influence tariffs, and fix prices." The trust disbanded after the passage of the Sherman Anti-Trust Act in 1890. One year later, it reincorporated as the American Sugar Refining Company—in New Jersey. (It was one of the original twelve stocks in the Dow Jones Industrial Average.) To get around the Roosevelt administration's anti-trust regulations, in 1900, American Sugar would diversify and create the Domino brand; the refinery continued to grow. By 1907, the Sugar Trust controlled no less than ninety-eight percent of all production in the entire country. That year, the Havemeyers built a pair of brick, steel, wood, and concrete buildings near the big refinery: a three-story, 21,000-square-foot warehouse on South Second Street; and a two-story, 44,000-square-foot structure on Kent, around the block. The former served as office space; the latter was a garage and stable. Ninety-nine years in the future, one would house the DIY establishment Death by Audio; the other would become the Glass House (later, Glasslands) and Paris London New York West Nile (later, 285 Kent).

American Sugar was the heavyweight of the Sugar Trust, and one of Brooklyn's biggest employers. At its peak, in the 1920s, the Havemeyer plant produced an eighth of all the sugar in the world; employed some 4,500 workers; and occupied eleven acres, or eight football fields. Still not content, and seeking lower costs, the Havemeyers threatened to move the plant to New Jersey after World War I. The government allowed the closing of two streets between the river and Kent Avenue as part of yet another big expansion. The iconic, forty-foot, yellow neon sign emblazoned with the name of Domino Sugar was erected in the '30s, and would become a lasting symbol for the borough of Brooklyn.

The Havemeyer legacy extended well beyond the shores of Williamsburg. In time, the clan produced a three-term New York City mayor (William) and a fortune in the hundreds of millions (Henry), which they spent on paintings by the likes of Rembrandt, Goya, El Greco, Monet, and Cézanne. In her will, Henry's widow, Louisine, bequeathed 140 paintings to the Metropolitan Museum of Art. Her children gave almost 2,000 more—to this day, the single biggest collection at the Met.

The sugar industry declined after the advent of artificial sweet-
eners during the Great Depression. The waterfront refineries would
close and gather rust in the coming decades. By 1969, the Havemeyer
plant employed 1,300 workers; by 1996, it was under 500. In 1988,
the company (by then, Amstar) was bought by Tate & Lyle, a British
multinational. Raw sugar was delivered to the plant by ship until 1999,
when workers went on strike after the company insisted on eliminating
seniority and sick days, cutting one hundred jobs, and contracting as
they saw fit. The strike would last for over 600 days, through 2001—the
longest labor battle in New York City history—and end in abject failure
for the strikers.

Tate & Lyle started liquidating the company's portfolio. They sold
the stable and garage on Kent Avenue and the offices on South Second
Street to Joseph Markowitz, the owner of an electronics business, who
told the *Times* he hoped to see the neighborhood rezoned for residential
use. "We have a problem renting to commercial," he said. "It's very hard."
In 2001, Tate & Lyle sold the company (by then, Domino Foods) for $180
million. In 2004, the new owners laid off the remaining workers and
closed the plant for good.

As industry gave way to the creative class in North Brooklyn,
Markowitz's hopes would be amply realized. In 2014, Mayor de Blasio
announced a deal with a developer, Two Trees Management, to build a
2.9-million-square-foot retail, commercial, and residential complex at
the Havemeyer site. Two Trees agreed to set aside 700 units as affordable housing; in return, they were allowed to build up to fifty-five stories,
twenty more than developers were usually permitted. (It opened as The
Refinery at Domino in 2023.) The plant itself would be demolished at
the end of 2014.

Also that year, the sons of Joseph Markowitz found a tenant, Vice
Media, who invested $20 million to renovate. The architect called it a
"balance between clean modernity and Brooklyn grit." (The company
received some $6.5 million in tax credits from the state after considering

a move to L.A.) They served eviction notices on the occupants: 285 Kent, Death by Audio, and Glasslands. The news was covered widely—among others, on vice.com, in a piece entitled "Why the Closing of 285 Kent Doesn't Matter." That same year, Kara Walker constructed a sculpture in the old refinery of a seventy-five-foot sphinx made of sugar. A sign at the entrance read:

At the behest of Creative Time Kara E. Walker has confected:
A Subtlety
or the Marvelous Sugar Baby
an Homage to the unpaid and overworked Artisans who have refined
our Sweet tastes from the cane fields to the Kitchens
of the New World on the Occasion of the demolition
of the Domino Sugar Refining Plant

Sea Ray (*Stars at Noon*)

Sea Ray were representative of countless bands who moved to Brooklyn in the early aughts. Their music was inspired equally by English and American guitar bands from The Cure to Sonic Youth. They shared a stage with artists who became both famous (Interpol, The National) and forgotten (Radio 4, The Stills). They toured extensively, made two LPs, and had their music licensed for commercials and TV. They paid the rent with freelancing, construction work, and part-time jobs. They organized their own affairs, and only got a booking agent toward the end. Although they didn't advertise it, as Vampire Weekend soon would, they were predominantly Ivy Leaguers and a product of the upper middle class. They symbolized an era when creative-minded young people were coming to Brooklyn in droves—when a career in music seemed possible, and less like winning the lottery. They found a measure of success in their adopted home, and could reliably fill the 250-capacity Mercury Lounge, but would remain a cult concern during their eight years of existence. They left a small but cherished legacy, and could have done a great deal more.

But then, there was always something peculiar about them. When most groups in New York had three to five Caucasian men, Sea Ray had a woman playing cello, several people of color, and a touring party of seven—as well as the requisite four white guys. In a scene that had an unofficial dress code of suits and ties, they walked onstage with all the panache of librarians. In a time when post-punk, garage, and electro were in vogue, they took their cues from atmospheric chamber pop, shoegaze, and space rock. Where many of their peers would write of nihilism or ennui, their songs were about the pursuit of happiness. The chasm separating Sea Ray from their contemporaries was what made them special—and also why they fell apart.

* * *

Most people can remember their first rock concert, but few can say it was a night they were onstage. Anne Brewster was the exception. She grew up in Seattle during the rise of grunge, but her taste ran more to Shostakovich. Her parents were enthusiasts of classical music in all its forms, from Renaissance polyphony to modern string quartets. Her mother was a writer and a pianist; her father was a journalist who founded an alternative newspaper, *Seattle Weekly*, and a performance space, Town Hall. When Anne was nine, she started playing cello. She practiced for hours on end and made her way to the Bach cello suites; she studied the recordings of the cellist Jacqueline du Pré. In high school, she and her friends got together for sight-reading parties; she joined a string quartet, a chamber group, and two different orchestras. At Yale, she was accepted as a student of the Brazilian cello great Aldo Parisot. It was a rigorous education in music, if one with limited utility for life in an indie band.

Colin Brooks, by contrast, had been in bands since the age of thirteen. He started jamming with his father—an amateur guitarist who revered Alice Cooper, T. Rex, and Funkadelic—at age seven. He was raised in Memphis, where he got his first drum set. Then his family moved to Little Rock, Arkansas, which had a thriving local punk scene. One of the first people he met was Jason White, who played guitar, and later joined Green

Day. They formed a band—the Numbskulz—and played house parties. If the scenes in Berkeley and Washington, D.C., were better known, the punk community of Little Rock was a fountain of all-ages DIY activity, producing dozens of accomplished and ephemeral bands, zines, and venues. After high school, he joined a string of groups like The Big Cats, Substance, and 2 Minutes Hate, who toured around the region. In 1998, he headed to New York to play with Skeleton Key, who had been signed to Capitol, and went on tour with Primus. When the band broke up, he found a place to live in Brooklyn. It was early 2001.

One day, a friend from Little Rock invited Colin to a party at 540 State Street in Boerum Hill, a block Jay-Z later immortalized in "Empire State of Mind." It was there that he met his friend's roommate, Jordan Warner, who was in a band called Sea Ray; they were looking for a drummer. Colin went home with a CD. "I wasn't super impressed," he says. "But I kept on going to these parties, and I kept on hanging out with Jordan, and we ended up talking about music." It clicked when he befriended Gregory Zinman, lead guitarist and bon vivant. "Greg's a very enthusiastic person," says Colin. "He's good at bringing people in and making them feel comfortable, whereas Jordan's kind of more the quiet type. And so after this one particular party, I said, 'I'll check out a rehearsal and see what you guys are up to. And that was when I first met I-Huei, who was on bass. And that was kind of how it came to be."

* * *

The band had formed in 1996, when Greg was in his senior year at Yale, and Jordan was a recent graduate residing in the East Village. They both were raised in Michigan, and shared a love of bands such as Teenage Fanclub, Yo La Tengo, and Spacemen 3, but little else. Jordan was from Leland, a tiny place (population 410) on Lake Michigan, and went to high school in a class of twenty. Greg was from a family of Jews-in-exile from Queens who taught political philosophy at Michigan State, in East Lansing. They met when they were randomly assigned to Branford, one of Yale's so-called residential colleges; that's where they met Anne. The music scene at Yale was dominated by dreadful a capella, but there were isolated signs of life. A band named Sunday Puncher signed with Turnbuckle, a label in New York, and would make an album with a young James Murphy. Singer-songwriter Mia Doi Todd was an undergrad; so was Bryce Dessner, later of The National. Jordan had a short-lived punk band, Tragic City. Greg was playing with I-Huei Go, a singer and guitarist from Shaker Heights, Ohio. The trio started writing and recording on four-track in the summer of 1996.

The songs were slow to come, and sounded more than slightly like their models: Pavement, Sonic Youth, and Yo La Tengo most of all. But other songs would show a band with some unorthodox ideas: the elegiac piano line in "Hall of Fame"; the sprawling, twelve-minute "Meet Your Match"; the unforeseen and extended coda of "Stray Dog's Got It Made." "We sort of jokingly referred to ourselves as the Michigan Space Rock Ensemble, and made fake signs and flyers, because we weren't playing shows," says Greg. "We weren't doing anything. But we were working up a bunch of songs."

In July of 1997, they went to Jordan's family's place in Michigan for the recording of their first LP. The album was produced by the eccentric Charles Francour, a journeyman who opened for The Rolling Stones and now was recording jingles. The session was a culture clash: "Jordan got a guy that he grew up with, Todd [Flees], to play drums," says Greg. "Todd was more of the hippie vibe . . . I remember he was like, 'Do you guys make music for people who are on heroin?' Then he broke out the djembe."

Jordan's family lived across from Lake Leelanau, and had a Sea Ray boat; the name seemed fitting. "We thought, 'That reminds us of being up there, and the times we shared,'" says Greg. "You could take the boat into town and dock. There were two bars: uptown and downtown. They were across the street from each other. The downtown one was where Tobin Sprout hung out."

Through a stroke of serendipity, they'd learned that one of their heroes, Tobin Sprout—the painter and musician, of Guided by Voices—had moved to Leland, where he had family. "We went to the gallery where he was showing some of his artwork," says Jordan. "This guy Malcolm was like, 'Oh, he's probably working on his parents' dock right now. You should go say hello.' We went over there, and sure enough, he was there, wearing a pink polo shirt, working on this dock. He was just a really down-to-earth guy."

"Oh, you guys are musicians?" said Tobin. "That's cool."

"We are such big fans," said Jordan, starstruck.

"That's cool. Love to hear what you guys are working on."

They handed off some rough mixes. Back in New York, they self-released their first LP and started playing shows, first with Rob Galligan of Sunday Puncher on drums, then with Rodd McLeod. In 1999, they got to make an EP produced by Tobin Sprout, "which was mind-blowing for us," says Greg. "We couldn't have been bigger fans. We were just flabbergasted, you know? Like, what dumb luck that he's up in this remote place, and that he's willing to record us." They started practicing that fall with Anne, whose cello would dramatically enlarge their sound. She overdubbed some parts when the band recorded with producer Peter Katis. "Originally, the idea was just to have her play cello on a few things, but we liked the way it sounded," says Jordan.

For Anne, who had decided against a life in classical music, it was transformative—especially in concert. "The first show I remember playing was at Luna Lounge. It was one of these itty-bitty places, and I was like: 'That was the most fun I have ever had.' It was just—I fell in love with it. I loved performing. I think it tapped into a part of me that classical music had never really reached. There was just something so much more visceral about performing rock music than there was about performing classical music."

By early 2001, Rodd McLeod had departed the group. Among the people to audition for his seat was Jeff Sheinkopf, who had arrived in town the year before to take a job at Elektra Records. "I wanted to be the drummer, and I went and played with them, and it was fun," says Jeff. "But then Colin came, I think the next day, and—I can hold my own, but there was no question that he was the one." Instead of leaving, Jeff started tinkering on the Rhodes electric piano, "and it just kind of fell into place that way," he says. "I was also drawn to the idea that they weren't just looking to add new members to the lineup and keep rolling along with their existing songs and existing sound. It felt more like the start of a second life for the band."

* * *

With Colin, Anne, and Jeff installed, the elements had fused into something unique. They had a formidable rhythm section; an arsenal of synths, effects, guitars, and pedals; and the cello, front and center. Through Jeff's connections in the music world, they started getting shows. The Brooklyn scene had yet to coalesce; for now, the action was entirely on the Lower East Side. The lineup made their live debut at Brownies in February of 2001 with Of Montreal. It was a heady time to be a New York City band. The Walkmen and the Yeah Yeah Yeahs released their first EPs that summer; The Strokes were on the cover of *NME* in June and once again in August, when DFA was launched. A few weeks later, in "NYC's Like a Graveyard," The Moldy Peaches joked, "You've gotta be cute if you wanna get far." It was a tongue-in-cheek remark that would have resonated for Sea Ray, a group that often seemed estranged from its more fashion-forward peers, and never quite agreed among themselves on something big: an understanding of success, or what exactly they were aiming for in the first place.

"I think Jordan and I-Huei had a different set of priorities," says Anne. "I think me and Greg and Jeff and Colin were like, 'Let's go as big as we can,' you know? Like, let's go for it, and if we need to wear certain clothes, or do certain things in order to make that possible—great! You know what I mean? Happy to do it. I think some of that, too, was because I hadn't grown up in this world, so I was like: you do what you gotta do to get where you want to be, you know? But I don't think Jordan felt that way at all. Jordan was in it one hundred percent for the music. He was not interested in wearing cool clothes, or being performative onstage, or anything like that. He was very pure. Like, 'I'm gonna play the music that I want to play, and if people like it, great, and if they don't like it, I don't really care.' So those two visions of where we were going as a band would occasionally kind of erupt. And then we'd all move on."

"When you think about the usual suspects of the New York rock scene, there was a certain cachet that bands had, that Sea Ray didn't have," says Colin. "Back then, it seemed like you needed to fit into a few different boxes, and we didn't fit into any of them, but we thought we could try, or we thought that's what we had to do to get noticed. And Jordan, to his credit, stuck to his guns, and was like, 'I don't want to do any of that.' I just wanted a career, like anybody. And yeah, sure—somebody wants you to put on a pair of Levi's, or wear a leather jacket or something—who's it gonna hurt? But Jordan wasn't interested in any of that, at all."

A major show took place October 12, 2001, when they shared a bill at Brownies with The Walkmen, Zero Zero, and Interpol. It was the annual CMJ Music Marathon, when industry professionals descended on the city for a week of showcases and networking—originally scheduled to start that year on September 12. "You could tell there was something going on at that show," says Colin. "I remember Greg and I sitting downstairs in what was the backstage area, and a couple of the guys from The Walkmen coming down, and it was almost like they didn't even notice we were there. They just ignored us. I think we might have even tried to say something to them. It was just like, 'We don't even notice that you guys are in a band, or that you're even in this room with us.'" In late 2001, the group recorded five songs with a producer, Pete Min, four of which were self-released on the *Revelry* EP the following summer. They played with Interpol again in the new year; the hype had multiplied. "I was next to Paul [Banks]'s girlfriend at the time, and she was like, 'They're going to be *huge* stars,'" says Greg.

The band would only play a dozen shows in 2002, and took their time composing new material for their second full-length. They practiced in the basement of 540 State Street. "Dark, musty, ceilings so low you could barely stand up, and, being an unfinished concrete room full of junk, less than stellar acoustics," says Jeff. Again, the songs were slow in taking form, but would reveal a group that had finally found its voice. In "Revelry," their best-known song—which they would license to a few small films, TV shows, and advertisements by Coca-Cola and Saturn—a pair of poignant verses yield to solo cello, and the band falls silent, as if in deference. In "Forge Utopia," they capped a melancholy, multipart arrangement with a wash of strings. With Brandon Derman, a visual artist, they started using colorful projections in their live show, and opened for Clinic, Radio 4, and The Church. They worked with a promotion company who sent the *Revelry* EP to college radio, where it was played on over one hundred stations; leading the charge was KCRW's Nic Harcourt. On Cincinnati's WOXY, "Revelry" went to number one in November, over The White Stripes, Sigur Rós, and Pearl Jam. "Sea Ray must be NY's biggest secret or why else wouldn't this band be signed?" wondered *Drowned in Sound*.

In January of 2003, they went to Tarquin Studios in Bridgeport, Connecticut, where Peter Katis worked and Interpol had made *Turn on the Bright Lights*. They captured three new songs, and rearranged two others from the first LP. "Quiver" was futuristic space rock, and easily their heaviest moment; "Swear to Your Face," meanwhile, was orchestral-country. "Sister Gone," "Forge Utopia," and "Nicholas Ray" were all about the lives of women who were finished with mediocre men. And over everything was the cello, which gave the group a center, a gravity, and a lightness all at once.

They recommended Katis to The National when they played with them that spring, and talked about a deal with the Dessner brothers' label, Brassland, that never quite transpired. In May, they signed with Self-Starter, a small indie with releases by Les Savy Fav and Lifter Puller. They also went on their first tour: a week around the South with Longwave, a band who'd signed with RCA and toured Europe with The Strokes. The stars were apparently aligning. "We're like, 'It's right there in front of us,'" says Greg.

They set a tentative release date for the summer, then the fall. On May 6, Kanine Records released *NY: The Next Wave*, a compilation highlighting twenty local bands, pop-oriented (Oxford Collapse) to experimental (Electroputas); as if to split the difference, the opener was "Revelry." They played with Broken Social Scene in June, and went on tour again in August. A few weeks later, in "The Music Issue," *New York* magazine included Sea Ray on a list of bands who were "changing the New York soundscape," next to TV on the Radio, Japanther, and Secret Machines. Finally, on October 21, 2003, the second Sea Ray album, *Stars at Noon*, was out in stores—a few of them, at least. *Time Out New York* hailed its "heart-stopping melodic beauty"; *Rolling Stone* called it "a gorgeous, bursting collection of rock songs"; and *Pitchfork* ignored it. They celebrated with another dreary showcase during CMJ with Dresden Dolls, the Starlight Mints, and Josh Ritter, and hit the road for most of November. Then they started getting sick of one another.

* * *

"I'd be like, 'We have to flyer,'" says Greg. "That's what bands do. Almost nobody would flyer with me. I was like, 'We have to go out. We have to see these bands. We have to inculcate ourselves into the scene. We need to make sure we're being seen when we're not playing.' I was completely in it, in a very obsessive way, and, I think, to a degree that wasn't entirely shared by everybody. I think some people would be like, 'Yeah, you're right, but I'm not willing to do that,' or 'I don't want to do that.' And I was like, 'It's not gonna happen unless we do X, Y, and Z.' And they're like, 'No, it should be a meritocracy.' And I was like—that's not how it works. Like, you need to play ball. That was always a discussion."

Without a manager or booking agency, the group relied on Jeff's unstinting work ethic. He phoned the promoters, and planned the tours, and settled up after the shows. "In addition to being an incredible musician, Jeff took on the brunt of all the managerial stuff," says Greg. "He did everything and designed everything. He made the flyers. He made the T-shirts. He kept track of sales. He organized a binder with directions from MapQuest when we went on tour."

To say that their accommodations were minimal would be stretching it. They slept where they could: in strangers' houses, on ant-infested mattresses, or in the van. On evenings when they sold a lot of merch, they sprang for a hotel and slept seven to a room. For Anne, the lowest point was in Toledo, where they were opening for The Brian Jonestown Massacre.

"We showed up at the venue, and there was just this sign taped to the door that said the show had been moved," she says. "So we drove here and there, and ended up in this bombed-out kind of mall, in this venue with this tiny little stage. That was always an issue, 'cause there were six of us onstage, and I was on the cello, and Jeff had, like, three different keyboards. I remember, it was the night of the Victoria's Secret Fashion Show, so that was on all the screens at this Midwestern bar that we're playing. The sound was terrible. I couldn't hear myself at all. And they're playing this Victoria's Secret show. All these boobs marching around while I'm like, 'What is happening?' That was a dark place. I remember pacing around the parking lot. I called an old friend. I was like, 'I'm done with this.'" The work was paying off, in terms of exposure—The Church invited them to open sixteen shows that spring—if less in terms of pay: divided six ways after gas, a $250 fee went only so far.

In May and June 2004 they went on tour with Metric and The Stills for seven weeks. The latter had their own tour bus, and a deal with Vice Records; the former had been cast in a film that went to Cannes. They played to an appreciative crowd in Detroit. Backstage, they met two guys who couldn't stop gushing—as it turned out, the Insane Clown Posse.

A show they booked by themselves in Toronto was less well-attended. "I'm pretty sure the only people in the room were the sound guy and the bartender," Jeff recalls. An invitation to open for Guster was the cause of some debate. Sea Ray was "fairly evenly divided between those who want to keep touring and those who want to hole up in the studio to work on the new record," said Jeff at the time. They licensed "Revelry" for an episode of *One Tree Hill*, as well as in an ad for Coca-Cola during the Summer Olympics in Athens, Greece. There was a string of dates in Canada, and then a homecoming show at East River Park. But for some in the group, the writing was already on the wall.

"We didn't have anything booked after the tour with The Stills," says Anne. "I think at that point, Greg was applying to graduate school. I applied to graduate school, and I just kept deferring it. And then The Stills were trying to poach Colin to be their drummer. And Colin was like, you know, 'They're going this way, and we're not.' So he was a little cagey with us, which I can totally understand. I think he was trying to make them both work. And then it was just more and more clear that some of us were willing to play the part, if you will, and some of us—like, Jordan did not want to play that part, and he has every right to feel that way. But at a certain point, it was increasingly clear that those kinds of differences were not gonna get resolved. That was when we started talking seriously about, 'What are we doing here?' It wasn't one conversation. It was more like a series of conversations. I honestly don't remember at what point we were like, 'Okay, we've made this final decision.'"

"I think we had two issues," says Colin. "One was, 'Will we be able to make another record? Is anybody interested in helping us make another record?' And then, should we do a tour with Guster or not? There were some who thought, 'We should do this tour,' and some who thought, 'We should work on songs and get a new record together. But who would put it out?' You could just see the back-and-forth, and round-and-round. People that had a way out, of—'I could go to grad school and get on with my life'— that's probably when those decisions were being made, I assume. So that's when it started to seem like, you know . . . kind of like life. You just can't move up in your job, for whatever reason. You can—stop trying, I guess [*laughs*]. That's kind of what happened to us. But then we also started to get on each other's nerves. People just saw other things they could be doing. You need money to eat and live in New York. Everybody does."

"We thought, you know: How long can we do this?" says Jeff. "Greg was getting ready to pursue his PhD. Anne was a teacher. I-Huei was teaching also. And everyone started to say, you know, 'We all see the potential of this, and we all want this to work, but we're also realistic, and we have lives to live. And there was also tension at times in the band about these decisions that sometimes were not always so pretty. Maybe we were offered a show where we thought, 'Okay, is it worth doing this, if it means taking off work?' The smaller decisions, where in the past we might have said, 'We'll do it, whatever it is.' Now thinking, 'What are we doing?'"

The ending would be bittersweet. On January 21, 2005, they played their final show, on Houston Street, at the Mercury Lounge—a few blocks from where Greg and Jordan had started writing songs together. Johnny Beach, the booker, brought a cake that said "PLAY ALL NIGHT." The hometown crowd was boisterous, if also a bit glum. "At some point we booked our farewell show, and emailed our list," says Anne. "I was totally heartbroken. Like, even with all the parts of it that were hard, I loved all of it, and did not want it to stop. But it just had this feeling of inevitability . . . like, you can't just work temp jobs and go on tour and be broke forever. I mean, you can. Some people do. But I—I knew that I wasn't gonna be able to do that for the rest of my life, and feel like I had done what I wanted to do with my life. I think other people were kind of in the same boat . . . I don't think Jordan wanted the band to break up. At the same time, I think he probably felt like his values and his purpose were pretty different from a lot of the other people in the band, and I don't know what he thought was gonna happen for him next." They reunited in New York for one final show in December of 2023, almost nineteen years to the day of their original farewell.

"It did kind of feel like we hit a rough patch, and we didn't survive it," says Jordan. "And we could have taken a break and come back to it, or started working on new songs. I'm sure there was an element of us being tired of each other. I definitely have mixed feelings in that regard. I'm sure that there was a way forward. It was not one hundred percent amicable, but it was pretty civil. And we remain friends. Not good friends, but still friendly. And it would have been nice to make a living from it. But the way I feel about it now, and the way I think I felt about it then, it was like, 'Yeah, if it happens, great, but it's not the be-all and end-all.' Which is maybe part of the problem. That I, or we, weren't hungry enough to really go for, you know, success. But really, my main thing is, I was trying to make some art, make some music that I enjoy. And if people respond to it, great. Hopefully, they do."

Silent Barn (I)

December 1960. Yoko Ono rents a fifth-floor loft on Chambers Street for
$50.50 a month. She builds a studio and living space using discarded
crates. A friend gives her an old piano. Along with the composer La Monte
Young, she hosts a series of events with avant-garde musicians, dancers,
and performance artists, attended by the likes of Robert Rauschenberg,
John Cage, and Marcel Duchamp; Young will get most of the credit. In
1968, at 131 Prince Street, Ornette Coleman founds the Artists' House, a
residence and concert space that launched a movement known as loft jazz.
Around the corner, at 647 Broadway, David Mancuso throws informal
parties at his home; he calls it The Loft. At his place on Centre Street,
Phill Niblock organizes shows by Arthur Russell, Laurie Spiegel, and
Julius Eastman. And in a living room at 228 West Broadway, a group of
artists from the Midwest host a series with composers and improvisers
Robin Holcomb, Butch Morris, Shelley Hirsch, and John Zorn. They call
the place Roulette, after the game of chance.

* * *

February 1980. Zeljko McMullen was born in Massillon, Ohio, a small
city south of Akron. His dad was from Florida; his mom was from the

former Yugoslavia; he had two older sisters. As a child, he liked to dance and roller-skate. When Zeljko was ten, his dad was diagnosed with cancer. "We found out in February 1990, and he died four months later. My mom tried to come up with activities to take my mind off it," he says.

He started frequenting a roller-skating rink. "And there happened to be this DJ there, Kevin Fowler, who was maybe eighteen when I was eleven, and he loved house music, and he loved industrial music, and I made friends with him. He would give me tapes to take home: Skinny Puppy, Ministry, Nine Inch Nails. So by the time I was twelve, I had pretty wild taste. He took me to my first rave when I was fifteen. One of the first concerts I went to was Nine Inch Nails, Marilyn Manson, and Hole, and it was the first show Courtney Love played after Kurt Cobain died. My mom would drive me to see Nine Inch Nails and sit in the car for hours while I was at the show."

He started throwing raves around the area when he was seventeen. "I'd borrow money from my friends' parents to book DJs. I would get faxes sent to me from Germany before I got on the bus to go to high school." He booked some of the inventors and pioneers of Detroit techno: Juan Atkins, Claude Young, and Derrick May. "Juan Atkins and his wife and daughter drove down from Detroit and they got a flat tire, and they called me to drive like seventy miles west of Cleveland to change their tire. At ten o'clock, in the middle of the party. So I drove my mom's car a hundred miles an hour and changed Juan Atkins's tire."

He wanted to apply to Oberlin his senior year. His guidance counselor said, "You'll never be able to afford it." As a result, he started working after graduation for a debt-collection agency instead. It came to be an education in itself—in ethics, economics, and late capitalism. "My whole job was sitting there for eight hours a day with a headset on, staring at a screen. I would be calling people and trying to get them to pay down their credit cards. I would call some old lady that bought a $40 tea set, and they would owe $300, but they had already paid $150, and my job was to get them to send us their minimum monthly payment, just to keep the balance going up.

"I drove a BMW. I went to Saks Fifth Avenue to buy clothes, which was some weird part of my life. I think it was a way for me to process the absurdity of doing that job. And then I just, like, snapped. I quit the job. Let the bank repossess my car. Applied to Oberlin. And then, like, would walk around Oberlin for the first year, looking for change on the ground, to buy a Snickers from a vending machine, to go back to the practice room, to make weird noise music. I was living on this porch that I rented in August, because I never filled out paperwork to get a dorm. The kids that started the Shinkoyo thing came over one time, and it was freezing, because I was living on a porch with no heat. And they're just like, 'You can move into our attic.' They came and helped me carry my synthesizer and desktop computer. It was not even two months of being at Oberlin. And then we had this huge clubhouse." They called it Silent Barn.

* * *

Imagine that the Wu-Tang Clan had been a group of raging dorks and instrument designers in the Midwest, and you'll begin to understand the Shinkoyo collective. In place of RZA, GZA, Method Man, and ODB, they had a sage (Peter Blasser), a mastermind (Matt Mehlan), a theorist (Severiano Martinez), a light and sound artist (Doron Sadja), and a classical metalhead (Mario Diaz de Leon). In place of classic kung fu movies, *Wayne's World 2*; in place of Staten Island, an old house in Ohio named Silent Barn. Shinkoyo was a label, a collective, and a set of ideals: collaboration, experimentation, and unpredictability. It was 2002. The president was pounding the war drums; the media was serving as stenographers; the nation's mood was steeped in retribution, obedience, and a permanent sense of crisis. "There was a need for a radical underground that says a lot, but without saying anything," Blasser would claim. "So made-up words are really good. They're uncensorable. And you can say a lot with them." Their catalog would range from ambient (Zeljko McMullen's *Disorder*) and synthesizer oddities (Blasser's *The Sound of Doves in a Cave*) to Philip Glass–inspired grooves (Martinez's *Clocks and Psandas*). Of all the artists that Shinkoyo would produce over the next twenty years, the one to make the biggest mark was Skeletons, a band led by Matt Mehlan.

* * *

You never knew what you were getting from a Skeletons production, both for better and for worse. "It's a mysterious package, this album," *Pitchfork* said of their debut, *Life and the Afterbirth* (2003). "Search though you might, you'll never find a tracklist or any kind of information about the people involved in crafting this record." They alternately billed themselves as Skeletons and the Girl-Faced Boys, Skeletons and the Kings of All Cities, and the Skeletons Big Band. They typically performed as a quintet—unless they were playing as a duo, or a nineteen-piece orchestra. Their sound could veer from Afrobeat to indie pop to noise, all within the same song; their lyrics toggled from nostalgia ("My friend took me to my first Bulls game / It was Jordan vs. Bird") to pessimism ("Let's fight about who wants to die more"); their shows could be transcendent or disastrous. The only thing that's cut-and-dry was that they played a major part in Brooklyn's indie boom, and then were effectively forgotten.

* * *

Matt Mehlan hailed from the suburbs northwest of Chicago. A middle child, born in 1982, his mother was a teacher; his father was a physical therapist. He begged for a guitar when he was in the seventh grade. "I was always balancing between my music friends and my normal friends," says Matt. "I had gotten into making four-track cassette recordings, and I would make these tapes and bring them to the cafeteria at lunch and sell them to people for three bucks. Everybody thought it was weird. It was like, 'Okay, you're into this. And it's weird you're into this.' And so getting to Oberlin was honestly—I met the people we started Shinkoyo with, and Skeletons, like, that first week of school. So Mario Diaz de Leon, I met him the first couple of days. Doron Sadja—I met him on the way to the dining hall. And by the end of the first week of school, I was asking people to play in the freshman open-mic night at the coffee shop."

Matt says, "As conservatory students we had ensemble requirements, within which you had to do a certain number of performances. We realized quickly there were all these ways to get those credits, which was important, as the sort-of outcasts who didn't necessarily play a traditional instrument. One thing we found is that we could check out the recital halls for concerts and put on our own shows. We would produce these ad hoc concerts, assemble a bill, and have a little show. We'd make flyers and post them all over campus. For one, we screened *Total Recall* atop all the performances, from beginning to end. For another one, we made flyers with women in bikinis, and their faces obscured. We were a boys' club, and critiqued by our classmates as such. By junior year, we all had records that we were making.

"Our department would have special guests each semester, and some of the students had conspired to bring Taylor Deupree, who ran the electronic-music label 12k. He came and talked really clearly and inspirationally about what it meant to run a label, and how it functioned, in simple terms, and how easy it was to get started—because there was genuine interest in the world for these niche communities of artists. We were all ambitious. We started having meetings to start a record label together. We found out we could get money from the school to do a project, which we used to make the *Music of Shinkoyo* compilation. I got a $900 loan from my dad, and Seve got a $600 loan from his dad, which we used to buy the spindles of CDs for the first three releases," says Matt. Among them was *Life and the Afterbirth*, the first official Skeletons LP.

"Matt's music immediately caught on at Oberlin when he started making the Skeletons records," says Jason McMahon, the band's guitarist. "He had made a name for himself as soon as he made the first Skeletons album, sophomore year. And by the time he made the second album for his junior recital, it was like, 'Matt's got something.' There were even people copying his music by senior year, which was a whole weird thing.

So there was buzz around Matt at Oberlin. There was a lot of excitement around the music he was making. All three of them—Peter Blasser, Seve—they had such an incredible energy and creativity about them. They each had their own style that was unique." By 2004, when Matt was still at Oberlin, Skeletons had opened shows for TV on the Radio and Animal Collective. By 2005, they'd signed with Ghostly International, an indie label in Ann Arbor, Michigan.

* * *

Meanwhile, Zeljko had spent a year in Williamsburg. "I moved to New York at the end of 2003. I did an internship through Oberlin with this sculptor and multimedia artist, Luca Buvoli. He gave me the most intense crash course on the New York City art-world scene. I was living on North Third and Kent in the middle of 2004, and I think Oneida had a practice space there, the Yeah Yeah Yeahs had a practice space there. And at the time in Williamsburg, it wasn't anything like what it was even just a handful of years later. It was pretty destitute, except for a few places. It was right around the time Brooke Baxter opened Glass House, which was around the corner, and Monster Island was there."

After graduating, broke, Zeljko moved back to New York in the summer of 2005. "I had no money. My friend Mario was loaning me money for cigarettes and bagels, because one bagel and cigarettes would get me through a whole day. I was like, 'I have to get some kind of job,' and I was on Craigslist, and randomly applied for a job that said, 'New York-based musician/photographer seeks office intern,' and this lady called me the very next day to come in for an interview. And she was like, 'I help this older artist, and I need some help, and you will never interact with this artist.' As soon as I opened the door, there was this giant six-foot-tall photograph of Lou Reed. I was like, 'Okay. Whatever.' I actually didn't know his work that much. I knew [the infamously discordant] *Metal Machine Music*." The opening was in Lou Reed's office. Zeljko was hired on the spot. "I was his assistant's assistant. I was supposed to handle the runoff when she was overwhelmed. 'Go get a space heater.' She had me digitize the Velvet Underground cassette archive. I was like, 'This is a cool song.' She was laughing at me."

"Shortly after I got there," he told *Interview* magazine, "she started looking for someone to replace her, because she was really stressed out by the job. He was kind of a difficult person, and somehow his assistant's role was to be the focusing energy point of all his grumpiness and desires." Despite what Zeljko had heard from the assistant, he and Lou Reed would end up interacting a good deal—as fellow music fans, and then as collaborators. "We actually got along quite immediately. At the time, he was doing this sort of meditation music and was getting into synthesizers and electronic music. He was impressed that I had studied music and could help him in the studio. I said to him, 'I love *Metal Machine Music*,' which was probably not something he heard from someone new. He would call me and say, 'I want to work on some music. Come over to my studio.' And the weird, demanding vibe he had about mundane things would switch over to, 'Let's go buy synthesizers. Let's go buy gear.' We started just making music in his house together, and it evolved from there. Eventually he said he wanted me to join his band as well, which I was excited about. I had sort of a modular synth rig made out of patched pedals with a mic on his guitar, and I would process his signal live. Some of it was contributing noise textures, but it became very reactive. How I would process the guitar began to affect what he played. This led to us going on a big tour of Europe, some of which were huge festivals—at the Isle of Wight, there were 80,000 people."

He helped his employer with more routine matters as well. "I was going to move his studio and office to this space in Williamsburg. I told him we could save him a ton of money, get all his gear out of storage. I was gonna live there. I was living at the time in Lou's office in SoHo, and showering at Lou's house in the West Village. When the realtor showed me the space that became Paris London West Nile, and later 285 Kent, I knew my future lay behind that door before he turned the key." He had a harder time convincing Lou. "He kept going back and forth about getting the space, and I had made the decision that I was going to take it anyway. I was at the airport with Lou, and I was faxing the landlords the lease when he told me he wasn't going in on the space with me. I took a cab from the airport back to the office, packed up my stuff, and moved to this giant concrete room in Williamsburg. Then I called my friend MV Carbon. I called my friend Doron Sadja. I was like, 'Do you guys want to move into this 2,000-square-foot warehouse?' I lived on that block for eight years." Because the building faced the western edge of Williamsburg—and as a spoof of the art world—they called it Paris London New York West Nile. It was 2006. "The landlord was this amazing guy named Joe Markowitz. He was not terribly interested in making a ton of money from this block. He let all this weird stuff go on because he liked the people and the creative energy."

It was an empty room, without appliances, heating, or walls. "And I was like, 'It can be where we live. We can have shows here, and we can do art shows, or noise shows, or whatever.' We spliced a line off the gas heater and hooked up a stove, and we built a kitchen, and we took water from the bathroom, and we used a sink we found in the garbage. I think we were there for six weeks before we had our first concert, which ended up being ten acts. We built a freestanding second floor, but it probably took six months to a year before it was done, and during that time we did kind of try everything. We had some vegan brunches that my ex-girlfriend cooked, and we would do art installations, and different kinds of shows. It was six people paying $500 each. The only thing I made a hard rule for was that I didn't want it to be a capitalist space. So we never charged admission, and we never sold alcohol. I got in arguments with everyone. They would say, 'This is stupid. We could be making so much money.' I was like, 'I'm sorry. This is my only rule.'"

Some of the many acts who played at Paris London New York West Nile were Tony Conrad, True Primes, Noveller, Sam Hillmer, Lea Bertucci, Black Pus, Nautical Almanac, Talk Normal, and Skeletons. "It was less about collecting money at the door," says Matt. "It never felt like a Todd P show—where there were people working at the bar, people manning the front. It was much more like, 'Hey, come on in. Have a glass of wine.' It was more like Phill Niblock's loft in a lot of ways. Phill would take the money at the door and offer you a glass of wine." Within a year, the building on Kent Avenue housed three more DIY establishments. "So there was a stretch of time when it was Paris London West Nile, Glasslands next door, Death by Audio, and Tom Arsenault's studio, So Many Fields, and they were all connected by these hallways in the back, so you could walk from one place to the next," says Matt.

"You could play at Glasslands, you could play at Death by Audio, you could play at Zebulon," said Tom Arsenault, who performs as Mas Ysa. "You could get these shows really quickly and always have a bunch of friends to play with. Tim DeWit from Gang Gang Dance lived there. Bruno [Coviello] from Light Asylum lived there. [Logan Takahashi from] Teengirl Fantasy lived there. Laurel Halo lived there. Nickle [Emmet] from Nymph lived there. [Publication and promoter] Ad Hoc was started there . . . Before there was an office, Ric [Leichtung] basically sat on the couch and did everything from there."

The business plan for Paris London New York West Nile was utopian, if not quixotic—and yet, they hung on until 2010, when the rent was hiked. They could have charged a modest ticket price for shows and kept themselves afloat, but Zeljko stood his ground. "I don't know why I was so staunchly anti–making money, because it would have been a lot easier if we had charged something. But for me, it was important to have a space where people could come all the time. So people brought a six-pack, or a bottle, and they would donate to the acts, and we would give it all to the performers, and all the bands would make a lot more money at West Nile, and we had the weirdest shows, and the only downside—and it was a plus to me—was that the whole place was a live/work playground. The fact that we never adapted and became capitalists was how we ended up getting priced out." Zeljko found a loft around the corner. The lease

would transfer hands a couple times, from John Barclay (soon to start
Bossa Nova Civic Club) to Todd P, who renamed it 285 Kent.

* * *

When Matt Mehlan moved to New York in 2005, abandoning his postcollegiate job in a Chicago mall, his reasoning was "as practical as it was
whimsical," he later wrote: "live with the band, wake up and hit record,
subsidize costs and share, build a self-reliant community for making art
and music in the City That Never Sleeps™." Matt and his wife Amanda
McCreary rented Zeljko's room at 184 Kent Avenue while he was back
at Oberlin. Matt started working three days a week in production at
Roulette, which had moved to Greene Street. He went on tour with
Skeletons in July. When he got back, he learned that 184 Kent had been
sold, to be converted to condos. "I was like, 'How am I going to make
this work?'" he recalls. "I need time to make music. I'm struggling here.
I can't afford a practice space. I can't afford recording studios."

Inspired by acquaintances from out of town, and facing imminent
eviction, he started looking for a place where they could live and work.
"Peter Blasser had become friends with Twig Harper from Nautical
Almanac and his wife, Carly Ptak," Matt says. "They had bought a former
dentist's office in West Baltimore, and they called it Tarantula Hill, and
they would do shows there. They built a little outsider empire there.
They always made it both their business and their living space and a
performance space and a recording space . . . 'What if we lived in a space
where it's cheap enough that all our rooms are $500 or less, and then
there's also space to rehearse and record?' I found a building on Craigslist
that was right off the L train, at 915 Wyckoff, on the edge of Ridgewood
and Bushwick. I had never been to Ridgewood, but it had a basement,
and that to me was like, 'This is the spot. We can put all our stuff down
here. We could rehearse here. We could put on shows down here. We
could do anything we want.'" The rent was $2,800 a month. They recycled
the name from Oberlin and dubbed it Silent Barn.

"We moved into Silent Barn with members of Skeletons," says Matt. "It was me, Jason McMahon, Tony Lowe, and initially Carson Garhart, who was our bass player at the time, and my wife, Amanda. And it was awesome—at first. Amanda's dad is a union pipefitter. He drove out with his utility van and all his tools from Chicago. And he was like, 'I can help you build walls. We're gonna build these bedrooms.' And he came out and showed us how to plumb-bob and frame out rooms and hang drywall. And we did all this demolition work, and went to Home Depot, and spent a bunch of money to build rooms, and it was great at first. We moved in, like, in October, so the weather was amazing, and it was super fun. We were excited by all the work we were doing to build it out, but Amanda and I quickly racked up a bunch of debt on our credit cards. And as the winter came, we started fighting with our landlord, because we didn't really think it through, and we had signed a commercial lease. As soon as it got cold, we said, 'The heat's not coming on.' And he was like, 'It's a commercial lease. That's your responsibility.' And every time you turned the oven on, the lights would dim in the whole place. That was the situation we were in. We were very naïve. I mean, I was twenty-three. I had all the ambition and desire to take on a space like that, but I had none of the understanding of what it actually meant. How you compel people to be part of what's a pretty large collective project. One of our roommates immediately left, and then finding a new roommate changed things, especially for Amanda, who would be alone when we were out on tour. It was chaotic and awkward for her to be the only woman, and for us to be a couple. I give her a lot of credit for lasting as long as we did in that place. I kept paying a little rent and using the basement for recording and rehearsing in the space after we moved out. Eventually, a whole new crew moved in."

Delia Gonzalez &
Gavilán Rayna Russom
(*The Days of Mars*)

In 1970, the English novelist Winifred Bryher wrote a memoir of her time in London during World War II. Though long a resident of Switzerland, she left her house, her husband, and her dogs to live with friends and share the hardships of the Blitz. She wrote about the bombing raids, the rationing, the many streets and structures reduced to rubble, the daily propaganda, the dread, and the duplicity of the government. "Periods of numbness were frequent at the beginning of the war, later they turned to disillusionment and rage . . . The one thing that united us was disbelief in any form of official pronouncement." The book was published as *The Days of Mars*. (Mars is the Roman god of war.) To Delia Gonzalez—whose parents were themselves exiles, from communist Cuba—it seemed a title worth repurposing amid a new war in Iraq, Afghanistan, on the airwaves, at the airport, and everywhere you looked.

* * *

The first two decades of the new millennium were something of a golden age for independent labels in New York. Stylistically, they ranged from gothic (Sacred Bones) to garage (Captured Tracks), symphonic (Asthmatic Kitty) to lo-fi (Woodsist), futurism (Software) to folk (Ba Da Bing). They specialized in moody pop (Frenchkiss, Kanine), metal (Kemado), modern classical (New Amsterdam), psych (Mexican Summer), soul (Daptone), dance (Fool's Gold), and experimental music (Tri Angle, Social Registry, RVNG). Of all the labels to emerge out of New York in the early aughts, the only one to win an instant worldwide following was DFA (Death from Above), the home of LCD Soundsystem, The Rapture, and The Juan MacLean.

Formed by James Murphy, Tim Goldsworthy, and Jonathan Galkin in 2001, they were in many ways the soundtrack of Michael Bloomberg's New York: immoderate, imperious, and gentrified. Inspired by the downtown scene that launched iconoclasts like Arthur Russell, ESG, and Talking Heads, they were at once a label, a production house, and an ingeniously marketed brand. Much like Sub Pop, Motown, and Dischord, they were synonymous with a city and a sound—a lively blend of dance and post-punk—starting with their very first releases, "House of Jealous Lovers" and "Losing My Edge," in 2002. Their reference points were cataloged in the latter: Can, Detroit techno, and the Paradise Garage, to name a few. They took a page from labels such as Wax Trax!, 99 Records, and ESP-Disk, which had a well-defined aesthetic—for better and for worse. Despite a roster that would include noise artists (Black Dice, Pixeltan), indie acts (Shocking Pinks, Pylon), and downtown elders (Peter Gordon, Liquid Liquid), the label soon became a shorthand for the genre known today as indie sleaze, epitomized by groups such as Franz Ferdinand, Cut Copy, and Justice. They started fielding inquiries about production jobs from the likes of Britney Spears, Duran Duran, and Janet Jackson. And for good reason: from *Echoes* to *Beaches & Canyons*, "Tribulations" to "All My Friends," few labels were as effortlessly hip, smart, and entertaining. Which may explain why some would be confounded by *The Days of Mars*: a fifty-minute instrumental composition in four epic movements that evoked Afro-Caribbean drumming, classical minimalism, acid house, German *kosmische*, and spiritual jazz, by the artists Delia Gonzalez and Gavin Russom, who changed her name to Gavilán Rayna Russom (Rayna for short) in 2019.

* * *

"Some of us are citizens not of a country but a landscape," Bryher wrote. Delia and Rayna were two such people.

Born and raised in Miami, Florida—an island off the cultural mainland—Delia grew up in a house where only Spanish was allowed. Her father was an anti-Castro dissident who took part in the Bay of Pigs affair and went to Guatemala for the CIA. He spent two years in a Cuban prison while Delia's mother raised her and her older sister. "My dad always wanted to go back to Cuba," she says. "He never wanted the United States to be his home. Miami wasn't a real city—it was totally empty. All these Cubans came in the '60s, and they transformed it into a Latin American city. I went to a Cuban elementary school, where all my classes, even my English classes, were in Spanish. So it was this really weird world, where you don't know *what* you are. I wasn't born in America. I was born in Miami. And so for me, America was this foreign thing. I always saw it from afar."

She studied film and visual art in college. She moved to Olive Street in Williamsburg in 1995. It was the year that Mayor Giuliani created the M.A.R.C.H. task force (or Multi-Agency Response to Community Hotspots), to fine and shutter bars, clubs, and restaurants for supposed infractions, with agents of the NYPD, Health Department, Fire Department, Buildings Department, and Liquor Authority. In tandem with a Prohibition-era law that made dancing illegal in any bar or club without a license—and was long used to target artists of color—the operation closed some fifty establishments in under two years. As a kind of response, and with her friend Christian Holstad, she started a guerrilla troupe and art project called the Fancy Pantz School of Dance.

"Giuliani brought back this law," says Delia. "I remember going to bars and wanting to dance, which was illegal. Bars were getting fined if people would dance. We were doing dance performances in the street. It was a depressing moment, where rents were getting really expensive. Where people were getting kicked out. It was a weekly thing. You'd walk around Williamsburg, and people would say, 'I got kicked out of my apartment,' or, 'My landlord raised the rent.' My landlord did try raising the rent a couple of times, because I paid $600. And basically, I would cry. I'd just be like, 'No, you can't raise my rent,' and I would cry, and he'd be like, 'Okay, okay.' He was kind of a softy . . . It started around 1997. It was around '98, '99, where you felt this really huge shift."

Williamsburg was a different country then. "A friend of mine had said, 'If you're really cool, you live off the Bedford Avenue stop [on the L train], and the further away you are from Bedford, you lose cool credibility.' I always thought that was funny, because you would go to Bedford Avenue at the time, it was just, like—everybody looked amazing. Everybody's dressed to the nines. It was pretty spectacular. There were so many characters. Every time you went out, you would bump into friends. Everyone had cheap rent. The greatest thing was that there was space, and there was so much time to just have fun. We didn't have to work so many hours. There were so many creative, crazy people around. It wasn't about, 'I want to be famous, and I want to shoot for this.' It felt like everyone was doing things because they loved what they were doing, and because they're doing something authentic. Because they have something to say. No one was doing what they were supposed to do. It was a time where everyone knew that the bubble was about to burst—you could feel it—and there was just this last little moment, and everything was going to be different."

Among the characters she met around town was a practicing magician, musician, and artist named Rayna Russom. "We met at a loft party," Delia says. "This is in 1998, when we talked. But we had been in performances together. There was a time that we crashed a Christmas parade unauthorized—like, seventy of us. When I met Rayna, she thought I was three different people. She didn't realize I was the same person, because I always had a different look. This was in January or February. I think that by the end of March, we were hanging out at a café one day. We bought a little notebook. We wrote down all the projects we wanted to work on. Some were hers, some were mine. A magic show. Performances. Sculptures. Art. Travel. And we were like, 'Let's do it together.' We came up with all this stuff, and we started working together. It was immediate. We wanted to create a universe."

* * *

One version of the life of Gavilán Rayna Russom might go like this. Born in Providence, Rhode Island, near the campus of Brown University—where her mother worked as a software developer, and her father taught Old English—she was consumed with music from an early age. "My mother used to get furious because I'd figured out how to make a trumpet from some pieces of the coffeemaker, and they were always missing when she wanted coffee," she said. "My dad was from Detroit and listened to a lot of R&B, Motown, and jazz." Her mother taught her how to sew as well as the importance of doing things yourself. Her cousins Mike and Bevin made music down the street, and later came to some renown as the composers Kelley Polar and Blevin Blectum, respectively. She studied music and religion at Bard, with professors such as Benjamin Boretz, who introduced her to the feminist composer-theorists Elaine Barkin, Susan McClary, and Meredith Monk. She moved to Williamsburg in 1997, at the age of twenty-three, and to Berlin in 2004. In the interim, she had a magic show called The Mystic Satin; a band with Casey Spooner called Sweet Thunder; a multimedia practice with Delia, in several forms of art and music; and a job at DFA repairing synthesizers—they called her "The Wizard." She played with LCD Soundsystem for the better part of a decade, performing at Coachella, Bonnaroo, and Glastonbury, contributing to the albums *This Is Happening* (2010) and *American Dream* (2017) before departing amicably in 2021.

Another version would go like this. "I came out to my parents when I was three years old, and that's not hyperbolic. I showed up one day in a dress and told my parents my name was Tina, and that I was their daughter, and that I didn't know what happened to their son. It was something I was very aware of, and, around eleven, I kind of knew that I was a girl, and I didn't know what to do about that, because there wasn't *anything* around me that spoke to that at all. The mob ran most of Providence in the '70s and '80s, and up through the '90s. There was a lot of sex work, and a lot of trans sex work. I mostly knew that because people in the punk scene would say terrible things about the people doing sex work, and some of them, especially skinheads, would beat on them. I was in an environment where people were talking about, that's what they're going to do for the weekend, was beat up trans women and cross-dressers who were doing sex work in downtown Providence," Rayna says.

Her high school years were marked by violence and bullying. "I was getting assaulted pretty regularly on the street and in school," Rayna says. "Just a brutal, brutal life of what I think was really queer and transphobic violence . . . I was a person that appeared very effeminate. I experienced a lot of violence and harassment. That was part of my daily experience. Sometimes, if they happened to be walking behind me at enough distance where they would read me as feminine, they would catcall me. Getting closer, they would see me as masculine and become very angry. I was assaulted on a number of occasions."

She found a kind of self-therapy in making music. "Before I had a consciousness about it, I gravitated toward certain sounds as a way of healing myself," she told musician Cosey Fanni Tutti in an interview for *Paper* magazine. "I just noticed that, 'Oh, I have this toy organ, and if I hold down all of the chord keys on it, this thing happens.' I now understand that feeling as harmonic density and temporal fluidity, but at the time I just knew, 'Something happens. I feel better.' So as a child, I learned how to create musical space in which I could heal, in which I

could feel whole, and find identity. . . . As I went out and tried on different identities and began unraveling this insane conundrum of being a
woman who was being told that she was a man, I continued to gravitate
toward aesthetic frameworks that really go back to my childhood . . .
toward technology that would do that and achieve it: reel-to-reel tape
machines, and feedback, and then, eventually, synthesis."

* * *

"Never expect morality or justice to succeed; it is the parasites who win
riches and a comfortable old age, seldom the worthy citizens," wrote
Bryher in *The Days of Mars*. "The longer a war lasts the more the extrane-
ous things drop away and it is only friends and perhaps a special corner
of a city that count."

"After 9/11, I was like, 'I *have* to get out of here,'" said Delia. "Every
time I turned on the TV to watch the news, it was like, 'We're going to
war with Iraq. It's red-alert day.' 'It's Halloween. It's red-alert day.' Or
orange-alert day. If they wanted you to approve of going to war with a
country, it was red-alert day. If it was a holiday where you might go out
and have fun—orange-alert day. To terrify you. Americans didn't see
this. You'd go to work, and people said, 'It's red-alert day.' I would just
sit there and be like, 'Don't you realize you're being manipulated? Turn
on the news. Look at all the billboards. All the movies that are coming
out are about the apocalypse.' Everyone was living in this fear."

By the fall of 2002, New York's new mayor Michael Bloomberg
was accelerating his predecessor's crackdown on nightlife. In just six
months, raids by the M.A.R.C.H. task force were up thirty-five percent
from the year before, and expected to rise. An assistant police commissioner told the *Times*, "If you listen to stories about what led to
this homicide or what led to this assault, you would be surprised how
many stem from nightclubs. We don't want those places in New York.
We make it very clear."

* * *

They had a metal band (Fight Evil With Evil), a disco project (Black Leotard Front), and a synthesizer duo (Delia Gonzalez & Gavin Russom). They made sculptures, drawings, collages, and installations. They were represented by a gallery in New York. They had their work exhibited in Zurich, Salzburg, Naples, and L.A. That doesn't mean that they could pay the rent. "At some point, I ran out of money," Rayna says. "And my one marketable skill was that I could fix vintage synthesizers and build custom analog synthesizers. I went through my inbox and found every music- and art-related email where a person had forgotten to BCC the recipients. I copied all the addresses and sent this email out to say, 'I'm available to do this.' One person wrote back, and it was James [Murphy]. He wrote back sixty seconds later and was like, 'We're the DFA, and we have this studio in the West Village, and it's full of equipment that we bought on eBay, and most of it doesn't quite work right.'"

She told an interviewer, "The first thing I got hired at DFA to do, James was like—it was 2002, I think. He said, 'I made this track, and it kind of seems like it's catching on, and I didn't ever intend to actually play live with this project, but it looks like we're gonna have to play this song live, and I don't know how to do it, because it was made on this crappy old Casio boombox. Could you build kind of a super-Casio that's super-tough, and I could take on tour?' That was 'Losing My Edge,' which at the time was a song that he thought was catching on a little bit."

"I didn't enjoy the job very much," Rayna says. "I would have been way ahead of the curve if I'd decided to be a synth designer for a living in 2004, but I just didn't enjoy it very much. Also, the impact on the environment, even at that sort of level—it's brutal. And it was honestly in a lot of ways very sad for me. I thought of myself as an artist. As someone who made music. Suddenly I was the person that the people who were making music went to, to fix their stuff. The years of working in DFA's basement—I think the initial time was quite an interesting experience. But then it became this odd thing where I was like, this feels very sad to me. And very classist, honestly. Like, 'She's the person we take our gear to.' I would think, 'I'm an artist too, you know.'"

Her fortunes would change in 2003. "James was on tour, and Jon [Galkin] and Tim [Goldsworthy] came to a screening that Delia and I were doing. We played a live soundtrack. And Tim was like, 'If you ever want to do a professional-quality recording, we could figure something out. You can rent the studio and record it here, or we could give you a record deal. Then we'd split it.' And, I mean: I always wanted a record deal. I was making these tapes and taking them to [indie record store] Other Music, and being like, 'Can you put five of these out? You don't have to give me any money.' I wanted to make music that people would hear . . . I think it was two years that we spent in the studio. Mostly me, Delia, and Tim."

The album was *The Days of Mars*. Along with releases by The Rapture, The Juan MacLean, Black Dice, and LCD Soundsystem, it was among the label's earliest LPs, unbeknownst to Rayna. "I did not know what DFA was. I didn't know what the scene was. There were a lot of things about New York that I did not know. I was coming from a very, very outside place . . . I basically hung out with this one person. Delia and I hung out and sometimes did dance performances with Christian [Holstad]. But I was just coming from a very different world . . . It was like, 'Oh, these people have a label, and it seems kind of cool, and they want to put a record out.' Later, I understood that it was part of building the story of that label. To be able to say, 'And we *even* have this.' And that was the role that I played as an artist on the label: 'We *even* have this out-there, psychedelic electronic music.' There was a very strong aesthetic of what DFA sounded like, and this was very different. But it was sort of used to build that story, to set DFA even further apart from the other labels at that time . . . I'd show up for work and sometimes James would be on tour and we'd get to work in the studio. Sometimes Britney Spears or Duran Duran would show up.

"There was this element, too, of, like—I'm trying to have a career. Not in a cynical way. I'm trying to find a balance between the artistic stuff I'm involved with, and the label, and the market. I'm working with a label that's very popular. Maybe the most popular label in the world at that time, at least in terms of independents. And that was something I was ambivalent about, but also excited by. Tim was a big part of that. Because, for better or worse, I think that was something he was very skilled at. He brought a lot to *Days of Mars*—of, how do we make this more accessible? In the way the music industry uses the term 'accessible.' More palatable to a wider audience. And, you know: how do we make this a successful album?"

* * *

If 2002 was when DFA grabbed the spotlight, then 2005 was when they lowered the boom. It was the year of debut albums by LCD Soundsystem and The Juan MacLean; remixes for Gorillaz, Nine Inch Nails, and The Chemical Brothers; and classic singles like "Daft Punk Is Playing at My House" and Hot Chip's "Over and Over." A few months prior, the label had signed a distribution deal with EMI. "When was the last time we had a great New York indie record label?" Simon Reynolds asked in the *Voice*. "The DFA sound flashes back to places and times when NYC's party-hard hedonism seemed to have both an edge and a point—Mudd Club, Paradise Garage—but never feels like an exercise in retro pastiche." It was in this context, in October 2005, that DFA released *The Days of Mars*—not that you could have forgotten.

"Investing in something that sounds like an amped-up version of Tangerine Dream is a bold move on the part of any label and that *The Days of Mars* has an EMI logo on its spine is a testament to the uncanny achievement of DFA Records," said *PopMatters*. "The DFA duo who don't play dance punk, noise, or death disco (except when performing as Black Leotard Front)," *Pitchfork* would write, in a 7.6 review. "By three minutes in, I was confused," said a critic in *Stylus*. "By ten minutes in, I was starting to get skeptical. Where was this *going*? Was it going anywhere at all? What would the next track be like? Where are the beats? This is on DFA?!?"

* * *

Bryher wrote: "I do not know if it is an advantage or not to see both sides of a situation (it is always uncomfortable), but I know from personal experience that it is rare for intense love to last an equal length of time between two people. We think it must endure for eternity; it is as ephemeral as a butterfly."

The fall of 2005 would see New Orleans hit by Hurricane Katrina; worldwide protests against the war in Iraq, then in its third year; and the conviction of an army reservist for her role at Abu Ghraib. Saddam Hussein went on trial as the U.S. death toll in Iraq reached 2,000. The president would nominate Samuel Alito for the Supreme Court. Alito met with Senator Ted Kennedy about his thoughts on *Roe v. Wade*. "I am a believer in precedents," Alito said, according to the senator's diary. "I recognize there is a right to privacy. I think it's settled." In *The Washington Post*, an exposé revealed the CIA's use of secret prisons in some thirty countries—"black sites"—where prisoners were subjected to sleep deprivation, waterboarding, and other forms of inhumane treatment. "Our country is at war," said President Bush, "and our government has the obligation to protect the American people . . . We are finding terrorists and bringing them to justice. We are gathering information about where the terrorists may be hiding. We are trying to disrupt their plots and plans. Anything we do to that effect, to that end, in this effort, any activity we conduct is within the law. We do not torture." In New York City, Michael Bloomberg won his second term as mayor in a landslide. And by late December—enabled by low interest rates, easy credit, and subprime mortgages—a record sixty-nine percent of all Americans were homeowners.

The Days of Mars was many things at once: a portrait of the country in a time of war, beginning with the two Confederates on the cover, drawn by Amy Gartrell; an effort to dissolve the walls dividing music for the body and the mind; a feminist work of art, in which fluidity between musicians and machines has gender and political dimensions. But most of all, the album was a snapshot of two voices, two styles, and two individuals, coming together and drifting apart. In *Arthur* magazine, Trinie Dalton wrote, "When you listen to it you feel like you're traveling to, well, Mars. But their music is really more about life on Earth." The veteran producer Carl Craig remixed the thirteen-minute "Relevee," delivering an instant DFA touchstone that all but overshadowed the original, and yet another double-edged sword.

The duo went their separate ways. The little notebook Delia and Rayna bought that day in Williamsburg would chronicle a decade's worth of art, ideas, and conversation. "I wish I would have recorded them all," says Delia. "We would have had books and books and books." She lived in Berlin for almost a decade before returning to New York in 2013. She kept making art, dances, and films. She had a boy and named him Wolfgang. They found a place on Kingsland Avenue, in Greenpoint, around the corner from her first apartment. "Culture shock," says Delia. "Nine months of complete culture shock." She moved to Greece in 2016, shortly after her first solo album, *In Remembrance*; a second one, *Horse Follows Darkness*, came soon after—both, of course, on DFA.

Rayna moved back from Berlin in 2009. She composed and improvised prolifically: as Black Meteoric Star, The Crystal Ark, and Gavilán Rayna Russom. She played synthesizers with LCD Soundsystem through their "final" show in 2011 at Madison Square Garden—her first time at the venue—and again for a reunion in 2015. She came out as transgender two years later. She changed her name and pronouns, and started taking hormones. She told *Pitchfork*, "I'm forty-three and I can identify that once a decade, I made a concerted effort to make my trans identity known. That includes a period of time when I was a child in the '70s, when I was going through puberty in the '80s, and then several periods throughout my twenties, thirties, and forties. What makes this time different is that I'm in a stable moment in my life. Working with LCD Soundsystem all last year and then having a solid block of time off to focus on self-care was really important for me. This is what came out of that. I don't like 'coming out' so much as a term, but sometimes it's the only way to say it . . . There may be people who are fans of either LCD or of my own music who really don't have any experience with these things. It's so easy to develop prejudices when you've never encountered a person in whatever group you're prejudiced against. I hope there's an opportunity to be of service and share my experience [in a way that's] true to the music." The news was covered by NPR, *Rolling Stone*, and CNN.

In March of 2020, she founded Voluminous Arts, an entirely trans-led organization that doubles as a community resource hub and record label. Then she did something for herself: she walked away from one of the biggest bands in the world. She told *The Quietus*, "My association with [LCD Soundsystem] was always going to negate me. So I had to leave DFA, legally and formally . . . I like those people and I'm friendly with those people. But those entities and those worlds are spearheaded by straight white men. They take up so much space and have such mass appeal. My affiliation with them meant people always saw that and not what I was doing.

"LCD was beneficial for me, sure; I went from playing shows for a handful of people in punk venues to a whole different scope and reach. But in the long term, I just got blasted out of context. I'd get booked for shows and people would have no idea what I do, or my discography. Bookers would ask me not to play the music I was playing. Over and over again. That was a decade of my life. People booked me because they couldn't afford James. It's so depressing. But there's a limit to the value of pulling it apart and analyzing it now."

Delia and Rayna are still making art and music—on their own terms. "What music means to me is not about being popular," Rayna says. "I don't care about making a record that people like. I'd like to make music that speaks to people. That's a different thing. I'm not interested in selling a lot of records or doing the things you have to do—the compromises that you have to make to be popular. I'm a folk artist. It means something to me, you know? It's how I create sense and meaning in this world, is to make experimental music. The process is the point. The recorded music that I've made is an archive of a spiritual evolution. It's an archive of a process. It's an archive of a life."

2009

"U.S. employers shed 2.6 million jobs in 2008, the worst year since 1945, and a rapidly deteriorating economy promises more significant losses ahead . . ." In California, Protests After Man Dies at Hands of Transit Police . . . Pilot Is Hailed After Jetliner's Icy Plunge . . . Few Israelis Near Gaza Feel War Achieved Much . . . "The time has come": Before vast crowd, Obama takes office with call to remake nation . . . *That tonight's gonna be a good, good night . . ."* Obama Orders Secret Prisons and Detention Camps Closed . . . Ticketmaster and Live Nation Move to Merge . . . "Rick Santelli, who reports from the floor of the Chicago Board of Trade for CNBC, unleashed a rant against Obama's newly announced housing bailout plan . . . 'Government is promoting bad behavior . . . Do we really want to subsidize the losers' mortgages? This is America!'" AIG to Pay $450 Million in Bonuses Despite Bailout . . . Tax Day Is Met with Tea Parties . . . Chrysler Files to Seek Bankruptcy Protection . . . U.S. Declares Public Health Emergency Over Swine Flu . . . Abortion Doctor Shot to Death in Kansas Church . . . Addressing Muslims, Obama Pushes Mideast Peace . . . Protests Flare in Tehran as Opposition Disputes Vote . . . After Years of Advocacy, Newly Renovated High Line Opens . . . *"Maybe sometimes? Make it easy?"* . . . U.S. Drone Strike Said to Kill 60 in Pakistan . . . A Star Idolized and Haunted, Michael Jackson Dies at 50 . . . Prominent Black Scholar Henry Louis Gates, Jr. Arrested; Cops call Gates disorderly; he says it's "what happens to black men in America." "Thousands of top traders and bankers on Wall Street were awarded huge bonuses and pay packages last year, even as their employers were battered by the financial crisis . . ." "Screaming constituents, protesters dragged out by the cops, congressmen fearful for their safety—welcome to the new town-hall-style meeting, the once-staid forum that is rapidly turning into a house of horrors for members of Congress . . ." "Joe Wilson, Republican of South Carolina, interrupted President Obama with a shout of 'You lie,' stunning both parties . . ." Obama calls Kanye West a "jackass" over MTV outburst . . . After Grizzly Bear's Brooklyn Show, Jay-Z Says He Hopes the "Indie Rock Movement" Will Inspire Rap and Hip-Hop Artists . . . Surprise Nobel for Obama Stirs Praise and Doubts . . . The New Facebook News Feed and What It Means . . . "One year ago today, we officially became a postracial society. Fifty-three percent of the voters opted for the candidate who would be the first president of African descent, and in doing so eradicated racism forever . . ." Bloomberg Wins 3rd Term as Mayor in Unexpectedly Close Race . . . U.S. Unemployment Rate Hits 10.2%, Highest in 26 Years . . . Obama Issues Order for More Troops in Afghanistan . . . Scores Dead as Car Bombs Rock Baghdad . . . The '00s: Goodbye (at Last) to the Decade from Hell . . . *Let's hear it for New York, New York, New York . . ."*

Pitchfork

In 1994—when a young Jeff Bezos started Amazon, and Yahoo! went live, and Netscape launched the first commercial browser for the World Wide Web—a friend of Ryan Schreiber's introduced him to the Internet. A recent graduate of Hopkins High School, in suburban Minneapolis, near Paisley Park, he was a fan of college radio, a sometime record-store cashier, and a voracious reader of the music press. From local zines (*The Squealer, Cake*) and the alternative glossies (*Magnet, Puncture, Ray Gun,* and *Spin*) to legacy magazines (*Rolling Stone*), the world of print, professional and amateur, was flourishing—an era when arts journalism and the written word held sway. "It was the height of '90s zine culture," he said, "so there were all these sort of DIY fanzines floating around." At a nearby Borders bookstore, there was an entire shelf of smart, opinionated publications like *Q* and *Mojo,* where he spent hours, engrossed. In 1995—when Match.com, *The Drudge Report, Salon,* and Craigslist all debuted—he started a webzine called *Turntable* from his childhood bedroom, using a dial-up connection. "All my friends were doing Xeroxed zines, and some small local papers were able to get interviews with artists that I really liked," he later said. "I thought, 'It can't really be that difficult if these guys are doing it. Why them and not me?'"

It was a monthly publication in its infancy. Before *Turntable*, Schreiber hadn't written much. He didn't know a single person at the record labels, so he improvised. He called the public library and asked if there were any listings in the phone book for a Sub Pop in Seattle, or a Merge in Chapel Hill—and then he sat on hold. Each number took twenty minutes. Several hours later, he had the makings of a list.

He started calling publicists for artist interviews. They asked where they should mail promotional CDs. "Once I found out that they could send me free music," he said, "I was like, 'Game over. This is what I'm doing.'" He interviewed a young band from Duluth named Low, as well as David Byrne, Ben Folds, and Modest Mouse. His parents had a fit each time the phone bill came, but he had found a vocation. He got himself on mailing lists for labels large and small, from Capitol to Kill Rock Stars.

It was a decade when the line dividing indie bands from major-label ones was all-defining, unambiguous, even a matter of allegiances: a stance the Internet was making obsolete. Around the time that Schreiber was discovering the Web, the Berkeley punk temple 924 Gilman Street would banish Green Day from its stage—where they had played as teenagers—for the infraction of signing with a major. In 1994, the zine *Maximumrocknroll* devoted a whole issue to the topic ("Some of Your Friends Are Already This Fucked: Everything You've Wanted to Know About Major Labels"), illustrated with a dark, demonic octopus to symbolize the major media conglomerates. When Schreiber was in high school, Kurt Cobain wore a shirt that said "CORPORATE MAGAZINES STILL SUCK" on the cover of *Rolling Stone*; Nirvana sold T-shirts that read "FLOWER SNIFFIN / KITTY PETTIN / BABY KISSIN / CORPORATE ROCK / WHORES." And in the pages of *The Baffler* magazine, the engineer-musician Steve Albini wrote "The Problem with Music," a jeremiad itemizing the exploitation of the major labels—and by extension, the corporate world at large:

> Whenever I talk to a band who are about to sign with a major label,
> I always end up thinking of them in a particular context. I imagine

a trench, about four feet wide and five feet deep, maybe sixty yards long, filled with runny, decaying shit. I imagine these people, some of them good friends, some of them barely acquaintances, at one end of this trench. I also imagine a faceless industry lackey at the other end, holding a fountain pen and a contract waiting to be signed.

It was the same debate within the indie world that would define *Pitchfork*'s trajectory in the decades to come. Was it preferable to have 100,000 diehard fans, or millions of casual ones? Should one aspire to the widest possible platform, or was there necessarily a compromise involved? Is it inherently unethical to get in bed with a massive corporation—or simply a concession to reality?

* * *

In 1996, the year he turned twenty, a CD-ROM company named Turntable sent him a cease-and-desist, "which scared the *fucking shit* out of me," Schreiber said. In keeping with the pugilistic criticism of the day, he changed the name to *Pitchfork*: a reference to the movie *Scarface*, where Al Pacino's pitchfork tattoo was code for an assassin. "When I started out, it was about really laying into people who really deserved it," he told *The Washington Post*. "To me, it underscored that we were going to be tougher as critics." *Pitchfork*'s origins in adolescent earnestness were most reflected in the weight assigned to grades. Much like *The Source* and *Rolling Stone*, the site evaluated records on a scale, but one designed for scientific precision. The scores were given as percentages initially: if seven out of ten tracks were interesting, it got a seventy percent. But then, the math was rarely so straightforward. The website's first review was of *Pacer*, by The Amps, a project of Kim Deal; it got an eighty-two percent. "Kim Deal set out to record a different kind of record and came out with one that's so terrific, it won't leave my discman [*sic*] for at least three days," Schreiber wrote. Percentages would soon become their signature two-digit score, on a scale from zero to ten. The *Pitchfork* era had begun.

It was a golden age for indie bands—Sleater-Kinney (8.3), Yo La Tengo (8.1), Neutral Milk Hotel (8.7)—and *Pitchfork*'s coverage reflected as much. Their calling card was Anglophone guitar groups of the '90s, but they also wrote about Steve Reich (5.8), Grace Jones (8.1), Albert Ayler (9.8), Noam Chomsky (8.5), Lauryn Hill (8.0), and Julio Iglesias (7.0). They championed melodic indie rock like *69 Love Songs* (8.0), *The Lonesome Crowded West* (8.9), and *Keep It Like a Secret* (9.3); innovative electronic music from Amon Tobin (9.8) and DJ Shadow (9.1); and Twin Cities groups like 12 Rods and Walt Mink, who both were given perfect 10s. They didn't shy from sacred cows: they panned The Flaming Lips (0.0) and Sonic Youth (0.0). They were particularly fond of The Dismemberment Plan's *Emergency & I* (9.6), which they picked for their "Top 100 Albums of the '90s" before it was even in stores. At times, their judgments were perverse, like when they wrote about *Pet Sounds* (7.5) ("passe and cliched [*sic*]") or *The Boy with the Arab Strap* (0.8) ("Maybe next time"). Reviews were penned by Schreiber and his friend Jason Josephes at a clip of two per day, and usually a single paragraph. The writing ranged from functional to incoherent. But on the whole, their taste was sound, their batting average high, and people noticed. One day, they got an email from a record store about a banner ad. Schreiber asked for $500. "They were like, 'Sounds great!'" He started calling magazines to ask about their rates.

There were some record labels keen to advertise—publicity budgets had yet to be slashed—but revenue was nominal, time-intensive, and a conflict of interest to boot. "Selling ads was just a slog. The ads were dirt-cheap," Schreiber said. "It was almost like asking for donations. And these were [labels] whose records we were already reviewing. It was kind of odd that you'd be talking to someone about ad stuff and then it would switch to editorial. It just wouldn't feel right." It was an ethical predicament at every level of the media: from Vice up to *The New York Times*, the long-established firewall that separated editorial from business would become increasingly porous.

They had 300 daily visitors after a year and more CDs than they knew what to do with, so they published a call for writers. Among the first to answer was Mark Richardson, a future editor-in-chief, and Amanda Petrusich, who went on to *The New Yorker*. The terms were onerous: reviewers had to file twice a week for six whole months without payment, aside from free records—at which point, they earned a fee of $20 per review, and $40 for a feature. (To be fair, it was the Mesozoic phase of the Internet; no one was making much.) Schreiber was twenty-three. He ran the website from his parents' house during the day, and worked at night in telemarketing. By 1999—when Napster went online, and Coachella had its first festival—the site had reached 2,000 daily readers. Using eBay, Schreiber pruned his records and moved to Chicago. He now could post reviews and features from some fifty writers, in genres that the site had long neglected: hip hop, metal, and dance, to name a few. He also had competitors: *PopMatters* (est. 1999); *Drowned in Sound* and *Chromewaves* (2000); *Tiny Mix Tapes* and *Glorious Noise* (2001); *Stereogum, Fluxblog, Cokemachineglow, Stylus,* and *Dusted* (2002).

What set *Pitchfork* apart? For one, their unflagging productiveness and drive. They published two reviews a day, then four, then five, which added up to twenty-five a week: a round-the-clock compendium of rising talent, sunken treasure, and emerging trends. They gave the art of criticism a significance and urgency. Where *Spin* and *Rolling Stone* would run reviews toward the back, by the classifieds, the *Pitchfork* team knew that a new album could still be an event, as was the case on October 2, 2000, with Radiohead's *Kid A* (10.0). A fan himself, Schreiber knew well how many were champing at the bit for *OK Computer*'s follow-up, and had been doling out a steady drip of articles before release. "It's clear that Radiohead must be the greatest band alive," Brent DiCrescenzo wrote in an extravagant review. Schreiber tipped off several fan sites in advance and watched as over 5,000 readers poured in. "I remember the date like a birthday," he told *Billboard*. "The web traffic was literally off the charts. I used a very small, local ISP and had a basic hosting plan, and the analytics maxed out beyond a certain point." By mid-2001, the site was up to 3,000 reviews, and 30,000 visitors a day.

They brought a palpable delight to the often-jaded world of criticism. The *Pitchfork* writers actually *enjoyed* listening to music—a rarer trait among the industry than one might think. What they lacked in gravitas, erudition, or grammar, they compensated for with absolute belief, exuberance, and desire for all things new. In "Top 100 Favorite Albums of the '90s," Schreiber wrote eagerly: "Since *Pitchfork*'s conception in November of 1995, I have been waiting patiently for the day when we would be able to bring you this feature." In a review of Yo La Tengo (9.7), Jason Josephes wrote, "The greatest band in the universe is back with their ninth studio release, *I Can Hear the Heart Beating as One*. What a terrible title!" They weren't afraid to plant a flag. In 1999—when *Rolling Stone* had Limp Bizkit, Kid Rock, and Eminem among their singles of the year—the *Pitchfork* year-end list included Godspeed You! Black Emperor (9.0), The Beta Band (8.8), and Bonnie "Prince" Billy (10.0). Where *Spin* would name Nirvana's *Nevermind* the "greatest" album of the '90s, it only came in sixth on *Pitchfork*'s Top 100—behind Guided by Voices, Liz Phair, and My Bloody Valentine, their number one. (At the same time, their "Top 100 of the '90s" had a single hip hop album—by the Beastie Boys—and, aside from Amon Tobin, not a single artist of color.)

But most of all, they did the work that almost no one else would do. They plowed through hundreds of promotional CDs and MP3s, one-sheets and press kits, day in and day out. They took a chance on groups that most had never heard of, based on simple curiosity. On February 2, 2003—when *Rolling Stone* had Shania Twain on its cover—Schreiber wrote about a recent discovery: a Toronto band named Broken Social Scene (9.2). "It's a bit late to be talking about New Year's resolutions, but mine was to dig through the boxes upon boxes of promos that arrive at the *Pitchfork* mailbox each month, and listen intently to hundreds of them in one sitting, in an attempt to discover those rare, impossibly great bands that would otherwise slip through the cracks." For all the wonders of the Internet, you had to sift through mountains of well-intended flops, misfires, and mediocrity—or find a trusted guide. In March 2003, the

Best New Music section launched, highlighting young artists such as The Books (8.4) and Sufjan Stevens (8.5); musicians in mid-career like Deerhoof (8.3) and The Wrens (9.5); and even the occasional pop star, such as Jay-Z (8.0), Cee-Lo (8.3), or Kanye West (8.2).

By 2004, the site was up to 115,000 daily visitors. The staff had grown with budding writers such as Nitsuh Abebe, Tom Breihan, and Julianne Escobedo Shepherd; the quality improved by leaps and bounds. *The Washington Post, The Guardian, Slate,* and *Wired* were writing of "the *Pitchfork* effect": the site's ability to lift an artist from obscurity at its whim. "Obviously, I never foresaw that it would get quite this big," Schreiber told the *New York Observer* in 2004. "I was sort of ambitious about it, but it's obviously gone so far beyond my expectations that it's hard for me to believe that this is my job." Meanwhile, the staff had raised concerns about their pay, or lack thereof. The tension boiled over when the site's financials were left on an unprotected server and posted online. They revealed that *Pitchfork* had been making more from ads than some were led to believe. The rates were raised to $80 for reviews and $110 for features. To grow the company, Schreiber hired his first full-time employees: Chris Kaskie, who sold ads, and Scott Plagenhoef, as managing editor.

A turning point in terms of real-world influence came on September 12, 2004, with an ecstatic review of *Funeral* (9.7), the second album from a rising band named Arcade Fire. "Ours is a generation overwhelmed by frustration, unrest, dread, and tragedy," wrote David Moore. "*Funeral* evokes sickness and death, but also understanding and renewal; child-like mystification, but also the impending coldness of maturity." It soon became the fastest-selling album in the history of Merge Records, and its first to reach the *Billboard* 200. An equally significant appraisal ran in late September, when *Travistan*—the awkwardly entitled solo effort by Travis Morrison, of The Dismemberment Plan—would notoriously receive a 0.0 rating. "One of the most colossal trainwrecks in indie rock history," went the review by Chris Dahlen, and with it, much of Morrison's career, as stores declined to stock the record, and college radio chose not to play it either. With an authority held once by *Rolling Stone*, the eight-year-old upstart could make or break an artist instantly, somewhat to their surprise. "I don't think it occurred to them that the review could have a catastrophic effect," said Morrison. "Literally, the view changed overnight."

By 2005—the year of *Illinois* (9.2), *LCD Soundsystem* (8.2), and *Silent Alarm* (8.9)—a Best New Music nod could catapult an artist to a worldwide following, or at a minimum, a semblance of stability. It meant the difference between an agency, a label scout, a manager—and, in turn, a license deal, a festival offer, another year to make a living from your art. It might have only meant a minimal amount of sales, in the age of file-sharing. But in the vacuum left by Napster, the MP3, and the decline of print, a different kind of currency emerged: authentic human enthusiasm. From music blogs like *Brooklyn Vegan*, *Productshop NYC*, *Largehearted Boy*, *Gorilla vs. Bear*, and *Aquarium Drunkard*, there was a feeling of opportunity, excitement, and disruption in the air—a sense that amateurs online would constitute a new and democratic A&R, untainted by the star-making machine.

With acts such as M.I.A. (8.6), Madvillain (9.4), Vashti Bunyan (8.5), Anohni and the Johnsons (8.6), and William Basinski (9.4) all getting Best New Music, *Pitchfork* elevated well-deserving artists old and new to a position of prominence. Not that they didn't slip: between buzz bands like Serena-Maneesh (8.6), The Go! Team (8.7), and Art Brut (8.9), the designation was sometimes puzzling. For young groups such as Clap Your Hands Say Yeah (9.0) or Tapes 'n Tapes (8.3), the hype could be a mixed reward, propelling acts before they had a record deal, or, at times, even played onstage. Born in part with *Pitchfork*, a comically accelerated cycle of anticipation and backlash led to groups with an abbreviated lifespan: just ask a flash in the pan like Voxtrot (5.9) or the Black Kids (3.3). For artists who were out of favor, feelings toward Schreiber were deeply personal. "You're so creative / with your reviews / of what other people do," David Bazan (4.7) sang in "Selling Advertising." "How satisfying that must be for you." Some pointed out that harsh reviews were nothing new. "They're entitled to write what they want," said Brendan Canning of Broken Social Scene. "It's kind of tragic for [Travis] Morrison, but if you get a bad review, you know, hey, that's showbiz."

But then again, how you interpreted the site itself would come to be a sort of Rorschach test. "Reading *Pitchfork* was kind of like talking to the guy at the record store," said Puja Patel, the future editor-in-chief. "It was the person who was a little arrogant—but possibly rightfully so. . . . In many ways, I've got to say, I didn't necessarily think *Pitchfork* was intended to be for me. But at the same time, I desperately wanted to know what they thought about things."

The site kept growing. In 2005, they were approached by organizers of Chicago's Intonation Festival, who wanted them to program two days' worth of acts. They chose some twenty artists from Four Tet (8.2) to The Decemberists (8.3), who played in Union Park for a crowd of 15,000. In real life, the site's aesthetic blind spots were obvious. "In the park as online, *Pitchfork* seemed to have trouble figuring out how to incorporate genres beyond indie rock," observed Kelefa Sanneh in *The New York Times*. "Dance music and hip hop still seem tangential to the *Pitchfork* mission." Advertising from American Express, Apple, and Toyota brought in $5 million of revenue. The following year, when they had reached 150,000 daily visits, the first official Pitchfork Music Festival was held at Union Park, headlined by the Silver Jews (8.5) and Os Mutantes (8.9).

In 2007, Schreiber moved to Park Slope from Chicago. He soon became a fixture at establishments like Glasslands, Silent Barn, and Death by Audio. "It was the peak of NYC DIY culture," he remembered. "There was always a show happening every single night." The Brooklyn scene would add a new dimension to his efforts on behalf of undiscovered bands. "Ryan was always a restless spirit," *Pitchfork* contributor Emilie Friedlander says. "He was not going to rest on his laurels. He was always looking for the next thing. When he came to New York, he was like, 'I want the rawest, deepest underground shit.' Kind of shifting from this world of things that are already on labels. He wanted to be catching stuff as it broke. More than a lot of *Pitchfork* staff, he was going out to shows, to all the venues, listening to what was happening, trying to find ways to support it." He founded *Altered Zones*, a site that brought together thirteen blogs with specialties across the musical underground, edited by Friedlander and Ric Leichtung, who would also book 285 Kent. Some pointed to a certain overlap between the groups that Schreiber hung out with, like DIIV (8.3), and those that got Best New Music.

As indie rock achieved unprecedented levels of renown and visibility among the public in the aughts, the site's hegemony had never been clearer. Among the groups to benefit from its largesse was the Toronto punk outfit Fucked Up (8.8). Some fifteen years later, guitarist Mike Haliechuk wrote about the day *The Chemistry of Common Life* (2008) was awarded Best New Music: "I went downstairs for breakfast. It's trite to say, but that was a turning point in our career, that morning. The score infected the room—we all knew that we could barely address it, but we all knew what it meant, we had to. Looking back you could say that one review is why we still have a career . . . Those numbered scores with the little decimals contextualized an entire generation of music." Others were more ambivalent. "It felt like *Pitchfork* was in control of the destiny of my career to an extent, because it did have this huge place in breaking or burying artists," said Nika Danilova, who performs as Zola Jesus. "The pressure as a musician got more to be *I better get a good review.*"

By 2008, their daily readership was up to 250,000. By 2009, they had a full-time staff of seventeen, and offices in Williamsburg and Wicker Park. They tried expanding with assorted sister sites—devoted to experimental music (*Altered Zones*), film (*The Dissolve*), and visual art (*Nothing Major*)—all of which would fold. They made the overdue decision to promote and hire editors and writers who weren't dudes from Minnesota. As Laura Snapes would write, "it was women and non-binary writers—Lindsay Zoladz, Jenn Pelly, Carrie Battan, Amanda Petrusich, Sasha

Geffen, Jill Mapes, Doreen St. Félix, Hazel Cills; the fearless editing of Jessica Hopper and then the most recent editor-in-chief Puja Patel, to name but a handful—who transformed the website in the 2010s." Their focus widened to auteurs such as Janelle Monáe (8.5), Miguel (8.4), Frank Ocean (9.5), and Kendrick Lamar (9.5), then to the world of pop. By 2013, the site was up to 1.5 million daily visits, a staff of forty-eight, and yearly revenue approaching $10 million. They won a National Magazine Award; they threw a festival in Paris. All the same, said Schreiber, "everything was on a shoestring budget."

* * *

For thirty years or so, the indie world defined itself in terms of distance from and opposition to the major media conglomerates and mainstream charts. In 2015—just shy of its twentieth anniversary—the site that Schreiber started as a teenager was bought by Condé Nast, the company that owned *The New Yorker, GQ, Vogue,* and *Vanity Fair.* He later said, "We were really enthusiastic and very excited about it in the beginning, because it felt like, here is a place where great journalism is valued, is prized, and we're now going to have resources to do that much more of it." The acquisition was a mismatch from day one. A Condé Nast executive would tell the *Times* it brought "a very passionate audience of millennial males into our roster," instantly alienating the *Pitchfork* staff. Another urged the Pitchfork Music Festival to boost its ticket sales by reuniting Oasis. Despite 8.5 million unique monthly visitors and 3 million followers on Twitter, the site's performance never satisfied the Condé brass—as Kurt Cobain and Steve Albini once foresaw.

"It became apparent pretty much immediately, when they laid out what the traffic goals were—well, how can I say this? I think our expectations were just different from what was delivered, and what was promised never really materialized," Schreiber said. He exited the company in 2019.

A few months before its thirtieth anniversary, in 2024, the world's most loved and hated site for music criticism was subsumed under the banner of *GQ*, the monthly men's magazine and "arbiter of cool for any-one who sees the world through the lens of taste and style." The staff was drastically reduced; the editor-in-chief was fired. Appreciations, obituaries, and analysis appeared in *The New York Times* (by Ezra Klein), *The Guardian*, and *Slate*, as well as on Substack, where music journalists—in the absence of paid writing outlets—had largely migrated. Some said that *Pitchfork* had betrayed its indie roots in favor of insipid pop such as Adele (8.2), Lady Gaga (7.8), and Taylor Swift (9.0); some said it was the end of music journalism as we know it; and for most, the tempest barely registered. The days when a review meant something seemed as ancient as the CD-ROM.

Or were they? On April 12, 2024, an album by the little-known and enigmatic artist Cindy Lee entitled *Diamond Jubilee* (9.1) was awarded Best New Music, and for the next few weeks, it was 2004 again. Like Broken Social Scene, the album had been quietly released, to almost no attention from the music press, or what remained of it. The music wasn't up on Spotify, whose CEO the artist called "A THIEF AND A WAR PIG." The shows on Cindy Lee's tour sold out overnight; the album ended up on countless critics' lists. In other words: you can't count *Pitchfork* out just yet. And in the fall, some former staffers founded *Hearing Things*, an "independent home for music and culture," funded largely by subscriptions. I signed up on day one.

Glasslands

The thing that I remember is the trek from Metropolitan. It was a twenty-minute walk from the subway. You had to cross a chaotic intersection; you braved the fumes from the Brooklyn-Queens Expressway. Then you saw the signs for Havemeyer, Roebling, Driggs, Bedford, Berry, Wythe, and Kent. Then south a few more blocks. You passed the people in the bars, the coffee shops, the restaurants—in conversation, or, increasingly, pawing their phones. The streets were emptier as you approached the waterfront. You saw a red-and-orange necklace of illuminated light on the Williamsburg Bridge. And when you heard the sound of amps and subwoofers from down the block, you knew that you had arrived at Glasslands.

According to my calendar, I saw more shows at Glasslands than at any other place in Williamsburg. From 2007 (Oxford Collapse) to 2014 (The Clean), I watched its evolution from a shaggy and ramshackle spot to one that rivaled any of its size (a cozy 300). I heard Americana (Woods), glitch (Zammuto), blue-eyed soul (Jamie Lidell), power pop (The Rock*A*Teens), hip hop (Das Racist), chillwave (Small Black), singer-songwriters (Mirah), neoclassical (Nils Frahm), and left-field electronic music (Prefuse 73). I wasn't there the nights that gave them bragging rights for life: the early shows and underplays with SZA and

Sophie, Mitski and Charli XCX, Lana Del Rey and Bon Iver. But then, the venue's reputation as a fountainhead of cool would always be at odds with its aggressively egalitarian and unassuming vibe. It was a place you stumbled into when another show had gotten out, and no one felt like heading home: a place for when your sense of time was growing indistinct. The feeling of suspension was accentuated by the artist Vashti Windish's paper clouds above the stage (2008–12)—declared a fire hazard by the city—and later, the design studio Hard Work Party's chandelier-like tubes (2013–14).

The bands at Glasslands struck a middle ground between the punk and rock of Death by Audio, around the corner, and the more experimental offerings at 285 Kent, just one door down. Out of the three, it was the most "professional" in terms of contracts, permits, or accounting, and the least devoted to the all-ages ethos. It was the likeliest to have a dance party, a sponsored open bar, or an audience that had come from Manhattan. For these reasons, it was a venue some would label insufficiently DIY, and they may have had a point. But anyone who says that Glasslands wasn't special is misleading you, or doesn't know the reason why it was the way it was.

* * *

Brooke Baxter was born to a family of entertainers. In the early 1900s, her great-uncles and -aunts were actors in a British vaudeville troupe. Her father, Billy Baxter, was a professional comedian—the youngest ever to perform at the London Palladium—and an associate of The Beatles. A headliner in the Jewish resorts and clubs of the Borscht Belt, upstate, he often brought his daughter to the Friars Club, on East Fifty-Fifth Street, the illustrious haunt of comics and celebrities. He made appearances on Ed Sullivan and *The Tonight Show*; he shared the stage with Liza Minnelli, Shirley MacLaine, and Tom Jones. "He was very much an artist in the way he lived his life, and how I spent my time with him," Brooke says. "We were constantly coming up with creative scenarios."

A native of New York, born in midtown, she spent her childhood in Connecticut before returning at age thirteen to the Upper West Side. When Brooke was still a teenager, she started sneaking out at night and venturing downtown, to Astor Place, Chelsea, and the Lower East Side. Her mother's only rule was not to leave the borough, which Brooke would mostly obey. It was the early '90s. David Dinkins was the mayor. The city was a more permissive place. At age fifteen, you could get into almost any bar or club; nobody asked you for ID. She went to hip hop and house-music parties; to underground gay bars on the West Side Highway; to downtown institutions like the Limelight, Tunnel, Life, and Lot 61. At the end of the night, she took the train uptown and quietly observed her fellow passengers: rich and poor, young and old, black and white. "New York is not a melting pot," the mayor had said, "but a gorgeous mosaic." From early on, she saw the city as a universe in miniature, where on every subway, sidewalk, stoop, and bench, there were individuals of every language, origin, and aspiration, each with their own story to tell.

At seventeen, she worked for Stretch Armstrong, a pioneering hip hop DJ and event promoter, handing out flyers. A year later, she rented her own place on the Upper East Side. She sent a check each month to an office in Williamsburg, which she had yet to see. Before she was of drinking age, she worked the door at clubs and learned the rules of entry—the art of keeping out the riffraff. If you weren't on the guest list, or a celebrity, you had to wait in the cold, like a peasant; if you didn't look a certain way, you might as well drop dead. The goal was making people feel bad: the worse, the better. The velvet rope, the VIPs, the utterly indifferent staff ensured an air of exclusivity, a buffer from the great unwashed. It felt demeaning, vacuous. "It wasn't fueling anything creative," she said. "I needed a change of scene."

* * *

In February 2000, *Time Out New York* published "The Bedford Files," an article about "arty East Village types" moving to Williamsburg. It was a neighborhood she knew little about, beyond the monthly rent she mailed to Bedford Avenue. She dialed her landlords. They offered her a two-bedroom on Roebling and North Eighth for $1,000 a month. She lived upstairs from a pierogi factory. She introduced herself to the neighbors and rode her bike everywhere. It was like living in a small town. At most, there were a handful of bars and cafés. She met painters, poets, and filmmakers; she went to readings, plays, and openings. "It felt like what I imagine college would have been like," Brooke said. "A small college campus, almost. It felt like I was at the start of something explosive, youthful, and fun. It also felt so small that it seemed anything was possible."

She didn't have much of a plan. She paid the bills by doing odd jobs here and there. She learned the dos and don'ts of show promotion at The Cutting Room, a venue owned by the lascivious Chris Noth of *Sex and the City*. She found part-time gigs through Craigslist. She worked as a nude model. She read books to a blind man. She befriended a calligrapher and started making books. She threw parties. She sold her poems on the street.

She met a sculptor who was renting out a space in 5 Pointz, a haven for graffiti artists in Long Island City, Queens. "There was a real collaborative spirit in that building," Brooke says. "Everybody's doors were always open." Among its residents was a collective named the Freestyle Arts Association, who thought that art was meant for everyone, not only the elite. She soon became the fifth member, and briefly moved in, "Which was hell. It's like showering in a sink. So from there we decided to open our own art space."

She registered her first domain name in 2004. "My hope," she wrote, "is to continue on the path of a poet, and to eventually get an art space that is open to all who are interested in creating art with each other." Just a few weeks later, she was walking up Kent when she noticed a "SPACE FOR RENT" sign hanging behind a window. Around the corner was a vacant warehouse on South First. It was an empty canvas: walls of cinder block, floors of concrete, and a malfunctioning, germ-infested toilet. "I thought it was beautiful," she said. The street was lined with warehouses, foundries, pallets, forklifts, and spray paint. Up the block, the Domino Sugar plant had just been closed. An overgrown and long-forgotten lot was visible behind a barbed and rusty fence across the street. The rent was $2,000 a month. The owner, Joseph Markowitz, was Hasidic, and something of a cad. "He rented it to me because I was a white, pretty girl, and young, and Jewish. It was not lost on me that it was my privilege that secured me the lease in the first place. If I had not been all of those things, I doubt I would have gotten a lease."

Her brainchild, the Glass House Gallery—a radically inclusive, anti-elitist art space—opened in the fall of 2004. Construction work was done by Brooke's then-partner, Lev, a.k.a. Leviticus, who also curated rotating installations. "His vision was very much behind the beautiful and chaotic space that was Glass House," says Brooke. They said it was a place "for artists to come together, support each other, and, above all, create together." Every Friday was an Experiential Art Night, where guests were free to paint on a 300-foot wall, or add a story to a "collective typewriter." They loaned the space to friends for poetry readings, performance art, dance events, screenings, plays, and fundraisers; they rented studios and rehearsal spaces; they hosted a monthly dinner party. They took the time to welcome anyone who wandered through the door. "I was looking for an almost utopian space, where no one is onstage," says Brooke, "or everybody is." Belatedly, they realized they weren't making enough money. And that was when they started booking bands.

The scene in Williamsburg was growing by the week. On Kent and Metropolitan in the spring, the Mighty Robot crew had founded Monster Island. On Wythe, around the corner, a Francophone trio had opened Zebulon, an artist-friendly bar and club. The year before, the video artist Montgomery Knott had started Monkey Town, a combination salon, restaurant, and concert space. At Tommy's Tavern, the Right Bank, and other makeshift venues, the DIY promoter Todd P had won a young and dedicated following. But even in a crowded field, the Glass House was unique. A Glass House regular, Thimali Kodikara, says, "To have a space that was not just about music—it wasn't created for music at all. It was created to bring people together and make art together. It really was rooted in social change and community-building. It was not about posing. It was not about who you know, because that scene existed on the Lower East Side. To me, the difference was that Brooke was a New Yorker. She grew up with people from all over. It wasn't like these kids who came from other parts of the country, and wanted to be around people that looked like themselves."

In the first few months, they hosted shows with friends from the neighborhood: Dragons of Zynth; Kyp Malone, of TV on the Radio; and a brand-new group named Grizzly Bear. By 2005, Kimya Dawson, Richard Bishop, Mary Halvorson, Carla Bozulich, and Dirty Projectors had played the Glass House, through Todd. Among the listeners out in the crowd was an aspiring musician named Caroline Polachek. "My central memory of being there was that I was going to be injured," says Caroline. "I was watching Japanther play from this rickety loft balcony that felt like a giant bunk bed attached to the wall, made out of two-by-fours. It was the best view in the house. I was like, 'I'm going to be hurt by the end of the night.' And even that was exciting. The opening act was a shirtless guy smashing a bike, and the toilet didn't work. I was twenty-one, twenty-two. And what more do you want when you're that age?" In hindsight, it was a moment that would rapidly be unrecognizable, before the tyranny of smartphones, social media, and Spotify. "It was a very pre-online era," Caroline says, "and there was such a strong, exciting feeling of *being there*, of being in these sweaty spaces where anything could happen . . . I've never seen anything remotely like that since. I've definitely had glimpses of scenes since then, but nothing that felt—in some ways, as big as that."

* * *

By late 2005, the limitations of the Glass House Gallery in terms of safety, space, and resources were apparent. "I wanted something a little more legit so I could find some longevity," said Brooke. "I called the landlord and he rented me a different space in the same building." In 2006, with the Taiwanese-American artist, musician, and Virginia transplant Rolyn Hu, she opened Glasslands, at 289 Kent Avenue.

Born in Washington, D.C., to a Taiwanese father and a mother who fled China by boat after Mao Tse-Tung came to power, Rolyn had lived in Canada, New Mexico, and Europe before landing in New York. Her family had weathered a succession of instability and mental illness. A grandfather died by suicide; her father was an abusive alcoholic, severely bipolar. At age thirteen, she had to call the cops on him and find a place for her and her mother to live. She chose to go to university in Toronto, lived in Montreal for five years, and moved to Bushwick in 2002. With a musician friend, Che Chen, she found a loft on Johnson Street, above a doll factory. They made music night and day; they formed a band, True Primes. She started throwing shows. Her first was with The Unicorns, Twi the Humble Feather, and Sharon Van Etten. "We were young, dumb, and happy just to be playing for our friends," says Rolyn.

With zero cash on hand or outside investors, they built the venue out in phases for the first few months. "Every show, we'd make a little money and use that to get better monitors, or put in a new toilet," said Brooke. The Yeah Yeah Yeahs played early on, in 2007. "We hardly play small venues anymore, but this one is definitely special and personal," Karen O told the *Times*. In June, they booked an up-and-coming band called Vampire Weekend, and in July, a young MGMT. Where most establishments gave minimal attention to diversity, they made a point of booking acts led by women and artists of color like Earl Greyhound, Magik Markers, Grouper, Celebration, and Okkyung Lee.

"We wanted to do something other than a bunch of sweaty white guys in a dark room," Rolyn says. "It was a huge part of my drive of making Glasslands into a real community space, not just an all-boys club where everyone stood around acting cool and pretentious. I was doing sound at Glasslands in the early days but would feign stupidity about gear just 'cause it was easier." As an Asian-American woman with a disability, she was an outlier several times over. "During that time, you would rarely see people of color working the bar at any music venue or DIY space. It was a predominantly all-white boys' club. I felt the pressure of homogenization even among the women as well. I was also still moving through the dynamic disability of six years of a serious autoimmune condition. Again, this was a time when disabilities were not discussed, and I held my tongue on that. It was before social media. We didn't have the language then to discuss this aloud, but I was deeply disturbed and also privately trying to disrupt the status quo, but in the funnest, kindest way possible. It was a struggle sometimes, and I definitely felt lonely in those early years—putting up with a lot of microaggressions toward me as a POC woman and Brooke also as a female."

Through Rolyn's work, the venue's musical identity would soon take shape. "Brooke didn't necessarily know a ton about avant music, or even have a clearly defined taste in music," says Cameron Hull, a decade-long bar manager, porter, and doorman at Glass House and Glasslands. "Brooke saw herself as bringing people together in a social sense, whereas Rolyn brought more of the avant-garde. She was responsible for bringing artists such as Thurston Moore. She also had a business acumen to her as well. Brooke and Rolyn got along really well, and they were always good to us, as a team. They complemented each other well."

* * *

Some would have tried to capitalize on a changing neighborhood, and many did. By 2007—when you could find silk muumuus for $318 or blue cheese at $43 a pound on Bedford Avenue—a local venue boom was underway. Club Europa, Studio B, Luna Lounge (formerly in the East Village), and Music Hall of Williamsburg had opened; Bruar Falls, Brooklyn Bowl, and the Knitting Factory (its third iteration) soon followed. In June, a group of preservationists would list the waterfront in Williamsburg among America's eleven most endangered historic places: "Today, Brooklyn's industrial heritage—a tangible link with the immigrants who struggled for new lives here—is in jeopardy as the waterfront falls victim to voracious developers anxious to cash in on the area's newly hip status."

But even as the area was bought up by developers, the venue would remain a home for artists, oddballs, and their extended circle. One night, police raided the place, only to find everyone dressed in costumes of the French Revolution. "The tchotchke-filled, mural-lined industrial space on a no-man's-land block in Williamsburg is something right out of the East Village's heyday," wrote *The Village Voice*. Where most promoters hardly gave the neighborhood a second thought, the founders tried to mitigate their impact as gentrifiers. They partnered with a local youth officer to start an arts-and-music program for teenagers; they sponsored after-school activities for kids from the community; they hosted benefits for free103point9 and the Willa Mae Rock Camp for Girls. In 2008 the *Times* wrote, the "Glasslands Gallery . . . holds concerts a few times a week, but also doubles, triples, quadruples and quintuples as a do-it-yourself art space, an after-school program, a lecture hall and a private party site. The ever-changing art that coats the walls gives a dreamy feel to the space, especially when it is rocking with groups like Heavy Trash, as it was on a recent weekend." Meanwhile—from Emeralds and Real Estate to Deerhunter and Oakley Hall; from Castanets and Yeasayer to Phosphorescent and Chairlift—the calendar comprised some of the brightest stars found in the indie firmament.

* * *

By mid-2009—when Jay-Z and Beyoncé came to Williamsburg for Grizzly Bear, right up the street—the team at Glasslands had accomplished what they set out to do, and then some. They started looking for an exit ramp. "I think age plays into it," Brooke says. "There's a beautiful time when you're an artist, when you're creating because you love to create. You don't have this compounding pressure to support a family. And then, I think, my group of friends—as we got older, things would change. It also came with record companies and promoters seeing the scene in Williamsburg, that there was money to be made. The neighborhood was changing so much. It was becoming something that didn't represent who I was anymore. Instead of complaining about it, I decided to jump ship. I was starting to raise children, which I wanted to become my focus. I needed to keep swimming. I needed to keep moving."

It was the year that Brooke and Rolyn handed off the booking to a pair of undergrads at NYU who called themselves Popgun Presents. As Brooke remembered, the Popgun team were "kind of a unicorn in that they were young and enthusiastic, but also had their shit together and were responsible." The starting salary was $225 a week, divided by two. Half went to a kid from Connecticut named Jake Rosenthal. The other half went to his roommate, Rami Haykal, who hailed from Lebanon, by way of Italy. As promoters, they got their start thanks entirely to the Internet, in the mid-to-late aughts, when bands and booking agents were a bit more reachable. "People were more open to having communication," says Rami. "It was an era when you could be a totally unknown person, and send one email, and you would get a response." They cut their teeth with shows by Passion Pit, Blood Orange, Disclosure, alt-J, Grimes, and Tame Impala. They also found a sanctuary of a sort. "After moving so many times throughout my life, Glasslands was the first place where I truly felt at home," says Rami. "I found a community of people who were always ready to help me without expecting anything in return. It was a sense of camaraderie and mutual support I had never experienced before—and yet, it also felt like its own protective, insulated bubble. And the entire time, being able to program a variety of music for the space never felt like a job." In 2011, Jake and Rami took over the lease. They would be the last of three venues in the building to close three years later, when Vice Media moved in.

* * *

By the age of seven, Rami had seen more of the globe than most will ever see. Born in Maameltein, Lebanon—a seaside town that dated to the fourteenth century, thirteen miles north of Beirut—his family personified the story of the modern Middle East. His great-grandfather had been a political appointee in Jerusalem. His grandmother was among the 750,000 refugees expelled from Palestine in 1948, resettling in Jordan. Both his father and grandfather had been educated in France, which governed Lebanon after the First World War; the family spoke English, French, and Arabic at home. When Rami was born, in 1987, the country was embroiled in a fifteen-year civil war, driving countless Lebanese to move abroad—among them, his uncle, aunt, and cousins, who lived in Westchester.

His father was an engineer who specialized in massive infrastructure—ports, canals, and bridges—often in remote, developing countries. In 1988, when Rami was an infant, his father's work took the family to Maiduguri, Nigeria. They led a cloistered life, on the equivalent of an army base, built by his father's company. It was a difficult place to raise a one-year-old. His mother missed her family; his father traveled all the time.

When he was two years old, the family moved to Cairo. He went to an Irish elementary school with a view of the pyramids. By then, he had a little sister, Tala. They moved again when he was six, to Doha, the capital of Qatar—according to *Lonely Planet*, the world's most boring place. (There wasn't much to see beyond a Sheraton hotel.) With average daily temperatures of ninety-nine degrees, everything happened after sundown: an atmosphere that lent itself to little more than staying indoors. He spent his days possessed by American music, sports, and culture: Michael Jackson, Michael Jordan, and the NBA. From the outside, at least, America was the envy of the world. In 1995, the family moved to Genoa, Italy, where they settled. He went to Lebanon to see his grandparents every summer, and every other year to see his cousins in New York.

He had a normal adolescence, if in "normal" you include an international school in Northern Italy. From the third grade onward, he had the same twenty classmates, all Italian, who had known each other since kindergarten. He, on the other hand, was an immigrant, as some of his neighbors were soon to point out. Beyond the confines of the school, he heard from kids that he should go back to his own country. At eight years old, he understood he was a foreigner—a fact he was reminded of in every airport in the West after 9/11.

His grandfather died prematurely in 2001. He had played an important part in Rami's fourteen years of age. He had attended hospitality school in Grenoble, France. He managed several restaurants and hotels from the '50s to the '70s—the golden age of Beirut, when it was known as the Paris of the Middle East—only to lose everything in the civil war. It was his grandfather who first instilled the idea of a career in hospitality: if not a restaurant, perhaps, then something adjacent. Rami didn't know it then—he couldn't have, at age fourteen—but his grandfather had bequeathed to him a calling.

* * *

In Genoa, he went to an experimental high school, with only six in his graduating class. The town itself was a retirement community, provincial and sedate. There wasn't much to do for teenagers. They hung out at the beach, they went to the movies, and they spent hours finding music on the Internet.

It was the heyday of the MP3. In January of 2001—by way of introducing Apple's new iTunes software—Steve Jobs told an audience: "This is a music revolution happening right now." Nine months later, the first iPod was unveiled. A U.S. judge issued an injunction against Napster, forcing it to close in July. To fill the void, a field of imitators sprouted, one more bizarrely named than the next: Soulseek, Kazaa, Gnutella, Morpheus, Audiogalaxy, and LimeWire. The services were swamped with ads and prone to viruses. The songs themselves were brutally compressed, a faint approximation of the source. Depending on your modem speed, it might have taken hours for a single album to download. And yet, for all their inconveniences, the networks were a priceless resource in a time of musical plenty: the year of *Oh, Inverted World*; *Is This It*; *White Blood Cells*; and the *Yeah Yeah Yeahs* EP, all of which he found on LimeWire.

Rami went to NYU in 2005. Before he left Genoa, his family told him not to attract attention or talk politics. He was there to learn—ideally, something lucrative, like banking. From a graduating class of six, it was a bit of an adjustment. His economics course alone had some 500 students; English was his third language. He had been randomly assigned to a dorm, with roommates. One of them was a skinny, half-Jamaican hip hop fanatic from Connecticut, Jake Rosenthal. They started going out to shows and parties in the East Village; they started meeting bands. The thing about New York, he found, despite its periodic surliness, was how quickly it felt like home—how tolerant, gregarious, and welcoming the city was, no matter where you had come from.

He flew to Lebanon to stay with family in the summer of 2006, much like always. He had just completed freshman year, and was feeling pretty good about himself. He had a group of friends at NYU. During his stay in Lebanon, he had an internship with a Lebanese bank. In Germany, the World Cup was underway. On the night of July 9, he was out celebrating Italy's win over France in the final. Three days later, he was at work when he first heard about an incident on Lebanon's southern border. Hezbollah militants had crossed the border with Israel, killing three soldiers and capturing two; another five were killed on Lebanese soil. Israel's prime minister, Ehud Olmert, said he was holding the Lebanese government responsible, and launched a series of ground, air, and sea attacks. The IDF imposed a land-and-sea blockade and bombed the country's one international airport, in Beirut. The currency was cratering. At his previously unexciting internship, there was a run on the bank; he had to limit customers' withdrawals to five hundred dollars, and then two.

Because his grandmother lived in a Christian neighborhood, they figured they were safe at first, and tried to wait it out. To some extent,

it was behavior born out of routine: for all its savagery, the civil war in
Lebanon had failed to extinguish the country's way of life. "The minute
a cease-fire took effect in one neighborhood," wrote the Beirut corre-
spondent Thomas Friedman, "the storekeepers cranked up their steel
shutters and life immediately mushroomed back onto the streets, as
people grabbed for any crumb of normality they could." By sheer necessity, the Lebanese had forged an instinct for survival, stoicism, and even
revelry amid the clouds of war. That same week, Anthony Bourdain was
filming an episode of *No Reservations* in a Beirut nightclub when the
Israeli counteroffensive began. On camera, his fellow clubgoers took in
the news, paused momentarily, and then resumed drinking. As Friedman
observed, "Even in their darkest moments, and maybe because of them,
the Lebanese never forget how to laugh." If anywhere embodied a philosophy of "the show must go on," it had to be Lebanon.

Israeli warplanes launched attacks on civilian infrastructure: bridges,
highways, seaports, and power stations. A hundred twenty Lebanese
were killed in the first three days of the war. Thousands in the south
of Lebanon fled their homes. Hezbollah launched some 4,000 rockets
into Israel, killing forty-three civilians. In mid-July, the IDF positioned
thousands of reservists at the border. The U.S. embassy was arranging
exits, which would have worked for most of Rami's family—but not for
his grandmother, who had a Lebanese passport. Israeli planes had started
bombing the suburbs north of Beirut. The time had come to flee.

They packed the car and left at four A.M. They made their way southeast, through the mountains, all on back roads—his sister, mother,
grandmother, and him. (His father was in Genoa.) At age eighteen, and
as a native Lebanese, he knew he was subject to involuntary service in
the army.

They drove by homes that had been flattened by missiles. They went
through villages that had been made into ghost towns, littered with glass,
ash, and debris. They sat in lines of idling cars and showed their pass-
ports at impromptu checkpoints staffed by men in uniform, with guns.

There was a nerve-racking exchange with an official at the Syrian border, along with a significant toll, so to speak. They drove through Syria, into Jordan. They didn't stop until they'd made it to Amman, where they had relatives. Just a few days later, Rami was on a flight to JFK. As the plane was speeding down the runway, he made a promise to himself, and to his grandfather. When he was finally back in New York—if it was the last thing he ever did—he would devote his life to hospitality, and the art of entertaining others.

Adam Shore (II)

July 7, 2007. Musicians from around the world united for an epic, one-time-only spectacle: Live Earth, a synchronized event with some 150 artists playing in locations on all seven continents. In Tokyo, Johannesburg, London, Sydney, Rio, and—uh—East Rutherford, New Jersey, the Black Eyed Peas, Metallica, Bon Jovi, Rihanna, Shakira, Alicia Keys, and Madonna drew attention to the threat of climate change. On CNN, Al Gore proclaimed, "It's the largest entertainment event in the history of the world." Before an audience that watched in 130 countries, celebrities urged governments and leaders to address the climate crisis. The British press would delightedly note that many artists came on private planes.

It was the second anniversary of the London terrorist attacks, and a week after attempted car bombings in London and Glasgow. In an address to the West Virginia National Guard, President Bush defended the invasion of Iraq, and called for "more patience, more courage, and more sacrifice." Iraqi and American casualties were at a monthly high. An NGO reported that a third of settlements in the occupied West Bank were built on Palestinian land. In Iowa, Senator Joe Biden campaigned for president. In cities small and big, people were camping overnight to buy the very first iPhone. *Transformers* took in $152 million at the box office. Economists were bullish: "It's premature to say the economy is reviving in a consistent way," one told the AP, "but I think it's safe to say the economy isn't going to weaken any further."

Meanwhile—between the Brooklyn and Manhattan Bridges, at Empire Fulton Ferry Park—a different sort of gathering and spectacle took place. At 7:07 P.M., for seventy-seven minutes, on Saturday, July 7th (7/7/07), an orchestra of seventy-seven drummers and kits was arranged in a spiral, like a serpent: one big organism, one giant instrument. The ensemble comprised members of Oneida, Lightning Bolt, No-Neck Blues Band, Sightings, White Magic, Excepter, Aa, and other pillars of the American underground. At the center of the spiral were the Boredoms, the fabled noise band from Osaka, Japan. Formed in 1986, the group consisted of three percussionists; a battery of mixers, organs, and synths; and the dreadlocked vocalist, sorcerer, and seer known as EYE. He used a custom-made contraption with seven tuned guitar necks, played with a satanic trident. "The 77 boa-drum," he wrote, "will coil like a snake and transform to become a giant dragon!" It instantly became the stuff of modern lore.

The word went out in June. Admission was free; capacity, limited. The first 4,000 people would be guaranteed entry. 17,000 had RSVP'd. It was a perfect summer day, blue skies and eighty-five degrees. At four P.M., the gates were supposed to open. By two o'clock, hundreds were waiting patiently in line. Some played cards on the concrete while others read paperbacks or magazines. The mood was equally expectant and concerned. The overmatched event staff huddled with their clipboards and walkie-talkies. The line stretched all the way down to Old Fulton Street, a few blocks south. As a measure of crowd control, cutoff points were instituted. When news began to circulate that most would be turned away, some pled their case to the staff; exasperated or incredulous, others gave up and chose to leave.

At 5:15, the gates were finally opened. Security guards did pat-downs. The crowd was orderly as we entered the park. In the words of a middle-aged blogger, it was a mix of "hipsters and hippies, rollers and stoners and euphoria seekers and experimental-music heads, friendly faces and free-show freaks, the sweaty, the scenesters, the nearly-naked, the curious, and me." There was a DJ set by Gang Gang Dance; there was food and alcohol; there was exquisite people-watching. The audience formed a crescent among the seventy-seven drum kits. Soft Circle and First Nation played. The park was maybe two-thirds full when the gates were closed; at least 5,000 people were turned away. At 6:45, we heard an announcement. "Drummers, if you're hearing this, you need to be at your drum sets *now*," said the event's producer, Adam Shore. "We remind the audience not to walk into the drum circle while the drummers are playing."

It was a simple and inspired idea. Every drummer would follow the pattern of the person to their right, one by one, passing swells or ebbs around the spiral, emanating from the Boredoms at the center. The skyline was in silhouette; the sun was coming down; the orchestra was waiting on its cue.

It started with a growing hiss of static from the cymbals—not a bang, but a whisper. Then a martial cadence: the sound of sacrificial ritual, of armies on the move. The pulse was steady, if just off-sync. Resembling a shaman, conductor, and mad scientist, EYE used his trident to play chords and cue changes. He hollered commands like a warrior in battle. The cymbals splashed and crested, spreading outward, to the end of the spiral. A military march was ricocheting off of warehouses and cobblestone streets on the perimeter of the park.

The magic was in the moments of unison. EYE raised his hands, and a crescendo built. The drummers flailed away; the crowd joined in, roaring, a chorus of Banshees. He played a long cathedral drone, and then a mushroom cloud of sound—like spaceships taking flight. On the East River, a passing booze cruise slowed to a crawl, clearly confused. On both the Brooklyn and Manhattan Bridges, hundreds watched from the railings. At the end of the show, EYE began to scream the word "Stand!"

The sun had set; the sky was painted orange-red. The Boredoms stood up, and so did the drummers, and so did the thousands in the crowd. It was an undisputed achievement—for the band, for the participants, and for the sponsors: Vice Media, Nike, Sparks, Sapporo, and Scion, a youth-oriented division of Toyota.

* * *

In a circuitous way, it was a moment many decades in the making—one dating back to the late nineteenth century, and the birth of the automotive industry.

"Dispense with a horse," the advertisement read. "No odor, no vibration." The year was 1898. The first American automobile was sold. The first fatality from a car crash was reported. And in the pages of *The Horseless Age*—the first magazine about "motor wagons," or cars—the field of automotive advertising was born.

The history of advertising cars is also a story of American consumerism. "Ford advertising never attempts to be clever," said Henry Ford in 1912. He changed his mind: in the '20s, Ford enlisted Madison Avenue to sell his new Model A. The first endorsements by celebrities preceded the Great Depression. In the decade after World War II, the car became an emblem of suburban aspiration, domestic plenty, and the American dream.

By the '60s, though—as seen in ads such as Volkswagen's "Think Small" campaign—that very sense of optimism was in doubt. To reach a generation that distrusted both advertising and authority, the car was yoked to youth culture—a road lined with speed bumps. In 1968, General Motors offered The Doors $75,000 ($675,000 today) to license "Light My Fire" for an ad; the deal enraged Jim Morrison, who vowed to smash a Buick with a sledgehammer. In 1985, Honda Scooters produced an infamous commercial with Lou Reed. Over the bass line of "Walk on the Wild Side"—a song about fellatio, amphetamines, and sex workers—the founder of the Velvets sneered: "Don't settle for walkin'."

By the Clinton era, the messaging had gotten savvier: the car became synonymous with subculture. In 1998, Mitsubishi launched its "Wake Up and Drive" campaign with the likes of Iggy Pop, Curtis Mayfield, and T. Rex. In a series called "Drivers Wanted," the elegiac music of Nick Drake was used to hawk Volkswagens. "On the road of life," we are told, "there are passengers and there are drivers." Not to be outdone, Ford licensed songs by Aretha Franklin, Bob Seger, Queen, and Alan Jackson; Jaguar had The Clash and Sting; Cadillac had Led Zeppelin; Buick had Stevie Wonder; Chrysler had They Might Be Giants; and General Motors had— well—Smash Mouth. Noticeably late to the game was Toyota.

* * *

In the early aughts, executives at Toyota faced a quandary. Perceived as stodgy and uncool, the company was losing ground with younger customers. The average Toyota owner was forty-seven years old, on par with Buick, Lincoln, and Mercury. An effort to attract young consumers, Project Genesis, had been a resounding failure. In 2002, Toyota launched a brand called Scion. Aimed at entry-level buyers, it was the automaker's attempt to enter the youth market. If Lexus was a rich man's car, then Scion was its slacker offspring: a car for the recession. At a starting price of $13,000, they were affordable, pragmatic, and easy to customize. Attempting to entice millennials—and in place of its regular agency—Toyota retained a number of firms that specialized in lifestyle marketing, a nebulous term at the time.

The person charged with making Scion cool was Jeri Yoshizu. A native of Southern California, she started out at Toyota in procurement and logistics before a move to interactive marketing. As she would readily admit, she didn't know the first thing about music, which only makes what happened next the more surprising. Her supervisors wanted to associate the brand with anything the kids were into, so she started with hip hop. She threw events with Wu-Tang Clan, DJ Premier, MF Doom, and Prince Paul. She sponsored shows at South by Southwest.

She hosted parties with the likes of Z-Trip, Miguel Migs, and Tony Touch. (A teetotaler, she was consistently the one sober person in attendance.) She started Scion A/V: a record label, website, zine, and video outlet. She printed countless CD samplers that were given out for free at auto shows, promoting acts such as Madvillain, Antibalas, and King Britt.

In her second year on the job, she asked about engaging Missy Elliott. The quoted fee was $250,000—a massive chunk of her budget. It was then that she had a thought. Instead of splurging for a one-off, she could divide that sum between a dozen projects. Instead of chasing stars, she could invest in subculture. That was when she pivoted to electronic music, garage rock, and metal. And that was when she would begin working with Vice. Her point person was Adam Shore.

"What Jeri noticed was, if you tried to work with the biggest names, there were a lot of brands vying for those artists," says Adam. "What she decided to do was narrow in on subcultures, and really own that entire ecosystem. When we did metal, we were very specific about doing certain subgenres of underground metal. We did the same thing with dance music."

It was a moment of transition for electronic music. The '90s techno boom had given way to what a later time dubbed indie sleaze, electroclash, and dubstep, from local scenes and record labels in Paris (Ed Banger), London (Hyperdub), L.A. (Dim Mak), and New York (Fool's Gold, DFA). For worse or for better, Scion's patronage would foster the dramatic rise of EDM in the aughts. They booked a rising Calvin Harris, Justice, A-Trak, Diplo, and Steve Aoki. They partnered with labels and promoters like Trouble & Bass, Mad Decent, and SMOG. They brought to North America the leading lights of U.K. dubstep: Skream & Benga, Rusko, Martyn, Joker, Actress, and Untold. When the recorded-music industry was on the ropes, they funded tours in smaller cities and so-called secondary markets. They even gave out thousands of Scion-branded socks, which soon became a collectors' item. In 2006, sales of Scion peaked at 173,000 for the year.

From hip hop and DJs to dance music was a logical progression. But metal and garage were a different story, tied in large part to the ascent of EDM. By decade's end, Glastonbury, Bonnaroo, and Coachella had a dedicated EDM tent, if not several. A festival circuit drew hundreds of thousands from Miami to Las Vegas. With the breakthrough of Skrillex and Bassnectar, the innovation of U.K. dubstep had coarsened into American brostep: a dizzying, belligerent assault, more Korn than Aphex Twin. "Dubstep in the U.S. has taken the place of nu-metal," said the producer Martyn. "An electronic-music rave in America is like a Limp Bizkit concert ten years ago." In St. George, Canada, a Skrillex show was canceled preemptively by the city council, who said that "the potential for disaster was just too big." A series of incidents and close calls had brought Jeri to the same realization.

Much as it was for dance music, the early aughts were a time of metamorphosis for metal. Previously a province of hair spray, spandex, and codpieces, the long-derided genre had a millennial renaissance. The label Hydra Head was home to bands like Isis, Jesu, and Pelican; Southern Lord had Boris and Sunn O))). Meanwhile—in the Midwest, the South, and on both coasts—Times New Viking, No Age, Jay Reatard, Thee Oh Sees, and Vivian Girls were leading a lo-fi revival. For all their differences, the metal and garage bands alike would benefit from a robust blogosphere, print publications from alt-weeklies to newspapers, and *Pitchfork*, not to mention brands like Scion, Converse, and Mountain Dew. In the age of indie, it had never been easier for corporations to target young consumers. The trickier part was projecting authenticity—something that Vice knew all too well.

* * *

Around the time that Jeri started at Toyota, in the mid-'90s, Shane Smith met Suroosh Alvi at a bar in Montreal. Smith was from Ottawa, a college graduate, and high on LSD. The son of Pakistani immigrants, Alvi was a recovering heroin addict, straight out of rehab, attending two meetings a day. "In treatment, we had a writing exercise," Alvi said.

"'What do you want to do when you're out?' I actually wrote, 'I'd like to work for a magazine.'"

Through a sponsor in Narcotics Anonymous, he got a meeting with a local nonprofit. As part of a government welfare-to-work program, they hired him to start an English-language newspaper called the *Voice of Montreal*. He soon recruited a cartoonist from Ottawa, Gavin McInnes, the child of immigrants from England, and the author of a comic book entitled *Pervert*. Their salaries were covered by the state, but the newspaper was financed by ads. To run the business end of things, Alvi hired Smith—nickname: Bullshitter Shane—a friend and former bandmate of McInnes's. "They were feral," said a friend.

In 1994, the *Voice of Montreal* debuted with an impressive get: an interview with Johnny Rotten from the Sex Pistols. To make it seem as if they had a staff, McInnes made up bylines and wrote most of the copy himself. Within two years, the newspaper was nationwide and entering America. In 1996, with $5,000 each from family, they bought the rights from the publisher. The *Voice of Montreal* became *VICE*, and went from black-and-white to glossy. According to McInnes, Smith would "call me at a payphone late at night and say, 'We're going to be rich,' into the receiver again and again like a financial pervert with OCD." By the turn of the millennium, it looked like Smith could be right.

In contrast to the style of the traditional alt-weekly, the magazine embraced a hateful, macho sensibility. Headlines included "Interview with a Black Guy," "Our Ten Favorite Psychopaths," and "The *VICE* Guide to Shagging Muslims." It published features like "Which is Cuter?" (with babies of different races) and "Gays or Girls?" (in which two men received oral sex blindfolded). Instead of classifieds, you could read "A Guy Who Was on Acid for a Whole Year." Instead of listings, you found "The Best High Is a Government High." (To be fair, it also carried interviews with musicians, writers, and philosophers; enlightening subcultural coverage; political satire; reviews of music, books, and movies; and above-average photography—now and again.) On the eve of the tech bubble, they bluffed their way into a $4 million valuation, and moved the company to Manhattan. "It's punk capitalism," Alvi said. "Staying who we are, yet wanting to do some business." They opened clothing stores in New York, L.A., and Montreal. "This is the first time young people have had a revolution that involves them getting paid," said McInnes.

In 1999, "The Racist Issue" depicted a Chinese man with fake buck teeth, an African-Canadian in a "mammy" pose, and a woman giving a Nazi salute with a KKK doll. The media was mesmerized. "In many ways," *The New York Times* explained, *VICE* "embodies the apex of hipsterdom . . . Think of it as a lad magazine for the Williamsburg set." *The A.V. Club* would add, "Beneath their antagonistic swagger, pieces like 'The *VICE* Guide to Eating Pussy' and 'Was Jesus a Fag?' hide a deceptively human heart."

The magazine would tap a certain vein of decadence in post-9/11 New York. "I'd never read anything like this magazine before," said Jonathan Galkin, cofounder of DFA. "It was irreverent and touched on all these subcultures that I loved and mainstream cultures that I loved. It had really good journalism. It was funny. I was passing my issue to other people to read, and they were reading it cover-to-cover. From the minute I opened that magazine, I was like, 'Holy shit, this wraps up a lot of stuff that's been floating around.'" By 2001—the year they moved their offices to Williamsburg—*VICE* was more popular with readers in their twenties than magazines with ten times the circulation. "It paid to be perceived as edgy," wrote Smith. They met with HBO executives about a show with David Cross. They published an anthology of their best articles with Warner Books. They signed a deal with Atlantic and started their own imprint, Vice Records. To oversee the label, they hired Adam Shore as GM and head of A&R.

It was a fantasy come true. "I thought it would be my last job. Like, this is it," he said. After seven years in marketing, publicity, and retail at TVT, he was finally running a label, and a good one. Off the bat, they signed Bloc Party, Chromeo, and Death from Above 1979; later, he added Justice, The Raveonettes, and Charlotte Gainsbourg. He started a reissue campaign for the Boredoms, which would lead to 7/7/07. He oversaw the stateside rollout of *Original Pirate Material*, by The Streets; *Silent Alarm*, by Bloc Party; and *Cross*, by Justice, three of the most celebrated albums of the decade. He also organized "Vice Kills Texas," an annual event at South by Southwest, sponsored by Scion. It was a fabulous time to work in music—except when it wasn't. "We have great records, but we're less sure than ever that people are going to buy them," Adam said to *Rolling Stone* in 2007. "There's a sense around here of losing faith."

The rise of piracy had overturned the business of recorded music. The industry was in an existential crisis. "I'm truly saddened because I think music has been devalued, so that it's just a file on your computer, and it's usually free," Trent Reznor said in 2007, when album sales were down by nearly twenty-five percent from 1999. MTV called it "the year the music industry broke." In January, the number-one album in America sold 60,000 copies, the lowest in SoundScan history. Both Musicland (who owned Sam Goody) and Tower Records filed for bankruptcy. A real-estate conglomerate acquired Virgin Megastores and closed it only eighteen months later. In Hollywood, the world-famous Capitol Records building was sold to New York developers. An estimated 2,700 record stores had closed since 2003. At least 5,000 record-company employees had been laid off since 2000. "The record business is over," an executive told *Rolling Stone*. "Here we have a business that's dying."

It's not that people weren't spending money on music, but who was profiting. Worldwide, consumers had purchased more than a hundred million iPods in the last six years. "ISPs, telcos, and tech companies have enjoyed a bonanza in the last few years off the back of recorded-music content," said Paul McGuinness, U2's manager, in a 2008 speech. (The band itself had authorized the "iPod U2 Special Edition" some years before.) The touring industry had a banner year in 2006; Ticketmaster alone grossed $1.1 billion.

Between the multiplying effects of illegal file-sharing, blogs and social media, home-recording software, and artist-friendly brands, the record industry seemed like a sinking ship. In early 2007, Paul McCartney left EMI, his label of four decades, and signed a deal with Starbucks. "It's a new world now," he said, "and people are thinking of new ways to reach the people, and for me that's always been my aim." In the fall, Madonna left the Warner Music Group for a $100 million deal with Live Nation, while Radiohead let people name their own price for *In Rainbows*. And announcing the end of his contract with Interscope, Trent Reznor said, "It gives me great pleasure to be able to finally have a direct relationship with the audience as I see fit and appropriate."

* * *

As album sales collapsed, the once-unthinkable became the norm. Adult Swim, Urban Outfitters, Vitamin Water, Red Bull, Coca-Cola, Mountain Dew, Bacardi, Converse, Dr. Martens, Nike, Levi's, Ray-Ban, Range Rover, Kia, Samsung, and even State Farm sponsored tours, one-offs, and festivals; commissioned singles, jingles, and videos; printed LPs; opened studios; and started in-house record labels—all geared at underground and independent music. "Artists are finding the only way to achieve any financial safety is to become a lapdog of the great corporations, just like the great painters did in the Renaissance, when it became impossible to sustain oneself as an artist without a patron," said the author Douglas Rushkoff. The old ideals had yet to fade completely: in 2006, The Thermals, a group from Portland, Oregon, declined a check for $50,000 from the Hummer corporation. "We figured it was almost like giving music to the Army, or Exxon," the band said. The following year, Wilco licensed several songs to Volkswagen, and felt embarrassed enough to post an explanation on their website. With the spectacular implosion of the economy, the job market, and the record business, a younger generation was less ambivalent. "It's almost pretentious to avoid the opportunity, especially in this climate," said Sleigh Bells' Derek Miller. On *The Colbert Report*, The Black Keys and Ezra Koenig of Vampire Weekend satirically competed in a "Sellout-Off," comparing placements of their songs by Sony

Ericsson, Tommy Hilfiger, and Victoria's Secret. "Music, in a way, has turned from being its own revenue stream into becoming added value for corporate brands," said Adam in the *Times*.

His higher-ups at Vice had reached a similar conclusion. In 2006, they started AdVice, soon to be Virtue, an in-house branding agency; one year later, they posted revenues of $28 million. With the director Spike Jonze—and a $2 million investment from Viacom—they started an Internet video hub, the Vice Broadcasting System, or vbs.tv. "We became a magazine when the barriers to making a magazine effectively became nonexistent," said Smith. "You could do desktop publishing on a Mac and print for cheap. Now you get a digicam and a Mac, and you can have something broadcast on the net within fifteen minutes."

They built relationships with HBO and CNN. They pitched an idea of *60 Minutes*–meets-*Jackass* to MTV. The end result was *The VICE Guide to Travel*, where they reported from dicey situations: brothels in Liberia, gun markets in Pakistan, and karaoke in North Korea. In the summer of 2006, at the height of the war, they went to meet the only heavy-metal band in Baghdad, Acrassicauda—named after a breed of scorpion common in Iraq. (They later helped the band resettle in the U.S.) Praised by the *Times* as "an intrepid, unlikely and altogether splendid feat of D.I.Y. reportage," *Heavy Metal in Baghdad* screened to wide acclaim at the Toronto film festival. The footage ended up on CNN's home page. "In the U.S., [the Iraqis are] just not being talked about," Alvi told *The Guardian*. "No one gives a shit here. All they care about is our troops and the forthcoming presidential election."

For Vice, it was an auspicious time to enter the news business. If 2007 was the year the music industry broke, a parallel emergency unfolded for journalism. In early January, in San Francisco, Steve Jobs revealed his most groundbreaking device yet. "iPhone is a revolutionary and magical product that is literally five years ahead of any other mobile phone," said Jobs. It was the year that Facebook tweaked its News Feed algorithm, and readers were discovering a site called BuzzFeed. *The New York Times* had publicly repented for its uncritical reporting in the run-up to the invasion of Iraq; its editor had been replaced after the Jayson Blair fabrication scandal. On *60 Minutes*, a story based on forged documents had forced the exit of news anchor Dan Rather.

With classifieds migrating to Google, Craigslist, and Facebook— and readers getting their news online—subscriptions, advertising, and circulation were declining sharply. The *Times* announced a plan to cut its workforce by 500 employees, close a printing plant, and shave the paper's width. The country's second-largest newspaper chain, Knight Ridder, was sold and soon dismantled. *The Village Voice* was bought by a conglomerate and went through five editors in the next two years. At *The Washington Post*, hundreds were laid off or took buyouts. The company that owned the *Los Angeles Times*, *The Baltimore Sun*, and the *Chicago Tribune* went bankrupt. In the wake of the economic crisis, nearly 170 newspapers went out of business, and 10,000 jobs were lost. "The newspaper industry exited a harrowing 2008," wrote the Pew Foundation, "and entered 2009 in something perilously close to free-fall."

"Readers are leaving newspapers, and people are having an even harder time getting to our demographic," Smith told *The New York Times*. While the world of newspapers was pondering extinction, *VICE* claimed to have a print circulation of 900,000; offices in fifteen countries; editions on five continents; advertisers such as Adidas, Nike, Xbox, Jeep, and Harley Davidson; and a following of millions online. They closed a $40 million deal with Intel for the Creators Project, a global arts initiative, engaging musicians such as Animal Collective, Interpol, Arcade Fire, Karen O, and M.I.A. "With each new territory that launches, our hold on the elusive and rare bird known as the 'tastemaker' grows," said the *VICE* media kit. "Together, we can grow drunk and bloated with power."

In 2007, McInnes sold his shares and left the company. He would chalk it up to a difference of opinion in *The New Yorker*: "Marketing and editorial being enemies had been the business plan." Many pointed to his history of racist and inflammatory comments. "I love being white and I think it's something to be very proud of," he told the *Times* in 2003. An immigrant himself, he said, "I don't want our culture diluted. We need to close the borders now and let everyone assimilate to a Western, white, English-speaking way of life." A year before, the *New York Press* asked him about living in Williamsburg. "Well, at least they're not fucking n****** or Puerto Ricans," he said of the historically Puerto Rican neighborhood, without apparent irony. "At least they're white." A turning point in his relationship with *VICE* came in 2006, when he attended a conference with hundreds of white nationalists and Klansman David Duke. The final straw was supposedly a photo shoot for *The New York Times Magazine* at which McInnes dressed in Nazi regalia. A decade later, he founded the Proud Boys—a far-right, anti-immigrant group that his native Canada would designate a terrorist entity, and the forty-fifth president would famously embrace.

* * *

Adam stayed at Vice Records until the fall of 2008, when sales industry-wide had fallen by one-fifth from just the year before. "All I ever wanted to do as a kid was work at a record store," he says. "So the idea that those don't really exist—who could have predicted that? As an adult, all I ever wanted to do was run a record label, and I got to do that. But by 2008, it was clear that my idea of a music company under Vice that also did management, publishing, and events was not the direction they were going in. Vice was doing brand and content deals, and recorded music didn't seem like it was part of the plan. Then, when I left the record label, Jeri called me out of the blue and said, 'Do you want to keep doing Scion projects?'"

He spent the next four years as a consultant for Scion, booking artists for festivals, showcases, and one-offs. "They had a weekly Thursday marketing meeting they required me to go to," he says. "So every Thursday morning I would take a six A.M. flight to LAX. I got in at nine and took a red-eye home. I did that for about two years." He booked the first Scion

Rock Fest in Atlanta in 2009. Thirty bands played: black metal, death metal, grindcore, doom, and thrash. "If you're a metal band and you're not playing this," said *Pitchfork*, "you probably suck." The second year's installment took place in Columbus, Ohio. "A festival with midsize clubs and good sound, surrounded by people who didn't have to pay admission and bands who'd been flown in, put up in hotels, fed and allowed to play sets of at least an hour," Ben Ratliff wrote in the *Times*. "This is a car company sponsoring a fairly extreme-metal festival. Why? What's Scion's gain?"

"It was a real moment in metal," Adam says. "The indie world, the *Pitchfork* world, and the blog world were all accepting that independent-minded metal bands could be part of the ecosystem. I was going to artists all the time. 'Can we commission you to record an EP? We'll press it up, and you can give it away at your shows. Can we commission you to make a video? You can direct it.' Then we did the same thing for dance music. We did a year of only U.K. dubstep. We were bringing artists from England over for the first time. Getting them visas so they could continue to tour in the U.S. Then we did a year of electro. A year of Detroit techno. We were able to do these things in these under-the-radar subgenres. We would become a benefactor to a whole ecosystem of musicians, and they would want to work with *us*. And then the artists that we *weren't* working with would then approach us, and that's really not the way it works with brands! It's usually, you go to artists, and you're pulling—but with this, it was artists pushing themselves on us. It was benefiting artists in a way I wouldn't be able to at a label." He worked for Jeri until 2012, when the Scion Rock Fest was held in Tampa. Once again, *The New York Times* flew in a music critic to report on an automaker's metal festival. "This is the upside of corporate sponsorship," Ratliff wrote. "It allows a festival to take chances." Adam would curate four annual Scion Rock Fests in total, and helped on a pair of Scion Garage Fests; he provided resources to over 300 artists. And that was when he got a call from Red Bull.

Parts & Labor
(*Mapmaker*)

Christmas 1984. The year's top singles are "What's Love Got to Do with It" and "When Doves Cry." The highest-selling albums are *Born in the U.S.A.*, *Purple Rain*, and *Thriller*. George W. Bush becomes the CEO of Spectrum 7, a Texas oil company. And in Massachusetts, an eight-year-old Dan Friel unwraps his present: a Yamaha PortaSound keyboard. He doesn't know it yet, but he's just found his life's calling.

Summer 1995. The year's top singles are "Waterfalls" and "Gangsta's Paradise." The highest-selling albums are by Hootie and the Blowfish, Alanis Morrissette, and TLC. At the United Nations, intelligence reports of an Iraqi weapons program make the rounds. And in Massachusetts, an eighteen-year-old BJ Warshaw quits conservatory. He gravitates instead to bands like Sonic Youth, the Boredoms, and Fugazi.

Early 2001. The year's top singles are by Matchbox Twenty and Nickelback. The highest-selling albums are by *NSYNC and Linkin Park. On a cold, rainy day in Washington, D.C., George W. Bush is sworn in as the forty-third president. And at a show promoted by The Twisted Ones at the Polish National Home in Greenpoint, Dan and BJ are in the audience for Lightning Bolt, Oneida, and Sightings. They start thinking: we should do this ourselves.

* * *

It's curious how little of the indie music from the aughts concerned itself with politics. Exceptions come to mind. But by and large—for reasons of aesthetics, acquiescence, or mental health—most were silent on a pointless and horrific war, "enhanced" interrogation, economic inequality, political division, fundamentalism, homophobia, misogyny, police brutality, or the stain of American exceptionalism. For all the ruptures, chaos, and tragedy of the Bush era—a legally contested election; a world-historical act of terrorism; an occupation of imperial folly—the cultural response amounted to a collective numbness, trauma, and grief. No music stood in contrast to this tendency more than Parts & Labor, the band of Dan Friel and BJ Warshaw.

* * *

Parts & Labor were a band for exactly a decade. They made their live debut on January 15, 2002, and played their last show on February 24, 2012. In the time between, they churned through four different drummers; recorded five full-length albums and a pair of EPs; started a label; and played 500 shows in Europe, Japan, and forty-four states, mostly self-booked. They survived a series of exploding amplifiers, blizzards, and busted vans. They toured or played alongside Battles, Matt and Kim, Fleet Foxes, Bon Iver, and TV on the Radio. Their paths converged with David Bowie and Brian Eno. The only thing they failed to do was earn a living wage. They understood that their music would never make them rich; their aspirations, accordingly, were modest. In a post-Napster landscape, the most a band could hope for was a livelihood—a feat that just a few would manage.

Much like their primary influences—melodic post-punk bands like the Minutemen, Hüsker Dü, and Fugazi—Parts & Labor was a marriage of opposites. They merged the binaries of melody and dissonance, order and entropy, acid and base. Their music was an exercise in counterpoint: between cacophony and calm, noise and pop, oil and water. Their songs were paradoxically absorbing and abrasive, polemical and personal, cathartic and controlled. It wasn't rare for noisy bands to win a following of open-minded listeners in the early aughts: Sightings, Black Dice, and Lightning Bolt all did. But only Parts & Labor could have written pop songs if they had chosen. They wove contagious hooks that in a different time would have been filed next to Green Day, and then obliterated them beneath an avalanche of atonality. By temperament, Dan Friel was drawn to dissonance, from free jazz to contemporary classical; at the same time, he had a gift for writing effervescent melodies. As a teenager, BJ Warshaw's taste ran more to punk and ska: a spirited, anthemic sensibility the band would make its rocket fuel. It was the yin-and-yang dynamic of Parts & Labor—in their sound, and their two songwriters—that made the band a marvel.

* * *

Dan Friel was born in western Massachusetts in 1976. He spent his childhood devouring guitar magazines, MTV, and classic rock. He was a fan of heavy metal—thrash, specifically—and the virtuosity of Rocky George, of Suicidal Tendencies. From shows on MTV like *Headbanger's Ball* and *120 Minutes*, he learned about Metallica and Sonic Youth. At sixteen, he joined a band called Squidlaunch, known for amplifying power tools, and played with them through college. His bandmates introduced him to the history of punk and jazz, which were seen as kin: "There was a thing in the early '90s of people who were into punk being obsessed with free jazz, so there was a fair amount of crossover there," Dan says.

BJ Warshaw hailed from a family of musicians. His parents were a folk duo in the '60s. His grandmother played piano; her sister was an opera singer; her husband was a concert pianist; his dad even played steel drum. The family record collection skewed '60s: Simon & Garfunkel; Peter, Paul and Mary. Born in Maryland, raised in Connecticut, he started piano lessons in the third grade, and saxophone shortly after. A '90s child, he soon discovered pop-punk and ska, which had entered the mainstream through bands like The Mighty Mighty Bosstones, No Doubt, and Green Day. In middle school, he joined the jazz band, a source of some hilarity to his peers. "I was a fucking nerd, you know, and kids were making fun of me for doing that," he says. "And then, by sophomore year in high school, you could play saxophone and be in a ska band, and that was cool." He joined a group called J.C. Superska that toured the all-ages circuit of the Northeast, and opened for the luminaries Desmond Dekker and The Skatalites.

BJ spent a year at music school; he found it clinical and soulless. After graduating from Tufts, in Boston, he moved to New York in the summer of 1998. He shared a one-bedroom place in a sixth-floor walk-up in the East Village. He started temping at BMG, the music publisher—a job he despised. "To give you an idea of the era, I had a stack of licenses, and I would have to stamp each copy, then file it." One of the components of the job was tracking down the artists they didn't have a contract for, to sign away their royalties against a nominal advance. "I would think: 'I'm stamping papers to take away money from musicians. This fucking sucks.'" He quit the job and started working at the Knitting Factory (the second and largest iteration, in Tribeca), under the publicist, sending press releases, proofing ads, and hanging flyers. Between the many print outlets in town that ran listings, features, and reviews—the *Times*, *The Village Voice*, *The New Yorker*, the *New York Press*, and *Time Out New York*—there was always something to do. One of the first people he met was Dan Friel, who helped the owner, Michael Dorf, booking tours—the same position Adam Shore was momentarily offered.

Dan moved to town in 1999. He had graduated from the University of Hartford, where he met a group of talented composers, improvisers, and instrumentalists: Jessica Pavone, Seth Misterka, Karen Waltuch, Mary Halvorson, and Tyondai Braxton. He spent a bruising eighteen months working for Dorf; the salary was $200 a week. By then, a lot of bridges had been burned. "Dorf spelled backwards is fraud," John Lurie told the *Los Angeles Times*. The jazz scene that had flourished in the New York of the '90s was a thing of the past. "There was a feeling that the Knitting Factory as a brand had reached its peak," says Dan. All the same, the job had its perks. "One of the first nights I was there, I saw Black Star with The Roots as their backing band. I saw The Master Musicians of Joujouka, The Ex, Don Caballero, Melt-Banana. A million awesome shows."

It was at the Knitting Factory that Dan and BJ hit it off. They shared a love for Sonic Youth, Fugazi, and the Boredoms; they bonded over Smog, The Flaming Lips, and Neutral Milk Hotel; they talked about the worlds of noise, hardcore, and avant-jazz. On afternoons, before the night's performers loaded in, they brought their instruments and messed around onstage. "There were a lot of conversations about things we like that are not rock music," says Dan. "That's a big part of what we listen to. But we want to have a rock band. How are we going to weave these things together? There was a lot of talking before we got around to doing."

* * *

Dan had a basement in Bed-Stuy where he could play without disturbing the neighbors. "Which, I did not realize how special that was at the time." He had his old guitar, from high school; his upright bass, from college; and his neglected toy keyboard—the Yamaha—which he hadn't used in years. He'd been listening to gauzy, glitchy electronic artists such as Amps for Christ, Le Tigre, and Oval. He was creatively adrift. "I had been amassing pedals and playing guitar and feeling like I'm not adding anything to the conversation." One afternoon in the winter of 2000, he plugged the Yamaha toy keyboard into his effects pedals. What he heard was a woozy, overdriven sound, like a Nintendo on the fritz—an act of serendipity that spawned the Parts & Labor style. "When I plugged that keyboard in, I thought: '*This* feels like I'm adding to the conversation.'"

In June of 2001, he self-released a solo EP, *Broken Man Going to Work:* a sixteen-minute compilation of "remote-control car joystick experiments, caveman synth shit, and boombox recordings." He did a one-week tour of the Midwest with Tyondai Braxton. When he got back to town, he opened at Northsix for the Yeah Yeah Yeahs, who had just released their own EP. "And that was kind of my first proper Brooklyn show," says Dan. "A lot happens very quickly right around then." The Yeah Yeah Yeahs started asking him to open shows, including one with Interpol in January.

BJ had left the Knitting Factory in 1999. He was collecting unemployment and looking for a change of occupation. "I felt very disillusioned because I wanted to work in music, and my first two jobs were at the Knit and BMG. I realized the industry is horrible to musicians, and I wanted nothing to do with it. I quit entirely. I stopped making music. I didn't know what I wanted to do with my life." A friend from college said: "You're good with computers. You should learn how to make websites." It was the apex of the dot-com bubble in New York; some were calling it Silicon Alley. "They just needed people skilled enough to learn on the job. They just needed bodies." He read a book and taught himself HTML. He started working as a web developer at $30 an hour. In the spring of 2001, wanting to see the world, he took a break from work and bought a one-way ticket to Japan.

In Tokyo, he got a job teaching English to kids in elementary school, where he would spend the next three months, the length of his visa. He traveled to Cambodia, Thailand, and Laos. He saw the fields of farmers pocked with unexploded mines, and fences made of casings from the American War, as it was known in the region. On September 11th, he was in Hạ Long Bay, an island chain in northeast Vietnam. The news reports were all in French; the footage was a few hours old. The next day, he found a group of fellow tourists at a nearby hotel. "We were just watching CNN collectively, dumbstruck by the whole thing."

He took a ferry back to the mainland, then a bus to Hanoi. He found an Internet café and started writing friends back home. He went by bus, train, and pickup truck to Phnom Penh. There was a stop in Bangkok, and a flight to Tokyo, where he had a job offer from a school, and nearly stayed. "Up to the day when I booked my flight, I almost didn't get on the plane. I was torn, because I loved my time in Tokyo. But to be honest, I really missed my friends. I missed New York, and so I felt pulled back."

In late October, BJ finally got back to town. There were American flags on every subway car, storefront, and street corner. Downtown, there were handwritten signs taped to walls, trees, and lampposts, with names and photos of the missing. Addressed to senators and news outlets, a series of anonymous letters with anthrax was found in the mail. The president had ordered the invasion of Afghanistan. The Patriot Act had just been signed. A flight from JFK crashed minutes after takeoff. "It was a fearful, fucked-up time. But there was also, like—in true New York fashion—a sense of community, and partying through the pain," BJ says. "I remember feeling extremely nihilistic at the time, and really helpless, but in other ways very energized to protest and be more politically active than I'd been before. That came from what I had seen on leaving the country, and seeing what America had done previously, and seeing what America was about to do again, and being afraid and ashamed of what seemed inevitable."

That fall, he reconnected with Dan. "I saw him do a show at Newsonic Loft in Williamsburg," says BJ. "His songwriting had come up to the next level. I told him: 'You could turn this into something more than just the solo keyboard stuff. These should be rock songs. We should make this a band.'" They started practicing that December with Dan's roommate, Jim Sykes, as their drummer, and BJ on bass. Their first show was in January.

It was an awkward time to be in a punk band. Between The Rapture and The Juan MacLean, Hot Hot Heat and !!!, The Bravery and Fischerpooner, the indie world had been subsumed by dance-rock, disco, and electroclash. Despite a climate of deception, jingoism, and war—or for that very reason—hedonism ("House of Jealous Lovers"), ennui ("Is This It"), and irony ("Losing My Edge") were ascendant, and songs like "Lose Yourself," "In Da Club," and "Hot in Herre" hit number one. "We were writing these songs in 2004 and 2005," says Dan. "A lot of what was happening in Brooklyn at that point was still the aftermath of the new-rock revolution. It was party music—a disco-punk, cocaine-mustache party. And we're in two wars, and this maniac has just been reelected, and there are these huge protests, and you just didn't see it reflected at all in the music that was going on around us."

* * *

Some bands are born complete and fully formed; some need years to find their footing. Parts & Labor were of the second camp. Their early songs are very much apprentice work—monotonous, repetitive, and beholden to their models: the density and drones of Amps for Christ, the tones and texture of Oval, the marching-band-on-mushrooms feel of Neutral Milk Hotel. Their first recordings were entirely instrumental, layered with noise and static; their first attempt at singing would take years.

They started by adapting Dan's solo music, trading synthesizer beats for a frenetic rhythm section, and turning up the overdriven keyboard, which alternately came to sound like an accordion, hurdy-gurdy, or bagpipes. They released a self-recorded EP and seven-inch with two of Dan's early songs in 2002. They hit the road in June, and played a string of DIY establishments in St. Louis, Cleveland, and Chicago, where they spent the Fourth of July. "I remember sitting on the curb after the show," says BJ. "Some kid riding by on his bike threw a firecracker at me, and it bounced and exploded in my lap as I was sitting on the ground, and people were lighting fires in the street, and Chicago cops are just rolling by like, 'Yep, that checks out.'"

When they got back from tour, their drummer, Jim Sykes, would be replaced by Joel Saladino, a gifted instrumentalist. On August 31, 2002, in a narrow alleyway off Kent, BJ helped to organize the Chester Fest: an all-day bacchanal with fourteen acts, including Les Savy Fav, Lightning Bolt, The French Kicks, !!!, and Forcefield. To their surprise, that very day, just a few blocks south, The Twisted Ones had booked the Yeah Yeah Yeahs, Oneida, and the Liars in a parking lot on Wythe. "It's our time, our time," Karen O sang. On every adjacent rooftop, a crowd observed the semilegal proceedings. It was the dawning of the early aughts in Williamsburg. "To me, that day, and that whole scene of people putting on shows in nontraditional spaces and not giving a fuck—it was exploding," BJ recalls. "It was also pretty lawless. We were selling beer. We had no liquor license, and easily a thousand people there."

"I remember walking around Williamsburg in 2002, and every person on the street is someone I know, from a band I really like," says Dan. "Obviously, it wasn't everyone. But you're twenty-five or whatever, and that's what you see. It really felt like a scene of all musicians and artists, and nothing else, and that was fascinating and cool."

Among the people in the crowd that day for Parts & Labor was Chris Weingarten, a recent transplant from Gainesville. He was a graduate of the University of Florida, a music journalist, and a drummer, who sometimes played "running around like a maniac, hilariously insulting the audience, playing the roto-toms, keyboards, and yes, the theremin," in the words of a reviewer. He had just moved to town that week. "This is the music I've been hearing in my head," he told them after the show. He saw them play again a few days later. "The sound system was maxed out beyond comprehension, the band was so sloppy they sounded like they were playing three songs at the same time, and a drunken BJ was pushing people and staggering all over a terrified audience," said Chris. "It was awesome." He started asking them to be their front man, half in jest.

On February 15, 2003, Dan and BJ were among the millions in New York, London, Madrid, and over 600 cities who marched against the imminent invasion of Iraq. Their first LP, *Groundswell*, came out three days later. They booked their first full tour: thirty shows in thirty-one nights. They drove all day, and slept on floors, and performed to single-digit crowds: a hand-to-mouth existence. The DIY community had an unspoken rule that touring bands would get the money from the door—if there was anything to split. "In most cases, a good night was if you made enough money to eat and put gas in the tank to get you to the next show," says BJ. "A lot of those shows in smaller towns, we were playing for a handful of people. Sometimes under ten, sometimes even less. Not very glamorous, but super fun."

Reviews for *Groundswell* were encouraging, in general. "The tracks on here—instrumentals all—wham their way into new post-free prog territory," Byron Coley wrote in *The Wire*. "About the only thing I can really say it recalls are some of the stranger, lesser-known groups of the later no-wave era." Some were more reserved with their praise. "Parts & Labor still show room for improvement on their debut," wrote Joe Tangari for *Pitchfork* (7.2), "but it's still a sharp salutation from a band that seems capable of creating some incredible mayhem." In *Dusted*, Charlie Wilmoth saw promise: "Parts & Labor might be a great band in my eyes, rather than simply a very good one, if they would spread out a bit"—with which they seemed to agree.

For *Rise, Rise, Rise* (2003), a split EP with Tyondai Braxton, they wrote "The Endless Air Show"—a comment on the Bush administration's case for war against Saddam Hussein, and one of two that featured singing. Just a few weeks later, the president would stage his landing on a navy aircraft carrier, before a banner reading "Mission Accomplished." Another breakthrough was "Probably Feeling Better Already," an irresistible earworm of melodic new wave. They booked their second U.S. tour in October, hitting destinations far and wide: Cedar Falls, Iowa; Eureka, California; and Shreveport, Louisiana. They played the basement of a house in Moscow, Idaho. "It was completely joyous, with people crowd-surfing and punching the ceiling," says BJ. "It was crowded with kids who generally don't get bands playing towns like Moscow, Idaho. In the early days, those were usually our best shows."

In 2004, they packed the van for South by Southwest. Somewhere outside Pittsburgh, they blew a gasket on the interstate, and had to be towed to the nearest hotel. The next morning, they bought an old, beat-up van from a used-car dealership, drove two days straight, and made it to the venue just in time. On the way back home, the engine died an hour past the Oklahoma border. They sold the second van for fifty dollars and a ride to the Oklahoma City airport, where they rented a car, packed up their gear, and drove for thirty hours straight back to Brooklyn.

They played with Saladino through the spring of 2004, and took four-plus months to find a replacement, auditioning over twenty drummers. When they invited Chris to try out, he was initially reluctant. On the one hand, Parts & Labor was his favorite band in New York; on the other, he had a full-time job at *CMJ New Music Monthly*, where he contributed reviews, columns, and features. He'd started writing for *The Village Voice*; his ambitions were less Robert Plant than Robert Christgau. "I swore up and fucking down that I would never play in a band again," said Chris. "I'd been playing in shitty, go-nowhere bands since I was fourteen and was sick of rehearsal spaces, power trips, tour vans that drove into oblivion, and the inevitable fact that everyone who puts you up for the night has a fucking cat." They ran a mix of songs at Sound City, their practice space on North Fourth Street, affectionately called Sounds Shitty due to a lack of soundproofing. "They apparently liked my drumming, offered me the gig, and, like a dipshit, I turned it down," said Chris. "Twice!"

"It felt like playing to a crushingly loud drum machine," says Dan. "He hit like a sledgehammer. We were like, 'You gotta do this.'" He sat in for a benefit on September 1, 2004—to the day, two years after Chester Fest. He knew the songs from having seen a half a dozen shows. He flogged the drums as if he had an extra set of legs and arms, as if he had an age-old vendetta. He lent a steadiness, precision, and unity to what had once been a rickety outfit. He was a veteran of metal-funk, power-pop, and punk bands, equally at home with postwar classical and old-school hip hop, and brought an omnivore's dimension to the group's two songwriters. With Chris in the drum seat, the band would find its secret weapon: a wrecking ball, who played with awe-inspiring velocity and vigor.

* * *

In the summer of 2005, the band recorded *Stay Afraid*, their second album, at Brooklyn's Headgear Studios. In many ways, it was their first mature LP, the first to unify the elements of bracing dissonance, anthemic melodies, and left-wing politics. It was the first to feature Dan and BJ's vocals throughout, and showed the band to have a pair of credible, complementary front men. A shroud of feedback, distortion, and digital effects fought for space with fractured harmonies, impassioned choruses, and head-banging sing-alongs. A creeping sense of dread, manipulation, and paranoia was reflected in the title, the songs, and the production. "We were definitely seeking to make a record that was more than just a collection of songs, where the lyrics and the sounds were cohesive," says BJ. "We also wanted it big and noisy and loud as hell."

In their lyrics, the band expressed its opposition to the politics of fear. "A Great Divide" was both a maelstrom and a metaphor for the red states and the blue: "the class divide, the urban versus the rural, the religious versus the secular," said BJ. The title track was "mostly a meditation on the patriotic and paranoid mood around the country in the last five years," said Dan. For "Changing of the Guard," they wrote about the first inauguration of George W. Bush: "It was raining and freezing, and there were so many protesters there ready to let loose, but the police presence was just unbelievable. Dark days," said Dan. In "New Buildings," BJ wrote about his neighborhood, which was being rezoned "to make room for high-rise apartment buildings. It's also more generally about bad decisions." The album cover paired a group of faceless bystanders against a fireworks display. "The 'shock and awe' campaign was marketed almost as if it were a celebration, albeit one of American prowess and military superiority, a show," said BJ. "I wanted the people to appear like spectators, like ghosts, immobile, unperturbed by the violence in front of them."

One door down, at Dave Sitek's studio, Stay Gold, TV on the Radio was recording their second album, *Return to Cookie Mountain*. "It was inspiring to walk by that door on the way to the studio and hear all kinds of oboes and weird clangs coming from behind the metal door," said Chris, who spent the week adjudicating arguments among his bandmates. "One thing you should know about Dan and BJ is that they're notorious perfectionists. Their attitude toward getting the exact right sound, the exact right melody, was both inspiring and infuriating. Those dudes were total sound nerds who loved to produce and tinker. I spent a lot of that session chilling on the couch while they tweaked."

One morning, the band received a visit from an eminent stranger. "At the time, I was reading *Hiroshima*, by John Hersey," says Chris. "I'm nearsighted, and I take off my glasses when I read. So when I saw this blurry figure coming down the hallway, I didn't recognize him at first. I *thought* I knew him, so I waved anyway. He waved back. I put my glasses on and saw that, yes, I did recognize him, but I'd never met him before." BJ, Dan, and engineer Scott Norton were hunched over the console, working out a song that was blaring through the speakers while the stranger watched from the door. Their concentration was total. "Our guest patiently played the wall, chilling next to me, dead silent for the few minutes it took for them to wrap up."

"Excuse me. Is David here?" their visitor asked politely, looking for producer Dave Sitek. Scott turned around, clearly caught off guard, and said, "Yeah, let me take you to him."

"This dude was pretty well-known around Williamsburg," Chris goes on, "so I was rather impressed by his presence at our humble session. BJ and Dan, however, were totally unfazed. They were older than me, they had played more shows, and they had made more records. I thought they were just over things like gossip and celebrities. I didn't want our guest and our producer to hear us talking, so I went up to my bandmates and started whispering."

Chris said, "You guys are too cool for school, huh?" They looked confused.

"You don't want to look like dorks? Is that it?" Again, blank stares.

"Guys, I'm talking about the amazing thing that just happened, that you two are pretending didn't happen."

"Chris," answered BJ. "What are you talking about?"

"That David Bowie was just in our studio."

* * *

From mid-2005—when they performed with a dozen other bands in a Queens parking lot, all booked by Todd P; successfully auditioned for Jagjaguwar at an Indiana pizza parlor; and found the time to start their own label, Cardboard Records—Parts & Labor would do little but perform, record, and write for the next two years. They went on four U.S. tours, and saw some 200 stages, squats, and living rooms; toured with Matt and Kim, ADULT., Erase Errata, Wilderness, Dan Deacon, and I Love You But I've Chosen Darkness; and performed with Mission of Burma, Girl Talk, Black Dice, Spank Rock, and The Juan MacLean. To celebrate the many artists they had met, they self-released *Love and Circuits (From Aa to Zs)*, a two-CD, fifty-seven-band compilation. *Escapers One* (2006) and *Two* (2008), a pair of EPs, collected several instrumental miniatures and fifty-one "grind pop" songs written in a single day, respectively. And in July of 2006, they made their masterwork, *Mapmaker*.

It was a moment of unusual artistic plenty in Brooklyn. Over the span of eight months, *Pitchfork* would designate releases from the Liars, Grizzly Bear, TV on the Radio, and The Hold Steady as Best New Music. On July 9, Dragons of Zynth, Les Savy Fav, Beans, and Holy Fuck played the inaugural Pool Party at McCarren Park. In Chicago, The National, the Liars, and Tyondai Braxton played the first edition of the Pitchfork Music Festival. The coming year would bring groundbreaking albums from Braxton's math-rock outfit Battles (*Mirrored*), Animal Collective's Panda Bear (*Person Pitch*), and LCD Soundsystem (*Sound of Silver*).

The band was driven by a newfound sense of urgency. Reviews for *Stay Afraid* had been polite, if not bemused. "A lot of people were like, 'I don't get this,'" Dan recalls. "It felt like the clock was ticking, somehow. Like we just needed to go as fast as we could." Dan and BJ had left their jobs, and Chris was filing copy from the road. They practiced in the same building as TV on the Radio, Animal Collective, and Battles; they saw firsthand how quickly things could change with a Best New Music from *Pitchfork*. "Being in Brooklyn at that time, you would see bands get that, and then just fly by you, in terms of the shows they were getting offered," says Dan. "And for us it felt a lot more like, that doesn't seem to be coming to us. So we're just going to tour as hard as we can, and keep cranking out these records. And that's the path that we'll pursue."

* * *

By mid-2006, Iraq was in the teeth of all-out civil war. July had been the deadliest month of the invasion, with nearly 3,500 civilians killed—an average of 110 a day. According to reports declassified in late September, "The Iraq conflict has become a 'cause célèbre' for jihadists, breeding a deep resentment of U.S. involvement in the Muslim world and cultivating supporters for the global jihadist movement." The president's decision to install democracy had galvanized "a new generation of terrorist leaders and operatives." *Mapmaker* was Parts & Labor's reply.

Released on May 22, 2007—the same day as *Boxer*, by The National, and *Mirrored*, by Battles—*Mapmaker* was the band at their most intelligent, exhilarating, and brave. The songs on the album veered between headlong sprints, whirlwind shredding, proggy tempo changes, and apocalyptic breakdowns. The melodies had never seemed as effortless; the hooks had never been as infectious; the virtuosity had never been more plain. The album was a Trojan horse: an antiwar polemic, in the guise of bubblegum pop-punk.

The lyrics showed a pair of writers in their prime, and themes of both political and personal malaise. The opening of "Fractured Skies" is unambiguous and abstract, all at once: "Don't you know that maps can't be drawn in a day? / They draw themselves." It peaks with a majestic brass fanfare—and for a moment, the band resembles an orchestra. "The Gold We're Digging" was a bravura showcase of Chris's rhythmic ability, a song about the pull of fortune and fame. It had the makings of a hit on radio or MTV in 1994, so much so that Dan believed it was "too pop." "I remember him lobbying at one point to leave it off the record," BJ says. "I'm glad we convinced him not to do that."

The album was recorded at The Brothers Studio in Greenpoint—and partially in BJ's bedroom—at a cost of $3,000. "I remember feeling the pace, and just *working*," says BJ. "As soon as we had twelve songs, we were like, 'Let's record this, and let's book the next tour, and let's put out another record, and just really pushing ourselves.'"

"I think it's the one we spent the least amount of time on," says Dan. "It's the least overthought record. We just went in and did it . . . I remember friends being like, 'Why? What are you doing?' It just felt like it was part of a broader project of pushing ourselves as hard as we could, to do as much as we could, in a lot of different ways."

* * *

Upon recording *Mapmaker* in July of 2006, they played eleven shows over eleven nights in the U.K. "It was very chaotic and very DIY," says Dan. "The first show we played in England was in Nottingham, and we hadn't slept in like a day and a half, and it was the first time I can remember going somewhere, and someone we didn't know in the crowd was singing along. Being sleep-deprived, and playing on another continent for the first time, and that happening." They played twenty more shows in Europe that October; a dozen gigs around the South after Thanksgiving; another twenty-seven dates across the U.S. in the spring of 2007; and, for good measure, a tour from Montreal to Manhattan, Kansas, that summer. The daylong drives, the hardwood floors, the shitty food, the endless setting up and loading out were more agreeable to some than others. "Touring," says Chris, "is one hour of the most life-affirming experience you could ever have, surrounded by twenty-three hours of absolute boredom and agony." Dan says, "Chris is a great sport, but he did not have the same desire to rough it. BJ and I were just sort of like, 'We will sleep anywhere. We will play a show every night.' He also had a way more demanding job physically in the band."

Meanwhile, Chris had left his job at CMJ to start a music site called *Paper Thin Walls*. It was an expertly compiled source of news, reviews, and profiles, along with daily MP3s. Unlike many, he made a point of paying his contributors, and soon attracted top-shelf writers such as Caryn Ganz, Douglas Wolk, and Jesse Jarnow. Musicians from bands such as Frightened Rabbit, Fleet Foxes, and Grizzly Bear served as guest editors. "We had all the best writers," said Chris. "We paid writers what they're worth to write."

It wasn't long before *Paper Thin Walls* was attracting suitors. After only nine months, in May of 2007, Getty Images bought the site for $850,000. The stakes were suddenly significant. Chris had to choose the life of a musician or a music critic; he chose the latter. He played his final show with the band that July, and started writing a book about Public Enemy. For the third time in less than five years, Parts & Labor announced an open call for drummers. "We're looking for someone who can tour a minimum of four months out of the year, starting this fall with trips in the U.K./Europe, as well as the U.S.," they wrote. "They'll have some difficult shoes to fill."

* * *

Joe Wong had been in punk and indie bands since middle school. A native of Milwaukee, Wisconsin, he was obsessed with Michael Jackson's

Thriller as a kid, as well as Prince and Depeche Mode. His parents ran a Chinese restaurant, where Joe was put to work cleaning grease traps. At age fifteen, he saw Fugazi on the *Red Medicine* tour. "They were the gold standard," he recalled. "I looked up to people like that—who made their own records, and figured out their own way of doing things." He won a scholarship to the Berklee School of Music in Boston and studied jazz for two years before returning to Milwaukee. He scored an independent film, which led to work in advertising and TV; he later joined the bands of Mary Timony and Marnie Stern. Through an old bandmate, he learned about the opening with Parts & Labor, of whom he'd never heard.

On August 9, 2007—Dan's birthday—Joe came by for an audition. "We had kind of resigned ourselves to our next drummer not being able to play the insane beats that Chris came up with," says BJ. "We had selected a handful of songs we definitely wanted to continue playing, like 'Fractured Skies' and 'Gold We're Digging.' Tryouts involved playing those songs with the prospective drummer, to see what they'd do with them. I remember us prefacing 'Gold We're Digging' with Joe, like, 'Don't worry about playing the beat exactly. Just do what feels comfortable.' Joe was like, 'Oh, you mean this beat?' and proceeded to play it, and the entire song, flawlessly. I don't recall considering any other drummers after that." He joined the band in mid-September, and played a European tour just a few days later.

*   *   *

It seemed as if every other week in 2007 brought a breakthrough indie album: Of Montreal and Deerhunter in January; Arcade Fire, LCD Soundsystem, and Panda Bear in March; The Field and Leslie Feist in April; The National, Battles, and Dan Deacon in May; Justice in June; Bon Iver and St. Vincent in July; A Place to Bury Strangers and M.I.A. in August; Animal Collective and Dirty Projectors in September. At the same time, a more accessible, anemic, and innocuous approach had been perfected by a pack of indie-yuppie types: anodyne one-hit wonders (Peter Bjorn and John), nostalgia acts (The Pipettes), blog bands (Voxtrot, Tapes 'n Tapes), and connoisseurs of cardigans (The Decemberists). "It felt like the beginning of a conservative pull within rock music," says Dan. "A Wynton Marsalis era—where being able to re-create something that came before is of more value" than "something that is trying to move the ball down the court and create something a little more singular. There were times in the 2000s where it felt like the scene—and critics, to some extent—had lost interest in the idea of developing new forms of punk and rock." In *The Village Voice*, LCD Soundsystem's *Sound of Silver* topped the year-end critics' poll. "The message was clear in 2007," wrote a contributor. "Being a 'rock star' is gauche at best, silly and anachronistic at worst." That the author had played drums in Parts & Labor was left unsaid.

For all their growth in terms of writing and recording, Parts & Labor had hit a ceiling. Five and a half years in, they were still sleeping on floors, still uninsured, and barely breaking even. Their friends and peers in the Yeah Yeah Yeahs, Matt and Kim, TV on the Radio, and Battles had all gone on to bigger things. "By 2008," says Dan, "the zeitgeist had solidly shifted toward chillwave, '90s revivals, and a more resigned, corporate music Internet, and I think we could feel it." Amid a context of increasing obsolescence, Parts & Labor chose to swing for the fences.

Recorded at four different studios, comprising eight heroic tracks, *Receivers* was their most expansive album yet. From "Satellites," the seven-minute opener, to the acoustic "Mount Misery"—a song about a former slave-plantation-turned-vacation-home, bought by Donald Rumsfeld—it was an album marked by slower tempos, open space, and long crescendos. They asked their fans to send them samples and recordings, getting over 600, all of which they used.

Released by Jagjaguwar in October of 2008, the album earned the band a profile on NPR. "Parts & Labor has spent the last six years crafting fist-pumping, operatic walls of sound with distorted electronics, scorching guitars, and lyrics you can sing at the top of your lungs on a cross-country road trip," said Liane Hansen. In the *Chicago Tribune*, Greg Kot pronounced: "Parts & Labor is now three-for-three in creating rock albums that everyone who cares about rock music should own." The question was: how many people still cared about the sort of rock music Parts & Labor were making?

By 2009, the Brooklyn scene had reached a tipping point, with the release of instant anthems from Animal Collective ("My Girls"), Dirty Projectors ("Stillness Is the Move"), and Grizzly Bear ("Two Weeks"). A dozen local acts were designated Best New Music: The Pains of Being Pure at Heart, The Antlers, Woods, and Bear in Heaven, among others. A younger group of artists from New Jersey (Real Estate, Vivian Girls, Titus Andronicus) and L.A. (Best Coast, No Age, Wavves) were seemingly ubiquitous. "You could tell that the Brooklyn bubble was starting to shift, and that we were not going to be a part of it, which meant that we had to think about if we could maintain the pace that we were working at," says Dan. "We were doing the label and we were touring all the time. I think that after *Receivers* came out, we felt strongly about what we had done. Enough that we felt like things were gonna get easier, and they did not."

The band had made an album a year since 2006. They'd pushed themselves to write, record, perform, and tour for nearly a decade. "There were no breaks," says BJ. "That pace is hard to sustain when we're going on these tours and not coming home with money to pay rent." There would be one more album—*Constant Future* (2011), for which they worked with engineer Dave Fridmann—and tours of Europe and Japan. But by then, the winds had shifted; the indie scene was in decline. "At that point, it felt like the world had changed in those couple of years," says Dan.

In the fall of 2011, the band announced a string of dates in which they played from *Stay Afraid, Mapmaker*, and *Receivers*, leading up to a tenth-anniversary celebration in February. "Following these performances, we're going to take an extended hiatus," they wrote on social media. "We'd like to thank everyone who's supported us, bought our albums, seen us live, offered us a floor to sleep on. We love y'all. As a token of our esteem, we're giving away a final song called 'No Nostalgia,'" which was recorded during the *Receivers* sessions, "but suddenly seems all too prescient."

They played their final show in Williamsburg at 285 Kent on February 24, 2012, down the block from where BJ had organized Chester Fest. They called up each of their four drummers, along with a full brass ensemble. There was a sense of muted grief and local pride among us out in the standing-room-only crowd. "That whole day is basically a blur up until we played the final drone, and it starts to sink in that it's the end," said Dan. "We've made it through this ninety-minute retrospective, brought up everyone who was ever in the band, and everybody starts tearing the stage apart."

Parts & Labor represents the best of the Brooklyn scene. Their albums were a cry for skepticism and dissent in a complacent age. Their legacy is one of unceasing innovation, restlessness, and hustle. The seven minutes of "The Gold We're Digging" and "Fractured Skies" encompass everything about the aughts in Brooklyn: the possibility, adrenaline, and spectacle. "I think that there was some success to what we did musically," says BJ. "I still wonder if we hit the thing that we were trying to hit. Even though I'm proud of everything we did together, I don't know if we ever did what we set out to do, in some ways, or ever did it fully."

They pushed themselves for years on end like mules without material reward, long after most would have called it a day. It's tempting to imagine a scenario in which they caught a break—a pinch of luck—like many of their peers. "There was a point where it seemed attainable, because people around us were attaining it suddenly," says Dan. "You looked around you, like: 'Well, that could be any of us right now.' Then you're like: 'Okay, how do I make that happen? What am I willing to do to make that happen?' That's pretty much where we were until probably 2010. It started to feel like, 'Actually, no. I don't think this is going to happen.'"

"We didn't have dreams of being Linkin Park, but we wanted to be Sonic Youth, where you could go out, play some music, release an album, and then when you come home, you don't have to work at a burrito place," says Chris. "Basically, a middle-class musician's life. Anyone who's a musician today will tell you that it's even harder now than it was in 2006. It's something that's been eroded more and more. We just wanted to play music for a living. And in today's economy, that seems like a pretty big dream. But we tried."

Silent Barn (II)

December 1979. An estimated 70,000 buildings in New York sit empty. An arts collective named Colab (Collaborative Projects, Inc.) asks the city for permission to convert a vacant property at 125 Delancey Street into a community art center. When the city decided not to respond, the artists cut the locks and built an exhibition called *The Real Estate Show*—an act of protest and a provocation, in a neighborhood where buildings sat unused while many struggled to afford housing. In a manifesto, the organizers wrote, "It is important to focus attention on the way artists get used as pawns by greedy white developers . . . a recognition that artists, living and working in depressed communities, are compradors in the revaluation of property and the 'whitening' of neighborhoods." The exhibition opened on New Year's Eve, and was up for only a day before the city padlocked the entrance. The organizers held a press conference. The *Times*, the *Post*, and the *East Village Eye* filed stories. "[The show's] basic ideological premise—that artists, working people, and the poor are systematically screwed out of decent places to exist in—could not have been brought home with more brutal irony," wrote the *Eye*. In the ensuing uproar, a compromise was reached: officials let the artists rent an abandoned beauty parlor at 156 Rivington. They used the letters from an aging sign and named it ABC No Rio—in due course, a gallery, print shop, darkroom, soup kitchen, zine library, and all-ages venue with one rule: NO RACIST, SEXIST, OR HOMOPHOBIC BANDS WILL BE BOOKED. In June of 1980, in a shuttered massage parlor, Colab staged *The Times Square Show*, with work from one hundred contemporary artists, including Jean-Michel Basquiat, Keith Haring, Jenny Holzer, Alex Katz, and at least one couple: Jane Dickson and Charlie Ahearn.

For its thirty-fifth anniversary, in 2014, a gallery would mount *The Real Estate Show Was Then: 1980*, revisiting the subjects of the original exhibition. The property at 125 Delancey Street had been absorbed within Essex Crossing, a six-acre, $1.9 billion megacomplex. "Then, the neighborhood was broken-down and filled with drug dealers and thug landlords," wrote a critic. "Now it's an upscale corporate development. This is worse." Others said the spirit of the '70s was alive and well. At the opening of *The Real Estate Show Was Then*, Jane Dickson noted that her son, Joe, had come of age around the Colab generation, and now resided at the Silent Barn, in Bushwick.

* * *

Joe Ahearn came from art-world royalty. His mother is a celebrated painter; his uncle is a sculptor; his father made the classic hip hop film *Wild Style*. His childhood took place amid the pornographic theaters of the old Times Square before his family moved downtown. "I always thought ABC No Rio was cool," says Joe. "Not because I knew much about its history when I was in middle school, but because I could go there to see hardcore bands and drink forties when I was fourteen." He trekked around the fifty states after graduating high school. "I didn't go to college. I kind of hitchhiked and made friends with a bunch of musicians at DIY spaces and ended up visiting every state in the country. When I got back to New York, I started getting questions from people who I had stayed on their couch, or I had met while traveling. There was a band that was touring to New York, and they were like, 'Do you know where I can play a show?' I felt I had this karmic debt," says Joe.

"I hadn't heard of Todd or anything in Brooklyn. This is 2006. Even though I'm a born-and-raised New Yorker, I hadn't been to Williamsburg. I was complaining to a friend. I was like, 'I want a place where no one's gonna complain that the bands are too loud.' And he was like, 'You should look for this guy. Todd P.' And so I went to Greenpoint for my first Todd P show, at Uncle Paulie's. It was pouring rain. And you have to walk like twenty blocks from the G train. And the whole way, I'm like, 'This is the coolest thing.' I hadn't even gotten to the venue yet. There's probably twenty people there, and Todd is sweeping water with a broom when I arrive, and I was totally enamored with the entire thing. I asked Todd, 'Could I volunteer for you? What can I do? I'll sweep the water from the venue. I want to be part of this.'"

He started working as an unpaid intern out of Todd's apartment in Long Island City—answering email, helping at shows, and listening to bands. He met Todd's posse of interns: Ric Leichtung, Mike Sheffield, and Alaina Stamatis. In 2007, he helped Todd launch *Showpaper*, a free biweekly publication that compiled every all-ages show around the tristate area, with a print run of 10,000. He worked the door at Silent Barn, in Ridgewood, and the newly opened Death by Audio in Williamsburg. He found a building for his friends The So So Glos and Todd to open Market Hotel in Bushwick. "I was trying to say yes to everything," Joe recalls. "I was like, 'I don't want to do any other work. I will figure out how to sleep in a bucket. This is what I need to spend my time doing.'"

He lived in the basement of Secret Project Robot when it was on Kent and Metropolitan. "Todd had a practice space on one side of the building. There was, like, a half-room that was underneath the stairs. I believe Dave Longstreth from Dirty Projectors lived right before me under those stairs. I was kind of the super. I would help collect rent. If it rained, I would make sure it wasn't flooding anyone's equipment. In exchange for doing all that, I didn't get paid, but I didn't have to pay rent. Which, in hindsight: it couldn't have cost more than $400 a month to live in a horrible situation like that. I got a membership at the YMCA in Williamsburg, because there wasn't a shower under the stairs." He lived there for a year, made friends with countless bands, and worked at hundreds of Todd's shows in 2007. "Sometimes Todd would book multiple shows in a night, so I would be responsible for some of them," Joe says, "and that was how I started doing shows of my own."

"This was when Todd's world was completely exploding," says John Chavez, booking agent and former Silent Barn resident. "In terms of the outside world paying attention to the bands that he had championed for a long time—Dan Deacon, Dirty Projectors, Deerhunter—all these folks that had been playing his shows for a couple of years were reaching a more mainstream crowd, and all of a sudden it became something where people were paying attention . . . This was the beginning of a multimillion-dollar industry [for indie rock]."

Joe was working seven days a week for Todd. He was done with life under the stairs. "I think I turned twenty-one under those stairs," he says. "I was going to a show every night of the week, and two of those were mine, and I was sick of moving PA equipment around. I really wanted a home base where I didn't always have to ask permission from other people to let me do stuff." A room was opening at Silent Barn, on Wyckoff Avenue, which had evolved into a working residence and makeshift venue after the Skeletons crew left. "I had been doing lots of shows there," Joe says. "And, you know—I love Dan Deacon. I love Japanther and all that wacky poppy stuff. But honestly, I was enamored with, like, weird noise music, and, to me—of all the venues that were around when indie was exploding, and everyone was paying attention to the scene in Brooklyn—I was much more interested in, 'What happens if we do a show for thirty people every night of the week?' And Silent Barn just seemed so much weirder than any other venue. I knew that this was where I wanted to live." His first month there was January of 2008. In time, his roommates were a game designer, Kunal Gupta; an artist, Nat Roe; and a musician, G. Lucas Crane, who played in the band Woods. Joe says, "That's when you saw the final transformation from

Matt Mehlan and Skeletons [who had left in 2006] to a show space that people were living in the middle of."

"We were having trouble because we had to change the configuration of the furniture in the living room on nights that we had a show," Joe continues. "If we didn't have a show, we were supposed to put the furniture back in resident mode or whatever. I remember us having a meeting where all of us were like, 'Well, it's really hard for us to keep track of when there is or isn't a show. So the practical thing is for us to make sure that there's always a show, every single night, and then we'll never have to worry about moving all the furniture back.' At that point, the people that were living there were crazy enough in that specific way where all of us were like, 'Oh, totally. We should have a show every night.' Our rule was basically: we wanted to be the venue that always said yes. We wanted to invite strangers to our home. We wanted to perform for them, and make food for them. The fact that it was happening in our home was key."

They hosted early shows with Future Islands, Real Estate, Vivian Girls, Das Racist, Kurt Vile, and Grimes, to name a few—in their kitchen. They volunteered their couch to hundreds of artists on tour. The basement served as a laboratory for the video-game collective Babycastles, cofounded by Kunal. "Three and a half incredible years," says Joe. And then they lost everything within a single weekend.

* * *

The summer of 2011 looked promising for Silent Barn. In May, they hosted shows with Wolf Eyes, RVIVR, and Dysrhythmia, among others. In late June, there was the inaugural edition of the Ende Tymes Festival— three days of workshops, screenings, and performances from forty noise artists—for which promoter Bob Bellerue had bought the venue an all- new sound system. Joe recalls, "We had a really shitty PA. A bunch of broken gear that had washed up at the venue. Bob was like, 'I want to do this festival here, but I need to have good gear. I'm going to buy a sound system, and in exchange for the space, I'm going to give you this PA.' So he had given us a new system that was beautiful, these huge subwoofers, and we had never had anything like that before." Exactly three weeks after the festival—on Friday, July 15—an audience of twenty was enjoying a performance by the synthesizer artist Steve Moore when the authorities came charging through the door.

"It was just this Voltron that came in, one by one," said Nat Roe. "Fire Department. Police guy. Health officers . . . Department of Buildings." The Barn had been raided by M.A.R.C.H., comprising agents of the NYPD, Health Department, Fire Department, Buildings Department, and Liquor Authority, en masse. Joe says, "It was an ambient show. The cops were like, 'Who are these people?'" They put a padlock on the door and ordered everyone to leave. Nat was standing in the street with his cat. He crashed with friends at a loft that itself had been raided one month prior.

"The landlord said, 'We'll sort this out. Don't worry about it,'" says Joe. "I don't think we ever thought that it would turn into what it turned into. So on Sunday, we had asked our landlord, 'There's a bunch of us whose stuff is there. Do you think it's an issue if we pop in?' They were like, 'Just don't mess with the padlock.' Kunal and I were the ones who first went to the space. I can still remember walking down the street and seeing from a block away that the front door was wide open. And, yeah—my heart sank. We walked in, and everything in the place was trashed. Pillows ripped open. Furniture upside down. It was hard to comprehend what I was looking at. There was a radio in one of the rooms that was playing really loud. The sound system was gone. Kunal went to his room and realized his computer was missing. A lot of the Babycastles gear was gone. Lucas's gear case got stolen. It had his entire life's work of these field recordings on cassette that he had been collecting his entire career.

"We called the police to file a report. The police, who were responsible for the M.A.R.C.H. raid a few days earlier. We said, 'The door's wide open. You guys padlocked it. The place is trashed. It looks like people have stolen stuff.' They send two people together, and they give us, like, the shittiest cop treatment. Where they were like, 'I dunno. You guys probably had a lot of enemies. Maybe your landlord was sick of your shit. Do you have receipts for any of this stuff? How do we know that anything was stolen at all? Maybe you guys trashed the place?' True to their history, the cops did nothing but make us feel like shit, and did not help us in the slightest." The losses came to $15,000 worth of audio equipment and personal belongings, and thousands in cash.

The following day, they wrote on Facebook: "This weekend has been incredibly heartbreaking for all of us at The Silent Barn . . . We've lost 7 years' worth of accumulated equipment, tools, and artwork donated and built by individuals from every end of the scene's spectrum, and we're still reeling with what this means for our own lives and the future of the space . . . We need your help to continue." By Wednesday afternoon, there was a fundraising campaign on Kickstarter. By Thursday, contributors had pledged over $18,000. It took another month for them to reach their goal of $40,000—but by then, it was apparent that their days at 915 Wyckoff were numbered.

On August 23, 2011, after speaking with a lawyer, they sent an update. "The Silent Barn will soon have a new address . . . To appeal our case to the local government would take nearly a year—in the time it takes to appeal, Silent Barn would fall into irreparable debt. Given the amount of support we've received through Kickstarter, we need to be certain that when we reopen Silent Barn, we will be able to keep our doors open for years to come." They started scouting properties in mid-September— right around the time that protesters were descending on Zuccotti Park for the start of Occupy Wall Street.

Dragons of Zynth
(*Coronation Thieves*)

Son House and Lead Belly, Lionel Hampton and Louis Jordan, Muddy
Waters and Sister Rosetta Tharpe. Fats Domino, Little Richard, and
Chuck Berry. Ray Charles, Odetta, and James Brown. Jimi Hendrix.
Curtis Mayfield. Stevie Wonder. Tina Turner. The Meters, Funkadelic,
Arthur Lee and Love, Sly and the Family Stone. Death and Bad Brains.
Prince. Tracy Chapman and Meshell Ndegeocello. Living Colour,
Fishbone, Body Count, and Rage Against the Machine. The roots of
rock are overwhelmingly in black American music. Then why was the age
of indie—The Shins, The National, Arcade Fire, Grizzly Bear, Vampire
Weekend, et al—so white?

It was an awkward and unspoken fact that few would argue with
today. But in the fall of 2007, the writer Sasha Frere-Jones incited a
major controversy with "A Paler Shade of White," a 4,000-word broad-
side in *The New Yorker*. He traced the lineage of what he called "musical
miscegenation"—where white and black traditions merged—and its
conspicuous decline among the bands of the '90s, like Pavement and
The Flaming Lips. He took the indie world to task for writing songs
that were both precious and pedestrian, with little sign of syncopation,

showmanship, or swing. "If there is a trace of soul, blues, reggae, or funk in Arcade Fire, it must be philosophical; it certainly isn't audible," he wrote. The magazine received more mail about the piece than any other in eleven years. The essay drew responses from the experts and the amateurs, the message boards and music blogs, the *Los Angeles Times*, *The Guardian*, *The Village Voice*, and even *Playboy*, who called Frere-Jones a fetishist and a racist. The piece's many critics noted errors, inconsistencies, and counterexamples: what about acts led by artists of color like TV on the Radio, M.I.A., and Bloc Party? In *Slate*, Carl Wilson said it boiled down to class, not race. In *The New York Times*, David Brooks would cite the essay in a column about "the era of fragmentation." Few, if any, found the argument held up. It was ironic, then, that *Coronation Thieves*, the first and only LP to date by Dragons of Zynth—an indie band of black and brown musicians, and therefore an exception to the rule—had been released the week "A Paler Shade of White" was published, and would exemplify its point as to the blind spots of the indie world.

*   *   *

According to the culture of the Ga, in southeast Ghana, the birth of twins is understood as a blessing from the gods. A symbol of abundance, health, and good fortune, twins are differentiated from other members of the tribe. For every set of human twins, there was a corresponding pair of spirits in the sky, who would inhabit human form when they were affronted. "Twins are feared, because when angry," wrote an anthropologist, they could invoke "the sickness, if not death, of the objects of their enmity." For males in Ga society, the first-born twin was named Akwetey; the second-born was named Aku.

Akwetey and Aku Orraca-Tetteh were born in the Bronx and raised in Ohio. Their mom and dad were both physicians who had emigrated after medical school in Ghana; their older sister had been born in Koforidua, near Accra. The family had to move around the parents' work, to hospitals in Massachusetts, New Jersey, and Connecticut. When the twins were ten years old, the family settled in Cleveland, where Aku and Akwetey attended an all-boys' school. They shared a love of basketball, the radio, and making art, but not much else.

In many ways, the twins were opposites as little kids. Akwetey was an introvert and virtually silent; Aku was student-council president in middle school and something of a prodigy. At age five, Aku was playing keyboard, writing songs, and making tapes of Janet Jackson. He starred in plays at school, and was cast for a local TV show. At six years old, by contrast, Akwetey barely spoke—until he joined his mom for church and started singing in the choir. Aku was studying piano at the Cleveland Institute of Music. Akwetey hated practicing and asked to quit. Like many families of first-generation immigrants, they were raised with great expectations, in a strict household. They fought like only siblings can, with savagery and spite; their arguments could lead to punctured walls.

Their paths converged as teenagers. By age sixteen, Aku had tired of conservatory and stopped playing. Akwetey started learning the guitar and singing in musicals. In 1998, the twins were both accepted at Amherst College, where they flourished. Aku was twice elected student-body president and studied law and social thought. Akwetey majored in religion and art history. Their classmates were compelling, talented, and fun. The atmosphere was inspirational. "There's something lyrical about that whole part of Massachusetts," says Aku. "Robert Frost. Emily Dickinson." He started playing piano again; he signed up for courses in jazz, voice, and songwriting. Akwetey spent his junior year in Chile. "I would take a Spanish flamenco guitar in a backpack. I would hop on a bus and go up and down the coast," he says. "I was getting into Chilean folk singers—Víctor Jara, and João Gilberto, from Brazil—so this style of guitar with the accented Spanish rhythm became woven into my playing." Senior year, they studied with the flutist, saxophonist, and composer Yusef Lateef, who taught a method known as "autophysiopsychic music." Like his friend John Coltrane, Lateef embraced a synthesis of

Western and non-Western music, classical and jazz, science and faith: an all-embracing mode of thought the twins would make their own.

"It was the most beautiful thing, to hear somebody like that speak," says Aku. "It's almost like a grandfather hugging you. He would want you to get into your mind, and your emotions, and find that connective thing. He said that 'jazz' was just a term the music industry had made for marketing. So it's really 'auto-physio-psychic music': 'auto' being self, the soul; 'physio' being the body; and 'psychic' being the psyche. The body, mind, and soul. But what it really means is, there are certain things you can do, if you practice all the time. I'm talking scales, drills. So you can actually know the space between each of your fingers, use the fingers you don't normally use . . . It was a great, safe place to develop those ideas, and having that support of making it actually real, because it seemed so impossible, at the same time—actually being a musician and artist."

Among the friends they made was a future bandmate, Jason Lucas, a student at nearby Williams College. A native of Chicago's West Side, his father was the director of a marching band. "He was a high school music teacher who played everything but drums," Jason recalls. "I was a drummer. Making music in the collective was always in the air. He died when I was twelve. So playing music became a completely different thing, and feeling like, 'If this is something that you're given, then you have to share it. You've been given it for a reason.' 9/11 was our senior year. I was getting ready to go into finance. I was an economics major. We were standing there, watching the world change. One of the last things with my dad was seeing Norman Schwarzkopf on TV and bombing Iraq [in 1990]. And I was like: 'If I were two years older, I'd probably have been working in that building. If that could have been me, I need to do what brings me joy every moment that I'm here, and that's making music.'"

The twins had an early aptitude for chutzpah. "I cold-called Ahmet Ertegun, the founder of Atlantic," says Aku. "I wrote him a letter. He's like, 'Yeah, come see me.' I went to meet him at this big office. And this is college, you know what I mean? I asked him about the state of the music business, and why they were putting out certain records. You know, 'You did The Rolling Stones.' He told me about trends, and how you have to go with them, or else you're dead, and how he doesn't dictate what those are." Aku was finding out about the power of proximity in New York, and creating your own opportunities. "If you could get your way into finding somebody, and presenting yourself, they were right there, and I knew I could do that."

A week before they graduated, in 2002, the filmmaker and alumnus David O. Russell came to Amherst for a talk. At the Q&A, Akwetey made an unintentionally off-color remark, and the room erupted in laughter. A few minutes later, he was approached by Russell's assistant. "You know, David thought that was hilarious," he said. "What are you doing after graduation?"

"So a few weeks later, I'm in L.A.," Akwetey says. "And at the time David was writing *I Heart Huckabees*, and I was kind of a speck on the wall in the office. They tasked me with reading scripts and doing some coverage to see how my development skills were. David was getting calls from Brad Pitt. I thought my ticket had come in, but I was in over my head. I think I felt a bit out of my depth as a twenty-one-year-old . . . When David asked me what I wanted to do with my life, I realized I had no answer. I was all façade and didn't have the courage to tell him. He invited me to yoga on a Tuesday and I left for New York the Sunday before. I didn't have the stuff that makes an artist, the stuff one experiences that makes ideas worth painting or singing about."

The siblings found a place together in Fort Greene. They went to parties thrown by friends from school. One of the people they met was Devang Shah, a drummer and an architect, with whom they had some things in common. Much like the twins, Devang was from a family of physicians and first-generation immigrants, from India. His father opened a Hindu temple in Queens. His mother's office was in Williamsburg. He grew up on Long Island, and spent his adolescence gallivanting downtown before he went to NYU. He played in bands, and listened to noise rock, free jazz, and hip hop. He started hanging out at Stinger Club, on

Grand Street, where he met a musician named Kyp Malone. He was living in Manhattan on September 11. "Obviously, my last name is Shah," Devang says. "It doesn't matter that we're Hindu. I feel the heat, you know? My family's putting up American flags on the car, on the lawn." He had an album's worth of noisy instrumentals when he met the twins. "I had a psychic bond with Aku," Devang says. "I was like, 'I can tell who you listen to. You like Jimi Hendrix, you like Shuggie Otis, you like Fela Kuti.' And he was like, 'Yeah.'" But it was with Akwetey that he started writing music in his parents' home.

Akwetey overdubbed a vocal using one of Devang's tracks. They called it "Labor Day Lung." "We automatically clicked," Akwetey says. "I started going out to Long Island and recording music with Devang in his mom's basement. Twice a week, I took the train, for about six months." Devang played the drums and made beats; Akwetey sang and played guitar. The sound was languorous, psychedelic, and utterly their own. They soon recorded a five-song demo under the name AD. They asked Aku to join, but he was skeptical. "I didn't want to play with them because I wasn't secure where they were coming from," Aku says. "They kept telling me, like, 'You gotta do this. We need you.'" The pieces came together for Aku when they played him a song entitled "War Lover." He improvised a synthesizer part. "He just laid it down in one take," Devang says. "We just look at each other. We're like, okay, you know: this is official now." They settled on a name: Dragons of Zynth. It was the fall of 2004—the year of M.I.A. and Diplo's *Piracy Funds Terrorism* and TV on the Radio's debut LP, *Desperate Youth, Blood Thirsty Babes*.

* * *

Aku was tending bar and working ten to six at Rawkus Records as an intern. Akwetey paid his share of the rent by interning at Spike Lee's 40 Acres and a Mule, script-supervising at the Public Theater, and freelancing in production at venues such as Hammerstein Ballroom, Irving Plaza, and Roseland. "I basically said, 'If I can work at all these venues, we'll figure out, like, how it rolls as a real band,'" says Akwetey. "So I'm sitting backstage in the office at Roseland, basically as a water boy, filling ice and coolers for the green room, and in walks a really tall African man—I can tell, just by his stature, you know? Wearing a newspaper-boy hat, with these thick, 1950s glasses, and he busts through the room right before the show where TV on the Radio opens for Interpol. And I swear to you—when Tunde [Adebimpe] walked through that door, in my head, I was like, 'This guy's the newsman.' He has this whole superhero-newsman energy." It was the night that Akwetey met TV on the Radio. "And this is when I really felt the shock wave of the music coming out of the city." He handed them a copy of the AD demo. He started seeing them around town. The bands immediately clicked. They soon were making music together.

"My brother brought me to the studio one day to meet everybody," says Aku. "That everybody looked like us—we could tell they were really smart—I was like, 'Wait a minute. It's like this?' Because to me, like: 'I could do this. They're doing this.' Once I met those guys, and I found Williamsburg, I felt like, 'I have to move here. I have to be *here*. This is where I'm supposed to develop my artist self.' Which it was. You know, it was like—school. It was like grad school. While my friends were going to business school, I went to rock-and-roll college." Aku would bond especially with Dave Sitek, the multi-instrumentalist and producer. "I learned so much, so fast, 'cause I spent every day with Dave. We had the same excitement about doing weird, cool, funky shit. It was a match made in heaven. Honestly, those days—I couldn't even understand it while it was happening. 'Is this even allowed? Like, this much fun? This much exposure to creativity?' You walk outside your house—the pool is down the street, that empty pool at McCarren, where there are huge rock shows. It's like, 'Is this even—it can be like this?'"

Jason Lucas moved to Brooklyn in 2005. "At the time, it was like, 'I'll see you at the show,'" he says. "And not because you were trying to be out. In Williamsburg, if you walked on Metropolitan, or if you walked on South First, you would see fifty friends in seventy bands, and forty of them were good. It was this amazing opportunity to reinvent. It was so catalytic."

"I think there was this energy in the neighborhood," Devang says, "where you would walk around, and when you're creating something meaningful for you, everyone notices, even if they don't know who you are, because there *was* something special. I really think it was some sort of psychic energy . . . And we're like, 'There's something happening here, and we're gonna make history.' That kind of attitude. That's what Dave [Sitek] was on, because he already had a gold record [from producing the Yeah Yeah Yeahs]. So he was like, 'We're gonna make history, guys.' Like, come along for the ride, you know? And this is after, like, four months of making music."

TV on the Radio evangelized on the band's behalf. They offered studio time and introductions to friends. "All of a sudden, they're setting up an expensive dinner," says Akwetey. "They had just signed to Touch and Go, and I think the first EP had just come out. Hottest band in New York, and they're coming to me, like, 'We're gonna fly to Chicago on Monday with your CD.' And I'm thinking, 'You guys have money just to fly to Chicago?' So they played the demo for the head of Touch and Go, and things started gaining momentum." They met with venerated labels such as 4AD before deciding not to sign with anyone for now. "I think we just wanted to be on a label with our buddies, because we kind of knew that they were working on a new deal [with Interscope] that was coming down the pipeline," says Devang.

The bands would navigate the world of indie rock like teacher and pupil. "By that time, the TV guys are touring," says Akwetey. "And they're coming at me, like, you know, 'We wanna make you shirts,' or 'Take this guitar,' or 'We're doing this show in two weeks. Can you guys do it?' They opened up their hearts in the biggest way a young musician could ever imagine. A sensei/student way of sharing this new space they're also in as this new band of color in the scene." They gave the twins a Fender amp, a vocal mic, a vintage tape-delay machine. They also served as models, mentors, and elder siblings. "Having those guys, watching how they were rising," Aku says, "I feel so lucky to have had that as a guide. Because it *is* also hard for black people in this—you know—zone. And I always knew that it was going to be. So the fact that we actually found people like us, I thought was like a one-in-a-million strike, like this is meant to be. And, yeah: I did like it that they were black. A lot. I like that I felt like I found, you know, people like me. And it's not to say it was a huge thing. But fuck yeah: I loved the image that was being projected—the beauty, and the songs, and the representation—because they're, like, the only ones. And that's a problem to me."

They played the Glass House Gallery, where they met Brooke Baxter. They played at Tonic, Union Pool, and the Mercury Lounge. "My whole M.O. was just, make sure you're working as hard as you can," says Akwetey. "So I'm walking from Brooklyn, crossing the Williamsburg Bridge with our CD, all the way to Attorney Street, knocking on the door of Sin-é and saying, 'This is why you should book us.' We did that all over the city." It was an uphill climb. "A majority of the scene around that time was predominantly young white bands, and a lot of the keyholders to the venues, the labels, and basically the scene," says Akwetey. "That's just how it rolled, right? So in a lot of ways, the whole indie universe was a shock to the system . . . I mean, we had bookers who, maybe on paper, everything looks great. But then for some reason they're saying, you know, 'I don't think you guys are the right fit.' It's like: 'What are you trying to say?'"

It was a mirror of the wider state of race relations in New York. During his three terms in office, Mayor Bloomberg oversaw a vast expansion of the practice known as stop-and-frisk. In 2002, NYPD made 97,000 stops, primarily young men of color; in 2006, there were more than 500,000. "The temperature in the city at the time was that the police were at war with black and brown people on the streets," said a public defender. In late 2006, in Queens, a twenty-three-year-old, Sean Bell—black, unarmed, and on his wedding day—was killed by fifty bullets from police. "To be class-, police-, race-, and foreign-policy-conscious in those days, it was not healthy, because society was so unready to hear all this stuff," says Devang. "I've been stopped in every state, every borough. I've been stopped walking down the street, talking on my cell phone. I've been stopped in Long Island, where my parents live. 'Why are you here?' 'We've lived here for thirty years.' 'Let's see your license.' So I kind of saw what black dudes are going through in this country. And then I saw what Muslims are going through in this country . . . So it's kind of like this clarity. I was like, 'All my black friends have been stopped by the police, and I've been stopped by the police, but none of my white friends have.' And they're looking at us, like, 'What were you doing wrong?'"

* * *

They started working on an album at Dave Sitek's studio, Stay Gold, in 2005; Sitek produced. "It was a beautiful time," says Aku. "We were recording our Dragons album at the same time that they were recording *Return to Cookie Mountain*." They went to London in the spring to work on music with Massive Attack. They met the former head of Virgin Music, Nancy Berry, who had been courting bands for her new label— among them, TV on the Radio. "I really liked her because she knew how to promote black artists," Aku says. "She worked with Lenny Kravitz and Ben Harper. That was a huge thing, because the music game, there's a lot of, like, 'How are you presented out there?' You know, something that's not just like, long-hair, guitar, white-guy stuff. So I was like, 'We might need to be presented in the right way, and she knows what to do.' And so, for a moment, everything seemed like it was gonna be—off into the sunset. But, it didn't."

The bands would find themselves at odds during recording sessions at Stay Gold. "An interesting thing happened in the studio," says Akwetey. "Devang and I had recorded the demo for 'War Lover,' and then my brother put keyboards on it. In our minds, the song was so minted that all we need to do is master it. During the last stages of recording, when we get to 'War Lover,' Dave and Kyp [Malone] are very interested in redoing the song from scratch. And here I am as a young artist, my inner voice is saying, 'No, dude.' Like, 'What do you mean? We already did the song. That's why we're here.' And I slowly began to realize that the situation was a little different." They tried the song as Dave and Kyp had suggested. "So Devang and I are in a room, overdubbing, making new sounds, and it's not really hitting at all. And we decided, okay, we're sticking with the original. Went to the studio and told the TV guys. And that was the beginning of a very different energy."

The argument became a source of hard feelings. "Dave was very much into this wall-of-sound thing that Phil Spector was doing, like 2.0," says Aku. "And that worked for his band, but our band—it did not work. We listened to it, and we're like, 'This is not our shit.' And yes, it is true that there was a severe response toward us saying we did not like the mix. It was very severe . . . And we decided to take it back. I mixed it with somebody else. There was this kind of, like, pressure to follow whatever they wanted, in a certain sense. I feel like we were sat down on the couch, or being talked to in the studio. In my head, I'm like, 'Fuck this. Hell, no. I'm not putting this out.'"

"And then, late-game scenario," says Akwetey, "the recording is finished, and plans are going full-speed ahead. I get a call from Nancy that summer being like, 'Hey, I'm really sorry. This is not gonna work out.'" When TV on the Radio went out on tour, Akwetey and the band would learn that they couldn't access their recordings for a few months. He says, "This was a very sensitive issue for a while. Because the guys who are setting us up to do well, they're also working professionals. So we weren't able to make the moves that we wanted for a little bit. And then I guess the real kicker is when *Return to Cookie Mountain* came out, the first seven words are 'I was a lover before this war.' When I heard that—you have to know—I completely died inside. I was completely crushed . . . So here I'm having flashbacks of this song 'War Lover' that I wrote two years before, shared it with the guys, had this falling-out . . . And for what it's worth—whatever it means to stick to your guns—not re-recording the song caused a sore spot. I didn't know how sore it was until I heard that single."

"I don't think we ever talked about it publicly," says Devang. "One time, Kyp was getting interviewed by *Rolling Stone*, and we're at this club with him. And then the interviewer said, 'I just *love* "I Was a Lover."'

That song is *so amazing*. What was the inspiration?' And Kyp just looks at us—Akwetey's on one side, and I'm on the other—and he's just like, 'I stole it from him.' There's two or three songs on the album they really kind of lifted from us. We kind of lost control of our own record. Like, it's our record, but Dave has final say on stuff, and that did not vibe well with us. And then the thing that bothered me was how the album said 'featuring David Bowie,' but our name wasn't on it. I was like, 'How do you steal these songs and not put our names on it?' It pissed me off, because we also lost the record deal, you know? Dave was always like, 'We can go to Interscope, but we're gonna go with this new label [with Nancy Berry] that we're gonna start and all of us are gonna be on,' right? When [TV on the Radio and Berry had a falling-out], we were left high and dry, and that's why the album got delayed. The interim hurt our momentum, and they got there first . . . They put the flag in the ground. So they were the creators, and we were the copycats. I guess that's some bullshit, but, at the end of the day, TV on the Radio gave us everything. Dave believed in me more than anyone else I met, maybe in my whole lifetime. So that's something I can't forget."

The album sat for twelve months—a year of endings and beginnings. Devang would leave the group for architecture school. "It was everything at once," he says. "You're living together, you're best friends, you're in a band. We hit a breaking point." They started playing with Jason Lucas as their drummer and the bassist FonLin Nyeu. They signed with Gigantic, an indie label in New York; they found a manager, a publicist, and a booking agent. In July of 2006, they played the first McCarren Park Pool Party. With Bad Brains and Mos Def, they watched Patti Smith perform the final show at CBGB. And on October 16, 2007—more than two years after it was finished—*Coronation Thieves* was finally released.

It was a record unlike any other to come out that year, an LP that made the critics reach for a thesaurus. Comprising forty-five minutes of glam ("Get Off"), soul ("Closer"), punk ("Who Rize Above"), metal ("Breaker"), doo-wop ("Rockin Star"), and psychedelia ("Anna Mae"), the album was reviewed in *Spin* ("insanely eclectic"), *Vibe* ("a blend of post-bop, Afrobeat, punk, the psych-blues of Hendrix and Zeppelin, and OutKast's high-tech-in-high-cotton thang"), and *Pitchfork* (7.0). The obvious comparison was to black rock bands Death, Bad Brains, and Living Colour; the more revealing one was to fellow Ohio eccentrics Devo and Pere Ubu. In certain ways—with its total disregard of genre—it was an album ahead of its time, anticipating mavericks such as Thundercat and Flying Lotus, unclassifiable, which may explain the narrative that rapidly congealed.

"Dragons of Zynth is a New York City band (transplanted from Cleveland) whose album . . . was produced by Dave Sitek," said *The New York Times*, "but they can make TV on the Radio's jittery music seem calm by comparison." "The knee-jerk reaction to hearing Dragons of Zynth is to compare them to their friends and mentors TV on the Radio," said *Pitchfork*. "Much of *Coronation Thieves* was produced by TV on the Radio's Dave Sitek," said *The Village Voice*. "It's a sonic connection the DoZ don't work that hard to deny: The first song on TVOTR's last record is 'I Was a Lover' . . . track one on *Thieves* is called 'War Lover.'"

"Then we were kind of like the buzz band," says Aku. They opened shows for Television, Grizzly Bear, Modest Mouse, and Little Dragon. They played the Siren Festival and Afropunk. They toured with Saul Williams and Yeasayer. Their name was on the cover of *The Village Voice*. Between musicians of color such as Santigold, Earl Greyhound, Apollo Heights, Ninjasonik, and Lightspeed Champion, the indie world was slowly evolving. "Around this time, there's the beginning of a lot more awareness of cultural diversity," says Akwetey. "M.I.A. and Santigold—all these projects are coming into view. But to be honest, the rock-and-roll scene—it was an uphill battle."

"We didn't really know anything," says Aku. "And I would say, if we had different people managing our lives, it could have been a very different story . . . We went to Gigantic, and the person that signed us got fired, and they got some new guy who basically was exercising his presidential world-power. We did not see eye to eye. Even our management, they could only go so far. We had all these people come to us, but it felt like—because of the press we were getting, the cover of *The Village Voice*—it felt like people were coming to find an opportunity for themselves to grow, too, which is fine, but it didn't blossom the way that I saw it happening for other bands."

Around the time the group would start recording their second album, Aku received an offer to play bass on tour with Santigold. He saw it as a temporary gig. "I just thought I was going to play with Santi," he says. "We're going to come back and pick it right back up. But when I left, I think the structure of the band vanished. I thought they would be able to keep the practices going—just keep it alive while I was gone. That didn't happen. So people left at different times. And once people started leaving, that's when it became hard to envision what the band was going to look like." The group recorded at least twenty new songs, but couldn't find a label that was interested. Akwetey left to start a new vocation as a painter in 2012. The band went on hiatus before a brief reunion in 2016. Aku would tour the world performing with Florence and the Machine. Jason holds out hope they'll still release the second album. He even has a title: *Cryptophasia*, or a language only understood by twins.

They patched things up with TV on the Radio. "I worked things out with Kyp, on a personal level," says Akwetey. "So that's been resolved. But, yeah—in a lot of ways, I think that whole thing really changed my feelings about music." (TV on the Radio did not respond to several requests for comment.)

The indie scene as it existed for Dragons of Zynth can often seem a more parochial time, when artists of color were a rarity. Nevertheless, its members have warm memories. "It's funny, because the indie world—it's the genre that has accepted me as I am," Aku observes. "I worked at *Vibe*, and interned at Motown, and there weren't open arms there. The indie world is what my life became." His brother adds, "I often like to say there was a halo over Brooklyn in those days, and if you were hip to it, you know, and could find a few guys or girls and a guitar, then the window was just wide open, and the spotlight was there."

"The scene in Williamsburg was a microcosm," Jason says. "It was a networking of bands, a networking of people. Because we didn't have many ways to self-identify outside of standing on a stage. It was a bubble of black freedom in an environment that was predominantly white. So there were individuals of color, who were black, who were Latino, who were not affluent, and that made the scene what it was. There were broke-ass, weed-smoking white kids with broke-ass, weed-smoking black kids, and Latino kids, and everybody's like, 'Yo, America is fucked up.' And we're miles from the smoldering wreckage of our disillusionment, when we thought America was shits and giggles and finance and Rolls-Royces. What are we saying about this? We can't go shopping like Dubya told us to. We gotta say something. So it was a space where, for me, with the individuals I knew, it was a predominantly black space, and whoever wanted to stroll in and have their life changed, we were down, because we wanted the army as big as possible—to push back."

Art and Commerce

I organized my life around live music in my twenties and thirties. I was a regular at Zebulon, Magnetic Field, Southpaw, Northsix, Pianos, Tonic, Maxwell's, Joe's Pub, Cake Shop, and Union Pool. I knew my way around the Knitting Factory, Webster Hall, and Irving Plaza: where the view was best, and where to drink for cheap beforehand. I saw Patti Smith and her band play *Horses* in an opera house; Frank Ocean and Bon Iver in a synagogue; The National and Beach House at Mercury Lounge; The White Stripes and Sufjan Stevens at Bowery Ballroom. I made pilgrimages to the Apollo Theater, Carnegie Hall, and the Village Vanguard. In Florida, where I was from, you had to drive an hour for a sign of something cultural, but in New York, you didn't know where to begin. Like a hot-dog-eating contest, I gorged myself on everything I could. From early May to late September, the city was engulfed with entertainment out-of-doors—concerts, screenings, and festivals—most of which were free. I got to know New York and its landmarks in this way: Central Park SummerStage, Battery Park, Castle Clinton, Judson Church. I used to have a rule: if someone invited me to something—a birthday party, a play, a concert by a friend of a friend—I went, no matter what it was. After all, you never knew who you might end up meeting.

A week before Thanksgiving of 2006, I saw Modest Mouse play at Bowery Ballroom. My expectations were inordinately high. It was my first time seeing the band, whom I had loved for a decade; they were touring with Johnny Marr of The Smiths. It had the makings of a memorable night—an underplay, in the city's best rock venue—and it was, if for unforeseen reasons. The room was oversold; the floor was filled with weekend warriors; the mood of the crowd was equal parts fraternity and *Fight Club*.

The little indie band a friend had clued me into as a college freshman had become unlikely superstars. The introspection of *The Lonesome Crowded West* (1997) had given way to the ubiquitous "Float On" (2004). They played it midway through the set: as if on cue, a '90s-style mosh pit briefly formed; a horde of baseball-hatted bros were leaping up and down; the floor was bouncing underneath your feet. I made it through the first eight songs before I started feeling antsy, and went downstairs to get myself some water. I heard them playing "Dramamine," an old favorite, and cursed my sense of timing. It was then that I saw someone I recognized—a musician named Serena. We had been introduced at a show a few months ago. She had a lighter in her hand. She was heading outside to smoke. Did I want to come with?

We climbed the stairs and had the inside of our wrists stamped with blue ink. The winter air was frigid, a crowd was milling on the sidewalk, and clouds of smoke were wafting in the light. She offered me a Parliament. A line of yellow cabs were idling right out front. The band was on their encore. The bouncers yawned and eyed their wristwatches.

We were making small talk when a guy our age appeared from out of nowhere. He was at least six-foot-two and had the swagger of a leading man. His hair was long and dark and tucked behind his ears. He wore a stylish coat and scarf; his shoes were anything but indie rock. I thought he might be asking for a cigarette. I thought he might have been a movie star. I didn't think the person I was meeting on Delancey Street would one day be my boss, and ultimately change my life. In the years to come, I would often wonder how things might have turned out if I hadn't gone downstairs when I did.

"Dave," said Serena. "Have you two guys met?"

We talked for maybe five minutes. He was a classical musician; we had some friends in common. The show was letting out. He asked me if I had a card. He said we should meet up some time; he said he had a project he was working on.

"For sure," I said. I didn't think too much of it. People in New York say all kinds of things.

*   *   *

I heard from him five weeks later, after New Year's.

Hello Ronen,

I don't know if you recall our meeting outside the Bowery Ballroom; Serena introduced us. I'm a composer and violinist. We rapped a while about music.

My business partner and I are opening an art venue/performance space and nightclub. The venue's programming will be deliberately eclectic, designed to reinvigorate the artistic landscape as it relates to young people, fusing popular and art cultures and celebrating art of multiple mediums and genres in an edgy nightclub environment. We are currently continuing capital raising and are looking to move in on a space by spring.

As programming is our top priority, we are currently meeting candidates for the Music and Art Director and his/her team. We are interested in meeting with people such as yourself . . . Provided there is interest on your end, I'd like to have you meet with me and my business partner.

We had coffee at the end of January. He came to Lincoln Center with the business plan. A little like a book report, it was encased in a transparent sleeve, in tasteful fonts, on heavy bond. Their pitch was fairly straightforward: a venue for every kind of music from Björk to Biggie and Brahms—a hybrid of a club, a concert hall, and cabaret. Their vision was expansive: a room that would offer seated, standing, and in-the-round configurations. For reasons that were never quite explained, the club was called (Le) Poisson Rouge, gratuitous parentheses and all—*en anglais*, (The) Red Fish.

I had a drink with David and his business partner, Justin. They were as different as chalk and cheese. David was an extrovert, a self-proclaimed aesthete, a natural born charmer. Justin, on the other hand, was a wallflower, a numbers guy, and a lovable schlemiel. One was articulate, self-confident, and suave, while the other was tongue-tied, fidgety, and ham-fisted. One was born with charisma, looks, and wealth, and one was mostly like the rest of us.

David had been raised in Manhattan. His parents owned a big apartment building on the Upper East Side; a home in Fort Lee, New Jersey; and "a modest place" in East Hampton. He had attended the Professional Children's School, by Central Park, which counted Carrie Fisher, Uma Thurman, and Yo-Yo Ma among alums, and geared itself toward young musicians, actors, and dancers. At PCS, he met the Culkins—Kieran, Rory, and Macaulay, or Mac, who soon became his closest friend—as well as Scarlett Johansson, who was his high school sweetheart. An only child, a smooth talker, he had a palpable magnetism, a senatorial charm: the kind that came from usually getting what you want. I later learned his Hollywood façade belied a crippling insecurity—a fear that he would amount to little more than just another trust-fund kid.

Justin's background was relatively down-to-earth, if not exactly working-class. He was raised in Fort Myers, Florida, two hours west of my hometown. The family was well-to-do. In high school, he played in a ska band called Supa Chicken. He studied cello at Manhattan School of Music, where he had met Dave. It was there—amid the snobbishness, entitlement, formality, and self-regard of the academy—that they first envisioned a venue that did things differently. He taught himself to code a custom site for concert ticketing. He had a head of curls, a slender build, a crooked smile. He dressed in cardigans, and drank absinthe, and smoked tobacco from a pipe. He liked post-punk, no wave, industrial, and outright noise.

They didn't seem to have any experience—but then, neither did I. At the time of our first meeting, I had produced only two shows, and booked another three. I could list my professional contacts on five fingers; I had a staff comprised entirely of volunteers. A part of me was petrified at the thought of booking a venue seven nights a week, and two shows every night. A part of me was nervous about gambling away someone's investment. A part of me was sure I'd never get a chance like this again.

I saw the space in the spring of 2007—a busy season for the local concert business. After thirty-two years, CBGB had pulled the shutters down for good. In April, the Knitting Factory went up for sale; Sin-é and Tonic closed; and Irving Plaza renamed itself the Fillmore. In May, Lou Reed would play the opening of the new Highline Ballroom, on West Sixteenth Street—around the corner from the Hiro Ballroom; a subway ride from the Nokia Theater, owned by AEG; and down the block from the Blender Theater at Gramercy, a new investment of Live Nation. In June, the city's leading independent, the Bowery Presents, announced the Music Hall of Williamsburg would open in the fall (in its past life, Northsix), and weeks later, another new venue called Terminal 5—a multistory cattle pen in Hell's Kitchen. A club owner told *New York*: "There's a full-scale concert-promoter war going on." And there was the matter of an economic meltdown heading our direction.

Our timing, then, left much to be desired. What we did have on our side was history. The spot that David and Justin found, at 158 Bleecker Street, had been a pivotal establishment of New York nightlife: the Village Gate. Founded by Art D'Lugoff in 1958, it was a hallowed stage for jazz, folk, salsa, and comedy for nearly four decades, presenting everyone from Duke Ellington, Miles Davis, and Albert Ayler to Charles Mingus, Jimi Hendrix, and The Velvet Underground. In 1961, D'Lugoff booked Aretha Franklin in her New York debut, trading sets with John Coltrane. Also that year, Nina Simone recorded a live album—*Nina at the Village*

Gate—with Richard Pryor opening the show. According to legend, Bob Dylan wrote "A Hard Rain's A-Gonna Fall" in the basement, and Dustin Hoffman waited tables before D'Lugoff fired him. Concert venues had been founded on less.

In May of 2007, they offered me the position of music director. The salary was almost twice as much as my job at Lincoln Center. The starting date was undefined. Between construction and approvals from the liquor board, Department of Buildings, and community board, the venue was at least a year away from opening. My pay would end up starting in six months; I kept my job at Lincoln Center in the interim. We strategized at Justin's place on nights and weekends over beer and Chinese food. We bounced around the names of artists we'd invite, the acts we'd have as regulars. We talked about the many ways we'd set ourselves apart. On good days, it was a forty-five-minute ride on the F train back to Brooklyn. I put my headphones on and asked myself if anyone had ever been so fortunate.

* * *

One afternoon at Lincoln Center, Norma, the executive director, asked me if I wanted some CDs that had just arrived in the mail. It was a package from her friend at Nonesuch Records, stuffed with new releases by the likes of Clint Mansell, Brian Wilson, and The Magnetic Fields; a retrospective box set from Steve Reich; a DVD of Wilco's Jeff Tweedy; and a reissue of *Shakuhachi: The Japanese Flute*, from the Explorer Series.

Salivating, I asked her, "Are you . . . sure?" The pile was the height of a shoebox.

"Enjoy," she said. "They send them every few months. I honestly can't keep up."

I ran my finger down the stack. At a minimum, it was a hundred dollars' worth of music.

"So they just *send* you these?"

"Well, Bob," she said, with a grin. "He sends them." She was referring to Bob Hurwitz, the celebrated head of A&R at Nonesuch. I had read about him in *The New York Times Magazine*. He was the man behind a number of unexpected bestsellers: the Buena Vista Social Club, Gorecki's Third Symphony, Bulgarian choral music. He had signed iconic musicians such as Caetano Veloso, Philip Glass, Astor Piazzolla, Kronos Quartet, John Zorn, and David Byrne.

"You *know* him?"

"Well, sure," Norma said. "Would you like to meet him?"

* * *

The office was across the street from Radio City Music Hall and Rockefeller Center. The building spanned a city block and stood some forty stories tall. The floors were polished to reflective quality; the atrium was walled in glass; the doors revolved counterclockwise and absorbed a human river. Curiously, a mural graced the lobby that depicted scenes of economic struggle during the Great Depression, by Thomas Hart Benton. Equally incongruent on the ground level was a record store, FYE, sprawling and soon bankrupt. It was a humid day in mid-July.

I had prepared by reading the encyclopedic history on their website. In 1964, Jac Holzman, the founder of Elektra, had realized there was a potential market for inexpensively produced recordings, just like the recent innovation of paperbacks. He bought the rights from labels and distributors abroad, in what was then exotic repertoire—baroque, medieval, Renaissance—and packaged the albums with striking, psychedelic cover art, in keeping with the times. He named the label Nonesuch, a word for something without equal.

For its first fourteen years, Nonesuch was run by a woman named Tracey Sterne. A former piano prodigy, she was a champion of high-modernist and difficult composers—Elliott Carter, Milton Babbitt, Charles Wuorinen—more admired than enjoyed. At the same time, she helped produce surprise bestsellers such as *The Nonesuch Guide to Electronic Music*, which spent six months on the charts, and Morton Subotnick's synthesizer classic *Silver Apples of the Moon*. She started the Explorer Series in 1967, with music from around the world. In 1970, with pianist and Bach scholar Joshua Rifkin, Sterne reintroduced the ragtime of Scott Joplin to a vast audience. She brought consistency to every element of a release from liner notes to album art; officially, her title was coordinator, but she thought of herself as an editor. Through Sterne's adventurous aesthetic and intelligence, Nonesuch became a home for uncompromising art, old and new.

Also in 1970—in what soon became an industry-wide trend—Holzman sold Elektra to a corporation, Kinney National, that later changed its name to Warner Communications. The spirit of the '60s yielded to the stock market, the share price, and the quarterly report. "Nonesuch is in business, and it is losing its credibility in its marketplace," Warner's chairman would tell *The Boston Globe*. "We can't make records that sell only outside the Russian Tea Room." In 1979, Sterne was abruptly dismissed. Her firing would prompt a letter in *The New York Times* signed by every artist on the label, and thousands more to the head of Warner. She died from complications of Lou Gehrig's disease in 2000, at seventy-three years old. I saw that her obituary in the *Times* had mentioned Norma, who confirmed her death; she left no survivors.

In 1984, Bob Hurwitz, then thirty-four, was hired as the president of Nonesuch. He came from ECM—a legendary jazz and classical label, founded by Manfred Eicher—where he had worked with Keith Jarrett, Chick Corea, and Dave Holland. After graduating from UCLA at twenty-one, he moved to New York, where he was hired at Columbia Records. He met Columbia's famed A&R man, John Hammond—who had signed Billie Holiday, Bob Dylan, and Bruce Springsteen, among others—as well as Goddard Lieberson, who had recorded the works of Copland, Ives, and Stravinsky. From these three men, he shaped his own approach to A&R, in terms of ethics, originality, and value. In a business run by MBAs and media conglomerates, he was one of the few executives, in the words of Stephen Sondheim, "who practice the making of records as a craft."

Part of me was awed as I entered the building. I waited for security to make a call and write my name on a sticker. The elevator had a tiny screen showing CNN, and footage from the weekend's Live Earth event. The logos of the Warner Music Group (Atlantic, Elektra, Sire, Reprise, and Nonesuch) met you when the doors opened on the twenty-third floor. Behind a door of glass, a young receptionist with headphones buzzed you in. The walls were lined with gold and platinum displays for Frank Sinatra, Ray Charles, and Joni Mitchell. The waiting room was furnished with a pair of plush leather sofas, a vast coffee table, a spread of music magazines, and a shaggy white rug. A double set of stairs ascended to a second group of offices; a floor-to-ceiling window overlooked the park. The industry appeared to be expending its reserves the way it always had: lavishly.

Another part of me was more ambivalent. For all the artists I admired on the Nonesuch roster, from Bill Frisell to Emmylou Harris, I was a product of the pirate generation: the first to know a time where music was divorced from ownership, and everything was free, or so we thought. My adolescence overlapped with the rise of file-sharing. By junior year in high school, friends of mine were sharing music with CD burners. By junior year in college, my school was one of three that Metallica would take to court for letting us use Napster—and use it we did. We downloaded entire libraries of album leaks and MP3s; we filled towers of Sharpie'd CDRs and external drives with digital contraband; we feasted at the grave of the record business. We didn't think of it as theft; we thought of it as being music fanatics. In the last five years, I could count on one hand the times I'd been in a record store. Among my group of friends— who actively attended shows, and even played in bands—no one I knew still paid for music, nor did they feel bad. The record industry had been defrauding artists over royalties since its inception; they had sued some 20,000 individuals for downloading from peer-to-peer networks. There was a certain satisfaction in seeing the major labels go bankrupt.

I could hear a Jersey accent down the hall. Gina, Bob's secretary, was garrulous and middle-aged, petite, with highlights in her auburn hair. She walked me down a corridor illuminated by florescent light, then another. It was after five. With the exception of a cleaning crew, the office was deserted. There was a row of desks and darkened screens.

As we rounded a corner, Michael Bublé and Madonna cutouts gave way to artsy portraits of Philip Glass and k.d. lang. She led me to a doorway with a poster from the opera *Nixon in China*. Someone was typing inside.

"Come on in," a voice said. "I'll be just a second."

There was an inviting light-brown couch against the back wall, an upright piano with a bench, a set of windows looking west, a stack of books, a modest chair behind a messy desk, and frames with black-and-white photographs on every surface. He was sitting with his back to me as he was typing on a laptop. I wasn't sure if I should sit or stand. His build was heavyset; his hair was thick and pepper-gray; his shoulders slumped beneath a rumpled suit. The sound of keys clacking filled the room. A solid ninety seconds passed. I took that as my cue to find a seat.

"So," he said, turning around in his chair. "What can I do for you?"

My hands were damp, my throat was dry, my shirt was dripping sweat. We sat in awkward and increasingly oppressive silence, punctuated by a siren from below; it might as well have been for me.

I wasn't sure what I'd been hoping for, or was even doing in his office. Norma had said, "It would be good for you to meet," but why? The club was opening within a year; it wasn't like I needed work. I had an allergy to anything that felt like being a nuisance—and by the look of it, I was doing just that.

"Bob?" said his assistant from the doorway. "I'm taking off."

"Okay, Gina. Have a good night." She waved and disappeared. A message flickered on his BlackBerry. He started scrolling, elbows on the desk. I shifted in my seat. A vacuum cleaner roared from down the hall.

"Hey—uh—" He was fumbling for my name. "Would you excuse me?"

I stood up from my seat, to wait in the hall, and give him some privacy. He waved me off and held the phone up to his ear. It sounded like a spouse. "We'll order in," he said. I looked around and saw a bureau with some framed family photos, a set of Éric Rohmer DVDs, an open score of Bach. The sun was coming through the blinds; the skies were blue and free of clouds. It dawned on me that I was keeping him from heading home.

"I'm walking out the door," he said, hanging up. "Where were we?"

In the eleven minutes that ensued—or so it seemed—I introduced myself and said I worked with Norma, writing grants; that she suggested we should meet; that I had long been an admirer. He said, "I heard," and checked the time. I told him I had booked a few concerts, including two of his artists, Glenn Kotche and Nels Cline. I told him that the music was a mixture of classical and more contemporary. I said that the idea came in no small part from Nonesuch, and that I probably owed him royalties, heh-heh. He didn't seem amused.

The conversation went in fits and starts, as though by messenger. I rambled earnestly about the club on Bleecker and the Village Gate. It seemed to break the ice: he said he'd been there several times. I asked if piracy was a concern, or if the Internet had been a boon; I asked how things had changed; I asked if he had any advice for someone in my shoes. He thought it over for a few seconds.

"I've been in this business for thirty-six years," he said. "Nobody knows what the hell's going on anymore." And so concluded our meeting.

I wouldn't say we hit it off, but I would have to live with that. He walked me to the door and shook my hand impassively. I said I'd be in touch about one of my shows some time; I think he wasn't listening. "Send her my best," he said.

* * *

I sent a thank-you note to Bob by email. He didn't respond, at first, which I assumed was only normal; it was mid-July. I went to work at Lincoln Center all that week. When Norma asked me how it went, I said, "Good, I think," and figured that was that. Forty-eight hours later, he wrote back:

Hi Ronen,

FYI, there is a spot opening up here, in the "editorial" department (no one knows what that means anymore) . . . starting around Sept. 1.

Is this something you'd like to talk about? (it would not preclude
you from doing Wordless Music btw)

Best,

Bob

* * *

I knew the owners of the club would be alarmed, and rightly so. The
venue was on track to open in the spring. In June, I'd signed a contract,
and would soon be on payroll. I'd given them my word. I even had a set
of business cards. I didn't need to speculate how they would feel about
me taking on a second job—or a third, if you were counting Wordless
Music. At the same time—or so I reasoned then—the venue wasn't open
yet, and still had months to go. A lot could happen in the interim. Didn't
things always get delayed? What if something fell through? And even
if we did open on schedule: wouldn't Nonesuch be a good relationship
to have? And *technically*, I told myself, I wasn't breaking any laws: the
contract said I had to execute my work. It didn't say I couldn't have a
second job—or, um, a third. As long as I accomplished everything the
owners asked, couldn't I do all three?

* * *

I joined the label in the fall of 2007, after several open-ended interviews in August. I had been asked to bring a writing sample and a few
CDs I thought were well-designed—a first for me. I had been asked to
meet four different times—a first as well. The job description listed my
responsibilities: communicating with musicians, managers, freelance
designers, and our printer, Ivy Hill; securing rights; assembling liner
notes, album art, and other relics of a bygone era. The salary was non-
negotiable and would involve a cut in pay from my job at Lincoln Center;
the benefits were generous, or so I heard; the title was editorial coordinator. To ease me in, I had a few days of training with my predecessor,
Robert, a twenty-eight-year-old who had a warm and kindly bearing

and a nervous way of speech. He was encouraging and patient as he walked me through the job.

The editorial position, I soon found out, was highly technical, and had as much to do with printing specs and legal lines as lyric sheets and liner notes. The label had a serpentine production process—one involving Warner distribution, publishing, operations, marketing, and publicity on several continents.

For every title (albums, singles, reissues), format (CD, LP, MP3), and territory (U.S., U.K., Japan), there was an assigned UPC, copyright, and catalog number. For every label in the Warner family, there was a representative in sales, who got the product into bookstores (Barnes & Noble), chains (Starbucks), big boxes (Walmart), and the remaining mom-and-pops. The company had offices in eleven countries, affiliates in fifty, and printing plants in four different states. For every new release, we printed hundreds of promotional CDs that went to journalists and industry by standard mail in bubble wrap, a system both archaic and wasteful. For all the innovation of the past few years—from digital delivery to smartphones—the record industry was stuck in 1987. As I took notes about watermarks and digipacks, barcodes and swinglines, O-cards and inlays, my eyes were glazing over.

"Well, feel free to call," Robert said.

My supervisor was a woman in her thirties named Karina, a curly-haired and Yale-educated native of New York. Karina was attractive and inscrutable, circumspect, intimidating. She looked at you with dark brown eyes and held your gaze until you turned away; she dressed in muted black and gray. She had an oval face; a long, thin nose; and a knowing smile. She struck me as the type who listened more than she would speak. She had an obvious rapport with Bob, for whom she'd worked since graduating college, fifteen years ago—longer than anyone in the office except Peter, the head of marketing.

It didn't take me long to learn the label had a culture of longevity that started at the top, with Bob, then in his twenty-third year—the patriarch, the godfather, and our benevolent dictator. His manner was avuncular: he liked to gather people in his office, holding court; he liked to walk the halls and check morale in the platoon; he liked to sit and shoot the breeze, our first meeting aside. Among the twelve employees at the label, few had been on staff for less than five years; some, over twenty. The feel of permanence extended to the roster. Its flagship artists—Steve Reich, John Adams, Kronos Quartet, Caetano Veloso—had been with Nonesuch since the 1980s. "It's not supposed to be the label celebrating itself," Bob used to say. "It's *always* about the artist." (This was sometimes not the case.) Like HBO or Tiffany, Criterion or Porsche, the label was synonymous with excellence, a blue-chip brand. It occupied a singular position in the business, neither major nor indie, but more of a boutique.

For all the label's reputation and prestige, it was an ominous moment for the parent corporation. In 2007, the Warner Music Group announced a second-quarter loss of $27 million, and 400 layoffs to "align the company's workforce with the changing nature of the music industry." The stock fell over fifty percent, to eight dollars a share. CEO and Chairman Edgar Bronfman, Jr., told investors Warner was becoming a "music-based content company with a more comprehensive approach to participating in artist revenue streams." That year, Bronfman drew a salary of $1 million, and $2.4 million in dividends; his deputy, Lyor Cohen, made some $4 million in salary, stock, and bonuses. This might explain why many in the industry were averse to change, and slow to stop the bleeding.

To some degree, we were shielded from these concerns. The budgets were a matter for Bob, who had to answer for the bottom line. He shuffled back and forth from the executive offices and never brought it up or showed the slightest sign of worry. The label had a couple big sellers keeping the lights on: The Black Keys, Wilco, k.d. lang. It had some artists with a large if hidden following: the Gipsy Kings, Pat Metheny, Thomas Newman. In any given year, it might have four to six albums sell 100,000 copies: peanuts, in pop terms, but just enough to stay afloat. They subsidized the opera, jazz, and classical recordings that won Grammys, and sold maybe 5,000—or once had.

We weren't entirely immune: among those laid off by Warner in the spring was Slim Moon, whom Nonesuch had hired only months before in A&R, and then been forced to fire. In 1991, Moon had founded Kill Rock Stars, the influential indie label from Olympia, Washington. He'd signed Elliott Smith, Sleater-Kinney, and The Decemberists—a track record Nonesuch had hoped he'd replicate. The label's two A&Rs, Bob and David Bither, were in their late and early fifties, respectively. They still went out to shows, and stayed abreast of younger musicians. But for how long would that be true?

We didn't discuss anything so vulgar as sales or revenue streams, at least in the production department. We gave the same attention to a Beethoven concerto as a new Black Keys LP; maybe more. We might have printed only 10,000 copies of the new John Adams oratorio, but it was packaged with a perfect-bound, bilingual, hundred-page libretto. My first assignment was a lavish, ten-CD box set for Philip Glass; my second was a DVD of the choreographer Mark Morris. As far as I could tell, the profit motive was, if not irrelevant, then certainly secondary.

My first week of work, Bob summoned us into his office for a meeting. We sat around him like a campfire. He said, "We have a new employee," and my face turned red; everyone applauded for me. He said he'd just returned from Burbank, and the room fell silent. He said he'd had a meeting with executives from Paramount for the release of *Sweeney Todd*, with Johnny Depp; the soundtrack would come out on Nonesuch. Bob said, "According to their research, only fifteen percent of moviegoers know the name Stephen Sondheim, but ninety-eight percent know Johnny Depp." The movie, then, was being marketed to women in their twenties, adolescent goths, and through a line of merchandise at Hot Topic. "Whatever that is." I'm paraphrasing.

He talked to us about art and commerce. "I said to them: 'Fifteen percent—you know, that's nothing to be embarrassed about. Fifteen percent is a *lot* of people. In the United States alone, it's *millions* of people, at least.' I said, forget fifteen. Take ten or five percent. There's nothing wrong with even five percent. Of all the people in the world, what percentage get in line every morning at the Museum of Modern Art? How many watch Paul Thomas Anderson movies? How many read *The New Yorker*? Is it more or less than five percent? It may not be Johnny Depp numbers. But it's perfectly honorable."

* * *

I hedged my bets and kept the news about my job at Nonesuch to a few close friends. I went to the office from ten to six, and cut my teeth collecting credits for releases from Youssou N'Dour, Rokia Traoré, Joshua Redman, and Terry Riley. I met with Dave and Justin once a week about the progress of the build-out, and stayed in touch by phone and email. It wasn't hard to juggle both, at least at first. The label job was regimented, orderly, with clear deadlines; the venue job, on the other hand, was undefined and all-inclusive, with few parameters. The label job engaged my sense of logic and design; the venue job, my more impractical, romantic, anarchistic side. The label had a legacy that spanned some forty years; the venue was a totally blank slate.

Meanwhile, in September—around the time I started at Nonesuch— the second Wordless Music season got underway with shows from the Canadian indie-orchestra Do Make Say Think, the French composer-cellist Colleen, and the Albuquerque-Brooklyn-Balkan band Beirut next to Bartók, Chopin, and Debussy. I booked a pair of shows with works from Bach and Ligeti before the electronic outfit Múm, a date with Grizzly Bear, and Max Richter's U.S. debut. I went to Minneapolis in late September for a show with the composer Nico Muhly, my first out of town. The day we arrived, we learned that Valgeir Sigurðsson, the co-headliner, had been detained by immigration at the airport and sent back to Reykjavik. At the soundcheck, a violinist saw her instrument fall flat on the ground with a sickening crunch; we found a loaner.

Two days later, Kris Chen, a friend who worked with Sigur Rós, inquired about a short acoustic set at Nico's show with Sandro Perri at the little church on Sixty-Sixth Street—in forty-eight hours. He asked,

"Is that something you would be okay with?" Among the 200 people in the pews were Sufjan Stevens and the Dessner brothers. I met Will Oldham in the church's makeshift dressing room and asked if I could look through his iPod; I didn't recognize a single name.

The crowds grew, as did our footprint. In January, with an assist from composer Caleb Burhans, at St. Paul the Apostle—a massive Gothic church by Columbus Circle—the Wordless Music Orchestra made its debut with Jonny Greenwood's first symphonic piece, *Popcorn Superhet Receiver*, as well as compositions by John Adams (*Christian Zeal and Activity*) and Gavin Bryars (*The Sinking of the Titanic*). The church was jammed both nights with 1,500 punters, and bathed in psychedelic light; *The New York Times* ran two separate articles; and several people asked where Jonny Greenwood was. (He was at home.) Dave and Justin of (Le) Poisson Rouge were there to cheer me on, as were Bob and David from Nonesuch—with notes about the volume, back at the office. The Whitney Museum got in touch about a show, as did Prospect Park, as did Lincoln Center.

In March 2008, I went with Dave to Austin for South by Southwest. We stayed together in a room at the dilapidated Radisson off the highway. We introduced ourselves around and brandished business cards. We trudged through shows with bands we instantly forgot. We traded rounds, and stuffed ourselves with barbecue, and talked into the night about our lives, our families, and our future. It felt like I had made a lifelong friend. It felt like we were onto something big. It felt like we were only at the start. Back in New York, we interviewed for openings in marketing and production. Dave and Justin hired a general manager, a chef, a PR agency, and an acoustic engineer, John Storyk, who had designed Electric Lady Studios. To help me fill the calendar with two shows every night, a second music director, Brice Rosenbloom, was brought on board to lend his expertise in jazz and international music. In mid-April, our application for a liquor license was approved. We started giving tours to booking agencies to build anticipation, and sending offers for a June opening. The second job began to weigh on me, less in terms of time than conscience. I knew I had to tell the owners sooner or later about Nonesuch, and hoped they didn't find out first.

* * *

I got to know my coworkers on the twenty-third floor.

The senior staff were mostly in their fifties. David Bither was VP of A&R and Bob's second-in-command. He'd signed the label's biggest acts—Emmylou Harris, Wilco, The Black Keys—and had an ear that kept us relevant and in the black. An unassuming, mild Midwesterner, he was compact, completely bald, and always dressed in Nehru shirts that buttoned just below the trachea. Peter Clancy was the VP of marketing and the office favorite. He'd been with Bob from day one, and led campaigns for every new release since 1984. He had a head of thinning hair, a booming laugh, an easy smile. Bob called him "the nice Peter Clancy." The website team, Samantha and Gregg, were in their mid-to-late thirties, as was our publicist, Melissa; they often went to lunch with Karina.

The junior and support staff were mostly in our twenties. Jocelyn was newly out of Wesleyan, and had been hired when Gina left for a new job. She was serene, diminutive, and scatterbrained, our first millennial; we were immediately pals. Eli worked with me in production, and oversaw the payments and recording sessions. He was sarcastic, prickly, and prematurely old; we bonded over our slight fear of Karina. Drew and Josh were both in marketing, but otherwise were opposites. The former was a ham, a raconteur and ladies' man; the latter was a self-effacing family guy and mensch. The five of us comprised a unit—the young and underpaid, content if vaguely restless. Some were angling for a job in A&R; some were interviewing with other labels. But all of us had independently arrived at the same unhappy conclusion: Nonesuch was a functioning antique, run by elderly men; the roster was embarrassingly out of date; the musicians we most cared about were signed to indie labels such as Jagjaguwar, Sub Pop, Warp, Domino, and 4AD.

It's not that Bob and David didn't welcome our suggestions for new acts; it's more that we were almost always overruled. Every other month, a few of us were asked to bring an album for a listening session. Drew had been an early advocate of Dirty Projectors; Josh had championed a still-unsigned Grizzly Bear; Jocelyn was never invited, but could have played her former classmates, MGMT. In every instance, Bob or David thought the artist wasn't up to Nonesuch standards, and they may have had a point: the Internet produced a different buzz band once a week. How many groups on *Pitchfork* had the smarts and humor of Laurie Anderson, the virtuosity of Chris Thile, or the timelessness of Ali Farka Touré? How many names on *Brooklyn Vegan* would be remembered in a year, much less twenty?

"John Adams was thirty-one when he wrote [the piece for strings] *Shaker Loops*," Bob liked to say. "What have these guys ever done?"

In moments of distasteful and malevolent shit-talk, the junior staff dissected our superiors, their faults and failures, imagined and real. They occupied our ninety-minute lunches and Thursday happy hours, our instant messages and drunken sprees.

"Do you think Bob gets a boner when he listens to John Adams?"

"It's David's latest crunchy singer-songwriter. She's awful."

"He gets a boner for Chris Thile, don't you think?"

"Another *Billboard* number one. Get ready, guys."

"Let me guess. Another ad in *The New Yorker*."

"Bob is so belittling to Peter. Did you hear him today?"

"He's belittling to everybody."

"Philip Glass was still in the womb when he wrote *Einstein on the Beach*. What have these bastards ever done?"

"You think Bob and Peter ever take mushrooms and listen to John Adams?"

"They didn't know who Animal Collective was."

"I can't *believe* they passed on Bon Iver."

"Dude: he didn't meet the Nonesuch standard."

* * *

It started getting hairy in the spring. The venue sent a press release in May 2008 announcing our soft opening, along with shows by Nina Nastasia,

Charlie Haden, Bill Frisell, and Simone Dinnerstein performing Bach. Our meetings moved to several times a week, sometimes at lunch, or when I was expected at my *other* full-time job. I often had to sprint from Rockefeller Center to West Fourth and back in time for an impromptu meeting with Bob or Karina, which took some finessing on both ends. The label had new releases from Jonny Greenwood, Steve Reich, Randy Newman, k.d. lang, and Brad Mehldau coming due. The Wordless Music series had expanded to Portland, Oregon; emails arrived at all hours.

For the first time in my life, I was doing what I loved and getting paid for it. The owners of the venue asked for my opinions—on everything from merch percentages and ticket prices to the protocol for mixing drinks during classical recitals; on who to book, and what was fair, and how to build a name. The label moved me to an office with a window and a view of the skyline. Every few days, Bob would casually stroll in and talk about whatever crossed his mind: Stravinsky's ballets with George Balanchine; Glenn Gould's philosophy of recording and performance; a biography of the editor Maxwell Perkins; the memoirs of Miles Davis; the symphonies of Mahler; the race between Obama and McCain. We talked about esteem: who had it, and who granted it, and who was overlooked, or couldn't catch a break. "There's no such thing as underrated," he would say. "An artist finds the audience that they deserve." For Bob—an old-school A&R—an artist with a mass following was doing something right; an artist with a cult following was doing something different. He talked about the devaluation of the art form: how an entire generation thought that music should be free. "I don't understand it," he said. "You wouldn't walk out of a store with a gallon of milk." He talked about the qualities that made an artist universal: the Sly Stones, the John Coltranes. He said that The Clash were "nothing special—just another punk band." "Ask yourself," he said of a CD that I had played for him: "Are they the real deal?" Despite my doubts about the future of the record business, it felt like I was back at school; it felt like I had found a mentor.

* * *

In June, *The New York Times* arranged a photo shoot at LPR. An article was splashed across the cover of the Arts & Leisure section on the day we opened—June 15, 2008—with a show by Damon & Naomi. The kinks would need some working out: the waitresses were struggling with the point-of-sale system; the front of house was understaffed; the air conditioner was drowning out the sound. The publicist we hired mailed to VIPs a dozen live red fish that showed up dead. Reviews were critical of the drink prices, ticket prices, and the clientele. The crowds were sparse for most of the summer. The calendar was filled with holes. As a result, we gave the space for much of August to a baroque-opera company. In an unforeseen twist, the *Times* ran both a preview and a rave, the word got out, and suddenly the lines were down the block; Monteverdi had put us on the map.

September brought the onset of the economic crisis, the fall of Lehman Brothers, and the stock market crash. I flew to Minneapolis for a Wordless Music show with the artist Fog. Rage Against the Machine and the Republican National Convention were in town; *The Daily Show* had sponsored a billboard on I-35 that read, "Welcome, Rich White Oligarchs!" Back in New York, LPR presented Lou Reed, Milford Graves, and John Zorn; Lykke Li; Flying Lotus; Deerhunter; and Steve Reich's *Music for 18 Musicians*, in the round. I worked on releases by Allen Toussaint, Toumani Diabaté, Natalie Merchant, T Bone Burnett, Wilco, and the soundtrack to *The Wire*. I edited a sci-fi novella from Ry Cooder (*I, Flathead*) and a manuscript about Imelda Marcos by David Byrne (*Here Lies Love*). I unknowingly shared an elevator with Michael Bublé. From ten to six, five days a week, I worked at Rockefeller Center, and from six-thirty on, six days a week, I went to work on Bleecker Street.

I made a few mistakes; they weren't minor. I unforgivably approved a PDF with a conductor's name misspelled. (It was entirely my fault—he was American.) The album had to be reprinted; Karina was annoyed, and she was right to be. I asked if I could have the cost deducted from my pay, but Bob dismissed it out of hand. Then, I inadvertently sent the wrong catalog number to a designer; that printing also had to be recalled. Eli overheard the two of them arguing one day. "Let's just give him a chance," said Bob. "He's distracted," said Karina. Another time, I overslept and missed a meeting. David gently pulled me aside. He said, "Is everything okay?"

The label helped me book a benefit for the Obama campaign at LPR in mid-October with Chris Thile and Brad Mehldau. I went upstate to Kutsher's Country Club and saw My Bloody Valentine in the Borscht Belt, staged by the London indie promoter All Tomorrow's Parties. It seemed like every night on the town was an occasion: LCD Soundsystem at Studio B, Vampire Weekend at Music Hall of Williamsburg, Frightened Rabbit at Pianos, TV on the Radio at Brooklyn Masonic Temple. The club was open seven nights a week. The food and drinks were on the house. The busboys, bartenders, waitresses, crew, and staff were all my friends. I kept a laptop in the office and a little perch by the soundboard. I did this for the next six years.

The night of the election, we bit our nails, and drank too much, and watched the returns as they came in from CNN, and heard the sound of horns and people cheering in the street. The sight of Sasha and Malia walking in between their parents at the rally in Chicago was an image for the ages: this was our new first family. In Williamsburg and Clinton Hill, Bed-Stuy and Fort Greene, Harlem and Times Square, the revelers were boisterous and briefly unified. I took the subway home and wondered if the world had changed.

Reluctantly, I left the job at Nonesuch in 2010. I had been juggling the club, the label, and Wordless Music for the better part of three years. I thought that I could do it all, but I was only short-changing others. The time had come to choose between the concert business and the record industry. As much as I would miss working for Bob, there didn't seem to be a future in the label world, so I went with live music—and for the next ten years, it seemed I had made the right call.

Bing & Ruth (*City Lake*)

When David Moore was growing up, in Topeka, Kansas, he and his dad went to Blockbuster Music on Sundays. "Their whole thing was, you could choose any CD in the store, and they would open it, and you could sit there with headphones and listen as long as you wanted," says David. "They were carrying a lot of film scores and soundtracks. So I got really into Thomas Newman." His dad was an amateur trumpet player and guitarist who worked in child welfare; his mom was in IT. He started playing piano at the age of six, and then the drums in school.

"I joined the jazz band in my high school as a drummer, and it was me and my buddy playing drums. There was this piano player in the band that was really good. Her name was Anna. Anna Riphahn. I'll never forget her. She was very sweet, a great piano player, and a really smart, lovely person. She was a children's-book illustrator and writer, the daughter of one of my old teachers that I adored. A wonderful person. She was killed in a car accident. My junior year. She was driving home from a Billy Joel concert. A driver hit a deer, crossed the median, and killed everyone in the car. My high school kind of fell apart because she was a really central figure. And when the dust settled, we were back in jazz band, and there was no piano player, so I was recruited to play the piano in the jazz band. Because Anna had passed away. I just got really into—you know—within six months or a year, I'd stopped taking drum lessons and put everything I had toward the piano."

David went to the University of Missouri–Kansas City for conservatory. "I had discovered that writing music was something I had a natural proclivity toward. So when I discovered that, I went on a tear. In the course of a year and a half, I think I wrote, like, 200 songs. I went totally nuts. They weren't necessarily jazz, but they were filtered through the language of jazz." The music was a strange amalgam of minimalism, ambient, and jazz—as if Erik Satie had shared a piano bench with Count Basie. In his second year, his mentor Bobby Watson pulled him aside. He said, "If you want to keep pushing yourself, I think you need to move to New York."

"He was a saxophonist who lived in New York for twenty-five years and played with everybody," David says. "He led the jazz program at KC, and he's the guy who kind of brought me in. If you wanted to be in the jazz program, you had to go through the classical department, and I had really blown my audition, my classical audition, and, I guess—I found this out later—the school had actually rejected me. Then I did my jazz audition, and Bobby went to bat for me, and talked them into letting me in, which—I'm not sure why, because I wasn't very good. So he encouraged me. I was just like, 'Fuck it. Let's go.'"

He transferred to the New School, with a scholarship. It was 2004. "One of my best friends had moved here the year before, and he had found a place. I was able to pack a suitcase, fly to New York, take a cab to Harlem, and move in with four roommates. My rent was $315." He lived there for a couple months before he moved to Bushwick in the fall. It wasn't long before he found his taste evolving. "It took two months of living in New York before I lost interest in playing standards. Once I discovered free jazz, and contemporary classical, and all that sort of stuff, my gear shifted to doing my own thing."

He started playing with some friends that he had made at the New School, eight people in all—a miscellaneous ensemble of acoustic bass, percussion, lap steel, synthesizers, clarinet, piano, cello, and voices—an ambient orchestra. "I invited them into a practice room in the middle of the day at school, and I brought three songs in. And the thing about school is—you have tons of resources, and everyone has time. It's this beautiful thing that doesn't happen unless you're very lucky. It only happens once in your life, where there's a bunch of really talented people living close together, and you have time to rehearse, and have good instruments. And not long after that, we broke into the school's performance space and set up two microphones, and that was our first EP."

It was an odd recording, less EP than concerto for chamber orchestra: three tracks, two of them ten minutes long, and a sixteen-minute opener. The easiest comparisons were to Brian Eno, Philip Glass, and Meredith Monk, of whom he had barely heard. "We played the songs, and I remember thinking, 'Damn, this is it. *This* is the sound.' I think if I had had more of a background in minimalism and contemporary classical, I would have done it differently, because I would have understood the conventions, but I only understood the conventions of jazz, and country, and folk music, and bluegrass. It was less of, 'I'm gonna orchestrate this.' It was more, 'Let's all get in the room and see what it sounds like.'"

He pressed 150 copies on CD. "What you hear on this recording was recorded on a Wednesday morning in May with two microphones and no overdubbing of any kind," he wrote in the credits. He called the project Bing & Ruth, after an Amy Hempel short story. The band ballooned to nine and then eleven members. He started looking for shows.

"It was a struggle to find anywhere to play, or anyone to give the music, you know, the time of day." For a museum-quiet band like Bing & Ruth, the conventional places didn't quite work. "If you're just starting out, you're playing small venues, and chances are, they're gonna be pretty noisy. Tonic was a bar. Zebulon was a bar. It was hard for us to figure out, like, 'Where do we fit in?'" They couldn't play without a piano, which complicated things further. "We had to go where the pianos were, and the pianos were at jazz clubs. They weren't in rock venues. Pianos [the venue] didn't have a piano. Jazz clubs wouldn't touch us. People got really turned off hosting an eleven-piece band, so I gave it a name I thought would help us. Like, 'Oh, it's a duo.' So I know for a fact there's a number of gigs we got because the promoter thought we were a duo, and we would show up with eleven people, and they'd be like, 'What the fuck?'"

The band found a residency at the 13th Street Repertory Theatre in the West Village. "It was this classic old New York establishment. The owner is ninety years old, and she's been doing the same musical for forty years, and it was pretty dysfunctional and falling apart, and a very cool place." They played every Sunday for months. "The funny sticking point was that they insisted we charge $20 for a ticket, and this is 2005—a time of $5 at the door—and here's a band nobody's heard of, playing their first real gigs. So it afforded us this weird opportunity where every week we had a place to play."

Some weeks there would be a few people there. Then the next week there'd be a few more. Then there'd be nobody there the week after that. "That was something Bobby told me: 'Find a residency. Play all the time. That's how a band gets tight.' Eventually, we had to stop. They weren't making money. I think they just wanted to go back to business as usual. So we did a bunch of shows and kind of figured out our sound. I was like, 'We have to figure out our own way of doing this. We can't rely on venues,' because I'd gone around. I'd been to the Tea Lounge, to Barbès, to Zebulon. Gave them our CD. Trying to find gigs. I don't know that anybody listened. Certainly, no one asked us to play. There were a few places we could get into. So we started doing our own shows, but also, we'd do a show at Goodbye Blue Monday in Bushwick, because they had an open calendar, and it was three or four bands a night, and you could sign up for a slot. And they had a piano."

They self-released their first LP, *Kentile Floors* (2007). They caught a break or two and opened shows for kindred souls like Max Richter and Múm. In 2009, David won a grant from Philip Glass's MATA Festival for young composers. He used it to record the second Bing & Ruth album, *City Lake* (2010). It failed to garner even one review. "I couldn't find a label that wanted to put it out," says David. "I mailed a copy to every label you could think of, and nobody wanted it. So we just said, 'Fuck it. We'll put it out ourselves.'" They self-released a run of 250 silk-screened double-vinyl. And that appeared to be the end for Bing & Ruth.

"We put the album out and went on hiatus," says David. "I thought we were done. At this point, we'd been slogging it out for a long time without much traction. I was getting older, and I got asked to join Langhorne Slim's band. I didn't have much else going on at the time, and it was an excuse to hop in the van and see the country. I was like, 'I'm gonna do that for a while.' And Bing & Ruth, we didn't do any shows for a few years, and, to me, the project was at the end of its life cycle, where we had done it for five years, and it had all kind of blossomed into [*City Lake*], and that was a fitting end, because we weren't making money, and the city was getting more expensive, and money was becoming more of a concern. So, yeah: we went on hiatus."

He spent the next six years as a sideman to the singer-songwriter Sean Scolnick, better known as Langhorne Slim. They played at celebrated stages such as Bonnaroo, Red Rocks, and the Newport Folk Festival; they went on tour in Europe with The Lumineers; they taped appearances with their fan Conan O'Brien. It was the lowest point of the ersatz Americana craze: Mumford & Sons, Of Monsters and Men, The Avett Brothers. "I joined the band after the sleep-on-a-stranger's-floor phase, after they bought a van and a trailer, and could afford to pay a salary," says David. "We were playing mid-size rooms. And then the Avett thing took off, and then the Mumford thing took off, and then it's like, 'It's come to this? Arena-folk anthems?'" Having been raised on bluegrass and country music, it was dispiriting to see the bands that took off and those that didn't.

"Like, whatever—make the music you want to make. But as some-one working in that genre, I couldn't help but be a little heartbroken, because I heard so many bands that deserved to see that kind of success." Not that there wasn't an upside. "I'd never played in front of that many people before, where I'm playing for an audience of 5,000, then 20,000.

We played massive shows, festivals, opening slots. The more people there were, the less nervous I was, and less in my head. There was something freeing about it being a mob of people that you couldn't see or make out but that you could start to have fun with. I got to play banjo a bunch. I got to travel. It was when I met my wife. It was a blast. But it's like a lot of stuff in life—like, it can work for a while, and then at a certain point, it's time to evolve, and find another direction. And that was when Matt Werth reached out."

* * *

If you had seen it in a film, or a novel, you might have rolled your eyes from disbelief.

In a divinely fated twist, the vinyl-pressing plant mistakenly had mailed an early version of *City Lake* in 2010 to one of its regular customers: RVNG ["revenge"], an indie label owned and run by Matt Werth out of his apartment in Greenpoint. It sat collecting dust for several months before he got around to playing the LP. "It was just a white-label test pressing," David says. "There were no markings on it. So Matt had no idea who it was, and he listened to it, and figured it out. He tracked me down and asked me if I wanted to reissue *City Lake*, and if I wanted to make a new album." And so began a second life for Bing & Ruth.

* * *

Matt Werth was raised in Little Rock, a product of the city's flourishing punk scene. His father worked in country radio, at KSSN 96, and helped to break the likes of Garth Brooks and Reba McEntire. In 1999—shortly after the deregulation of radio ownership—the station was acquired by Clear Channel, so his dad resigned. "He was like, 'Fuck this. I'm not gonna work for Clear Channel,'" says Matt. "It was this weird parallel to my punk stance. He left the station for another job, and then *that* station was bought by Clear Channel as well. They were buying stations all over the country. He eventually got out of the business completely."

Beginning as a teenager, he played in bands, wrote a zine, ran a label, and helped produce shows—among others, with Colin Brooks, who later joined Sea Ray. "Little Rock was different from other places," says Matt. "It was a very young, nurturing, generational scene where kids were embraced and no one had anything better to do than to be productive and participate in this community and culture." He moved to Philadelphia for college, where he started RVNG with his friend, the party promoter Dave Pianka. He played the bass in bands like Aspera and Favourite Sons, who signed to Vice Records. RVNG's first releases were a series of mixtapes in the early aughts by DJs such as Julian Process, Tim Sweeney, and Justine D. They followed it with FRKWYS ("freak ways," a play on the Smithsonian Folkways label), pairing artists young and old: Excepter with Chris and Cosey (2009), Arp with Anthony Moore (2010), Laraaji with Blues Control (2011). Their breakthrough came with *Ekstasis* (2012), by Julia Holter—around the time that David heard from Matt.

It was the unashamedly emotional unguardedness of *City Lake* that touched a nerve for Matt. "The test pressings were mistakenly sent to RVNG from Brooklyn Phono," he says. "I called them, and I was like, 'What is this music? This is incredible. What's the deal?' And Leandro [Gonzales], who had cut that record, told me, 'This is Bing & Ruth.' Eventually, I was like, 'I'm going to get in touch with this guy and just see what the deal is.' He was composing a new album, so the conversation morphed into, 'Let's make a record and reissue *City Lake.*' I think it was the right time and right place for RVNG and Bing & Ruth. There was something happening with ambient music around that time in 2014. I wasn't even thinking about it as an ambient record, but a lot of people did."

* * *

A funny thing transpired circa 2014, when David phoned his friends from Bing & Ruth and made *Tomorrow Was the Golden Age*. With the redis-covery of first- and second-generation pioneers (Laraaji, Suzanne Ciani, and Stars of the Lid), archival compilations (*I Am the Center: Private*

Issue New Age Music in America 1950–1990), and a wave of ambient-adjacent composer-producers (Grouper, Sarah Davachi, and Kaitlyn Aurelia Smith), ambient and new-age music were enjoying a revival of a sort, one that began in earnest around 2010—coincidentally or not, when left and right alike were losing faith in the direction of America, and visions of equality, opportunity, and justice were foundering. "It was a time when ambient was bubbling up into the mainstream," says David. "Our album came out when people were hungry for that sort of thing. Culturally, it felt like—I mean, it hasn't settled down since then, but—in a way, 2012 was the last semi-normal year, and everything after that felt like madness."

The cultural environment worked to Bing & Ruth's advantage. "By 2014, I was a few years out from Bing & Ruth even being a thing," says David. "I thought the band was done at the time . . . I had been operating in the experimental world, and RVNG was in this zone between experimental and indie, and then the indie thing became more genre-less, where eccentricity and weirdness were being celebrated, and the bands that were becoming successful were all weird and interesting in their own way—Animal Collective, Dirty Projectors, The Antlers—the pillars of late-aughts indie rock. It was a really interesting time, where the indie world and the experimental world started colliding. The indie scene in general seemed a little more curious about what the weirdos were doing."

RVNG released the album on October 14, 2014. Reviews were near-unanimous. In a rave for *Pitchfork* (8.1), Larry Fitzmaurice called it "one of the finest left-field releases of the year." *Fact* magazine named it one of the year's best: "a suite of penetrating, deeply emotional music that nevertheless remains appealingly indeterminate." In *Resident Advisor*, Andrew Ryce would claim, "From its rumbling lows to its ethereal, resonant highs, *Tomorrow Was the Golden Age* is one of the simplest and most beguiling albums of its kind since Stars of the Lid's landmark run on Kranky in the '00s."

"It was the first time that I'd ever gotten some kind of attention for what I had been working on," says David. "There was all this stuff that I wasn't super familiar with, because I wasn't operating in that kind of more mainstream world. We got a great review in *Pitchfork*, and I barely knew what *Pitchfork* was at the time. We got an NPR First Listen, and I was like, 'Cool. We're on NPR.' Not realizing that, like—that was an insane honor. The day after the *Pitchfork* review came out, I started getting calls from booking agents and managers, and suddenly I was in the belly of the biz." Its songs appeared in indie movies and ads for brands; they soon became a fixture of the "Ambient Essentials" playlist on Spotify. In 2016, it placed at forty-nine on *Pitchfork*'s "50 Best Ambient Albums of All Time." The band would make their European debut at the Royal Albert Hall. They signed with 4AD for the release of *No Home of the Mind* (2017) and *Species* (2020), but it didn't quite work out. They're still recording for RVNG.

"I think David was destined for greatness," says Matt. "Hearing *City Lake* for the first time, in my heart and mind, I felt something so great in it, so mature, and so inclusive, with so much emotional and musical gravity. It was so undeniable to me." On the one hand, Bing & Ruth's belated recognition was an example of true serendipity; on the other, it was a logical conclusion of Matt's adolescence back in Little Rock. He says, "It goes back to these fundamental qualities. Like—Philip Glass and Steve Reich, yes, those came to mind. But for me, I heard, like, a version of punk rock. That's where I came from. Whether it was Jawbreaker or Rites of Spring, I was always in search of that emotional quality. So I'd like to think that, you know—it would have found its audience regardless."

2014

"Bill de Blasio was sworn in as the 109th mayor of New York City early Wednesday, at two minutes past the stroke of midnight . . ." 285 Kent, the Williamsburg Club, Gives Its Last Party . . . Philip Seymour Hoffman, Actor of Depth, Dies at 46 . . . "My plan was to never get married. I was going to be an art monster instead . . ." "Millions in this country feel like strangers in this land—you recognize that, don't you? An older America passes away, a new America rises to take its place. We recoil from that culture. It's foreign to us. It's offensive to us . . ." *"Clap along if you feel like a room without a roof . . ."* Malaysia Airlines Loses Contact with Jet Carrying Over 200 . . . Putin Reclaims Crimea for Russia and Bitterly Denounces the West . . . Supreme Court Strikes Down Limits on Federal Campaign Donations . . . Enrollments Exceed Obama's Target for Health Care Act . . . *Times* Ousts Jill Abramson as Executive Editor, Elevating Dean Baquet . . . "What I'm talking about is more than recompense for past injustices— more than a handout, a payoff, hush money, or a reluctant bribe. What I'm talking about is a national reckoning that would lead to spiritual renewal . . ." Facebook Tinkers with Users' Emotions in News Feed Experiment, Stirring Outcry . . . Vice Media Moving to New Williamsburg Headquarters . . . Sunni rebels declare new "Islamic caliphate" . . . Staten Island Man Dies After Police Try to Arrest Him . . . Israel Exits Gaza as Truce Begins . . . "The fatal shooting of an unarmed black teenager Saturday by a police officer in a St. Louis suburb came after a struggle for the officer's gun, police officials said Sunday, in an explanation that met with outrage and skepticism in the largely African-American community . . ." "Death by Audio, the Brooklyn rock club and musicians' workspace that sprang up in a Williamsburg warehouse in 2007, will be closing on November 22 . . ." Flint issues boil water advisory for section of the city after positive test for total coliform bacteria . . . *"But I keep cruisin', can't stop, won't stop movin' . . ."* Airstrikes by U.S. and Allies Hit ISIS Targets in Syria . . . *New York Times* announces plan to cut 100 newsroom positions . . . Police Shoot, Kill Knife-Wielding Teen on South Side . . . "Vice Media is behind the closure of Williamsburg venues Death by Audio and Glasslands, *Billboard* has learned . . ." Riding Wave of Discontent, GOP Takes Senate . . . Obama Plan May Allow Millions of Immigrants to Stay and Work in U.S. . . . Comeback by Bill Cosby Unravels as Rape Claims Reemerge . . . Twelve-Year-Old Boy Dies After Police in Cleveland Shoot Him . . . Wave of Protests After Grand Jury Doesn't Indict Officer in Eric Garner Chokehold Case . . . Many Feel the American Dream is Out of Reach, Poll Shows . . . 25,000 March in New York to Protest Police Violence . . . Obama hails "new chapter" in U.S.-Cuba ties . . . *"And my band 'bout that money, break it down . . ."*

Death by Audio

If you had entered an unmarked warehouse at 49 South Second Street in Williamsburg from 2007 to 2014, you might have met a soft-spoken, teddy-bearish individual named Edan Wilber, or spotted him across the room. He was a permanent fixture, impossible to miss, not merely for his signature Old Testament/mountain-man beard.

You saw him in the evening, when the bands were loading in, and the entire place would smell like beer from last night's show. You saw him right before the doors were opened, setting up the bar, box office, and—in the loosest sense of the word—backstage. You saw him there at front of house, mixing sound for the headliner, the opener, and everyone between. You saw him there at five A.M., cleaning the bathroom, sweeping floors, or paying out the staff. And if by some odd chance you found yourself at Death by Audio in the daytime, it's likely he was just across the hall, working in bed—the living space was too small for a desk—advancing shows, and placing holds, and fielding emails from insistent agents, bands, and managers.

It's difficult to overstate the legacy, example, good will, and importance of Death by Audio among the universe of independent rock, punk, and left-of-center pop. For seven years and some 2,000 shows, they gave a stage to countless up-and-coming acts, from Liturgy, Future Islands, and Ty Segall to Prince Rama, Vivian Girls, and School of Seven Bells. From those that found a mainstream following to those that never got their due, from those that headlined festivals to those that never left New York, it was the rare performance space in Williamsburg or otherwise to book established and emerging artists every night, invariably all ages, and rarely more than five or ten dollars. But it was more than that. It was a place where people listened, blew off steam, and tempered their inherent disbelief as New Yorkers—where everyone was invested. It was a place you went when you had no idea who was booked, a place you always saw someone you knew. Some DIY establishments were trendier (Glasslands) or sexier (285 Kent), but DBA felt like a friend's house, because it was: the "dressing room" was in their kitchen. In retrospect, it might have been a place a newcomer would find off-putting or insular; it certainly skewed pale, male, and straight, onstage and off. At the time, though, there were few who welcomed its untimely demise. We all knew Death by Audio's eviction at the hands of Vice had marked the end of an era, and that the one responsible for its improbable endurance was Edan.

* * *

He was a native of St. Petersburg, Florida, its fifth-largest city, on the Gulf of Mexico: home of the first commercial flight, a Salvador Dalí museum, a dozen sports facilities, and the world's oldest shuffleboard club. That he would leave at the first opportunity was preordained.

His mom and dad were from Chicago and Syracuse, respectively. He had a younger sister, Devan. The family was working-class. They had a house on St. Petersburg's south side, which was historically poor, black, and segregated. To send the kids to private school, his parents each had multiple jobs: during the day, at a frozen-fish plant, or cleaning houses; nights and weekends, in restaurants, for tips, serving and bartending. "They switched off at night, and once I was old enough to watch my sister, it was the two of us," he says. "I never saw them buy a thing for themselves."

One of his mom's regulars at the bar worked at Jannus Landing, a small outdoor venue downtown. Its offerings were frightful in those days, reflecting the culture at large: post-grunge (Collective Soul), '80s relics (Vince Neil), and third-wave punk (Less Than Jake). Nonetheless, it was a safe environment where a kid could spend a few hours unsupervised—no small thing in Central Florida. His mom had got to talking with her customer about his line of work. She told him, "My son likes music." That was how Edan got to see his first concert, in 1996—The Presidents of the United States of America—as well as Everclear, Reel Big Fish, and blink-182. It was the year that the Philips corporation sold the first CD burners for home consumers, a jaw-dropping invention for those with access to one. He and a neighbor would spend hours duplicating albums, burning them to blank CD.

He was an awkward, introverted teen, and struggled to make friends. In the ninth grade, he transferred to a magnet school that focused on technology. Every morning, a student-run TV show, *Fast Forward*, did a fifteen-minute broadcast of news and funny sketches. He started sitting in, and helping out, and making people laugh; he was a natural on camera. The show went on to win a national award for students from the Emmys, and the attention of college recruiters. He thought about a job in movies or TV.

At the time, there were only a few schools with programs in film production. One was the University of Miami, one was USC, and one was NYU—all private universities that then charged $30,000 a year. He was accepted at all three. But only NYU had teased the prospect of a scholarship. When he applied, a financial-aid officer informed him that—because his parents made less than a year's tuition, room, and board—his expected family contribution (EFC) would be zero. It didn't end up working out that way.

He mailed in his acceptance letter. Then he learned there was a catch. The scholarship that NYU had pledged was generous, but wouldn't be available until his junior year. If he could find the $60,000 for his first two years, the university would fund the second two in full.

It sounded pretty dubious to him, and not exactly what an EFC of zero would suggest. When he expressed some hesitation, the financial-aid officer explained how he could easily apply for loans—as much as $30,000 a year. She talked about the school's professional placement rate of ninety-five percent. She talked about deferring the repayment after graduation.

The figures were bewildering to him at seventeen years old. The documents they had sent him could easily have been in Greek. He couldn't shake the sense it was an awful lot of debt for a degree. But then, he thought, the university had given him their word: he simply had to make it to his junior year. He signed the paperwork. In August of 2000, he and his dad drove up the coast from St. Petersburg. The next five years would alternate between semesters of stability and the prospect of financial ruin.

* * *

His freshman year, he lived near Washington Square Park. His sophomore year, he lived in Chinatown, on Lafayette Street. He was on the way to class one morning when the first plane hit the north tower. It was the opening week of fall semester. When a plane crashed into the Pentagon, his film professor said that they should stay calm, and make their way outside, and that was when they saw the south tower fall. The streets were fogged with clouds of ash, emergency sirens, first responders, and people running in distress. He started heading north, with friends, to find a hospital, where he donated blood. He walked from Greenwich Village up to Chelsea, into midtown, then west to Lincoln Center. By then, the subway was running. He made his way downtown, but learned that no one was allowed south of Canal. The area reopened a few days later. There was a checkpoint where he had to show ID. A lot of kids left school. He heard that one of his professors had a child who didn't speak for months. He found a welcome distraction in the weekly routine of his classes—especially the one in audio engineering.

He started venturing into the East Village. At the intersection of Houston Street and Avenue A was the epicenter of the New York rock revival: the Mercury Lounge. The Strokes had been in residence in late 2000; The National and Animal Collective were regulars. There was a small performance space behind a curtain, and a long, inviting bar up front. Because there wasn't a backstage, a band would start the show by walking through the audience. It was the coziest club in Manhattan— provided, of course, that you were twenty-one. He pleaded with security the night the Liars and the Yeah Yeah Yeahs were there, to no avail. Another time, he asked them to put Xs on his hands, which got a laugh. He tried emailing bands to see if they would add him to their guest list but was always turned away. The staff got used to seeing him on Houston Street, consistently forlorn.

He looked for places people under twenty-one could go. There were occasional events produced by NYU. There was a colorful dive in Tribeca, Nancy Whiskey, where the bartenders didn't check ID, despite the police station next door; it's still around. And a few blocks south, on Leonard Street, there was the Knitting Factory, where shows were sometimes eighteen-plus. It was there, in 2003, that he saw a band called Parts & Labor. It was exuberant, tumultuous, and deafening: exactly how he liked. The show was in the Tap Room, downstairs, capacity 200. There was a low ceiling and a bar to the side; the stage was one foot high. As soon as Parts & Labor said good night, there was a band that started playing at the far end of the room. Their instruments were set up on the floor. They were also a noisy three-piece, but different: the keyboardist banged her head; the drummer flailed away; the singer howled, barked, and yelped into the mic. The audience was going bananas. It was his introduction to the Coachwhips, from San Francisco, and to the rabbit hole of underground and independent music. "That was the jumping-off point," says Edan. "It was me trying to see that band, and finding out about these other underground sources, like Todd's website." He signed up for Todd's weekly newsletter, and started frequenting all-ages shows at Tommy's Tavern, in Greenpoint; Woodser, in Williamsburg; and Flight of the Buffalo, in Bushwick.

He took a mix of classes in film production, history, and theory. He juggled class and work, with campus jobs in the equipment room and as a teaching assistant. He got along with his classmates, for the most part, even if they existed in different worlds, different realities. Once a term, there would be a stressful meeting with a financial-aid officer. Once a term, there would be a call from the bursar's office about an overdue balance. The thought of next semester's likelihood was always weighing on his mind. He came to dread the very sight of NYU letterhead.

He moved into a squalid loft on Morgan Avenue in Bushwick in 2003. "It was a 2,000-square-foot raw space they had built out: two rooms that were full-size, and then two rooms on top of that, and that was where I lived. Both rooms on top were compromised for height, so I could not stand up straight in that room." He lived there for the next three years. He had some roommates that he liked, and one who was dysfunctional at best, so he went out most nights when he was done with work. The shows he saw were either at the Knitting Factory, where he knew someone who could get him in, or at whatever bar, garage, or parking lot that Todd had commandeered in Brooklyn or in Queens.

By junior year, the scholarship that NYU had promised him turned out to be a smattering of tiny grants and further student loans. He weighed his choices. If he left NYU now, he was four semesters shy of a degree, and $60,000 in debt. He looked into a transfer to a school in Florida, but they would only take a number of his credits, so he signed the forms the financial-aid office put in front of him. A year went by, a loan fell through, and he was forced to take a leave of absence. It also meant he lost his campus job and health insurance.

He moved in with his girlfriend and her roommates in the East Village. He found a job in midtown at a call center for tourists, right upstairs from Sardi's restaurant. Now that he wasn't underage, he spent his nights at places like Northsix, Glasslands, Cake Shop, and Union Pool. He spent his afternoons arranging tickets for *Spamalot* and *Avenue Q*. When things were quiet, he read the music blogs: *Brooklyn Vegan, Ultragrrrl, Productshop NYC*. He started a blog of his own: *The Pirate Hat*, after a keepsake from his dad. He took pictures of the shows he saw, from Matt and Kim, Les Savy Fav, and Lightning Bolt to Gang Gang Dance, Mount Eerie, and Oneida. He saw Japanther play accompanied by synchronized swimmers; Arcade Fire at Judson Church; and the acoustic barbecues that Todd produced on Roosevelt Island every summer. He reenrolled at NYU and finished his degree, tens of thousands in debt; like many of his contemporaries, the student loans the school had offered him would rack up interest for the next two decades. He kept on working in midtown. He went to South by Southwest in 2006, where he spent most of the weekend at Todd's unauthorized showcase. But it would take a full two years of seeing Todd across the room before he summoned up the nerve to introduce himself.

It was a show with !!! [pronounced "chk-chk-chk"], at Shangri-La, in Greenpoint, in February of 2007. Edan had overheard somebody say that Todd was not presenting any shows that year at South by Southwest, so he asked him about it.

"I really liked your shows in Austin last year," said Edan. "I'm sad that you're not doing it again."

Todd said, "No, I am doing it."

"Man," Edan replied. "I guess it's probably way too late for me to try to go now."

Todd said, "If you want to come with me, you'd be welcome."

And that was how he ended up with Todd and his enthusiastic intern Joe Ahearn in the van to South by Southwest; and it was also how he ended up among the troop of volunteers who worked at all of Todd's events—at Silent Barn, Don Pedro's, Uncle Paulie's, Studio B, and a place called Death by Audio.

* * *

The floor was checkerboard, in black and white, like in the painting by Vermeer. The wall behind the stage was checkered, too; the art changed frequently; the last few months, it was two oversized and disembodied heads. The ceiling was a rickety mosaic made of ancient fiberglass panels, several missing. To your left, there was a mural in magenta, orange, black, and teal; to your right, a painting of a pair of tigers and the words "YeAH RigHT." On two sides of the space stood a monolithic stack of speakers. There was a room with someone selling cans of beer and booze in plastic cups for four or five dollars; to say it was a working bar would be a stretch. The stage was maybe two feet high; the front of it was decorated with a bed of pillowy white clouds. Capacity was 200 or so—except on nights when it was double that.

The arc of Death by Audio would parallel the strange career of indie rock in Brooklyn and the country as a whole.

The year the city council authorized a plan for the rezoning of the waterfront, in 2005, a group of friends and transplants found an empty building on South Second Street in Williamsburg. They spent the next few months converting it into a multi-level rehearsal space, office, workshop, and five-bedroom home. It was the vision of guitarist-gearhead Oliver Ackermann—whose pedal company, Death by Audio, gave it its name—and brothers Greg and George Wilson. To pay for the construction, they threw rent parties: $5 for five bands and unlimited beer. The first was in the spring of 2007—around the time the blog *Hipster Runoff* (a poker-faced satire of the indie world), Bandcamp (the independent retail site), and *Showpaper* (Todd's free, biweekly print publication for all-ages events) would all be launched. They hosted 65 events in 2007; 170 in 2008; just under 300 in 2011; and an abbreviated 250 in 2014. (Each show would feature anywhere from two to twenty acts; you do the math.) The reason for its meteoric growth was a preponderance of young, determined bands and open-minded listeners. But it was also inextricable from Edan stepping up and shouldering the endless work of venue management, production, sound, and booking at the end of 2007. That year alone, they welcomed Thurston Moore, Vivian Girls, Dan Deacon, Future Islands, Magik Markers, Tony Conrad, Mary Timony, Mika Miko, Kyp Malone, Frightened Rabbit, Skeletons, and Dirty Projectors. The sound would drastically improve; the walls would be covered with art; in time, even the bathroom was presentable. By June of 2013, a profile in *Noisey*, Vice's music vertical, would say, "For over five years, Death by Audio has been pretty much the best and weirdest DIY venue in Brooklyn, if not all of New York." (There was an irony in this.) The building on South Second Street would be a temporary home for some, but the one constant was Edan at the console, house-left—pogoing, headbanging, and mixing 5,000 sets during the venue's existence.

"It's a funny thing about Edan," says Greg Saunier of Deerhoof. "It was very easy to just assume that he was simply nuts for wanting to be there mixing every band at every show. No one sane could endure that much loud music night after night . . . It was dedication, a conscious decision, made by a sane and reasonable person, with rational reasons. I relate to it in a way, because I can become similarly fixated on something I truly love. Mixing [sound for] bands, ones he also helped to book, because he was their fan, is his love language."

"What makes him singular is that he never once aspired to the loftiness of being called a 'curator,'" says longtime friend Zan Emerson. "He wasn't trying to 'be' somebody in the music business. To this day, he is driven by a love of the music itself. In an industry that spits even the deepest lifers out, his work ethic and idealism are I think what makes him who he is."

"He does it all for the love," said Future Islands' singer, Sam Herring. "And that's the thing that comes through. He loves music. He loves to do sound. He loves to watch bands. He loves to dance and have a good time . . . Death by Audio allowed us a taste of something that was really sweet, in a place that we didn't belong. We didn't belong in New York

City. But we immediately felt, 'This is like where *we're* from. These people are like us.'"

* * *

I only saw a dozen shows at Death by Audio, so I can hardly claim to be an insider. I caught a sweaty and frenetic set by Thee Oh Sees; a predictably spectacular display from Deerhoof; and an exceedingly rare solo show with Jawbreaker's Blake Schwarzenbach, an all-time favorite songwriter. I saw a psychedelic group named Aa playing maniacal percussion in the living room. I saw when Parts & Labor played their album *Mapmaker* in full. And I had friends among the staff when word got out that Death by Audio was closing in the fall of 2014. A post on *Brooklyn Vegan* said it all: "Well this one hurts."

The last eleven weeks at DBA were a defiant show of independence, gratitude, and pride, if also one that was tinged with sorrow. The news would make the rounds in early September—a little less than eight months after 285 Kent closed. In a statement, Edan wrote:

> When we first moved onto South 2nd Street the only things on our block were a used police car lot and several empty buildings. Now there are a half-dozen expensive restaurants, bars, a daycare center, and a new condo building (that was an empty lot when we moved in). All-ages DIY music venues are almost by definition temporary, and we feel fortunate to have lasted in this space for this long. We knew from the beginning that it couldn't last forever and we are extremely grateful to everyone who has performed or attended any of our shows . . .
>
> Our closing party starts Wednesday, Sept. 10 and we will have great programing for these last 75 days. We are looking forward to putting on some really incredible shows to send off what has been one of the greatest undertakings of our lives. We hope to see you there.

They listed some performers for the closing weeks, but kept a few surprises up their sleeves. A couple of nights were promoted simply as "Special Guest (a good one!)" The shows (with Woods, Speedy Ortiz, Protomartyr, Future Islands, Screaming Females, and METZ) all sold out anyway. The final week or two, a line would stretch around the corner long before door time.

A documentary was filmed, entitled *Goodnight Brooklyn: The Story of Death by Audio* (2016). It opens with the grand finale, on November 24, 2014, when Lightning Bolt, A Place to Bury Strangers, Grooms, and JEFF the Brotherhood closed out the place. It cuts between immersive footage of the venue's last two months and its eviction at the hands of Vice, who had received $6.5 million in state tax credits to build their $20 million headquarters: "a freaky, space-age utopia that will give today's creative visionaries a place to produce astonishing stories and leave their indelible thumbprint on the annals of history." (You watch a biblical ordeal of flooding, sewage, and harassment during the construction that caused tens of thousands of dollars' worth in damage to DBA's inhabitants.) At times, the documentary can make it seem as though the place was always full, and there were lots of nights like that. But Edan was the rare promoter who would book your band if they could sell twenty tickets or a thousand; if he liked your music, that was reward enough.

"It wasn't really a venue as much as a hangout zone," says Greg Saunier. "Where you knew you'd see your friends and meet other people in your city who shared your ability to tolerate incredibly loud and harsh-sounding music . . . It was the tail end of that neighborhood being remotely affordable or cool, before being completely taken over by real-estate speculators and yuppies. Everyone knew it was the end but wanted to drag out the scene's survival as long as we could . . . It was a fight to the death. It was impossible to separate the musical experience from the human one and the sociopolitical one."

The writer Michael Azerrad recalled, "When you have a place like Death by Audio that cares about the musicians more than profits, and actually wants to foster a scene, because it's fun—not because they want to be rich—bands find a home there, and really interesting things come out of that. Alliances form. New kinds of music are allowed to foster even though they may not make money at first."

"Bands felt like Death by Audio was a second home," wrote Noah Kardos-Fein, who makes music as Yvette. "It was the kind of place where a small fledgling band had a good chance of playing on the same bill as a much bigger, touring band. And one day, that fledgling band might just become a headliner. You tended to get just as much as you were willing to put in: if you attended or played shows there regularly, there was a good chance you'd get to know the staff there, as well as other regulars."

More so than most, the crew at DBA was very much a family, if not a gang—if by a gang you mean a group given to extended bear hugs. There was a universal sense of shock when we found out 285 Kent and Glasslands were closing, but I'd wager that, for most, the coup de grâce was Death by Audio. "To have a space like that in Williamsburg at such a late date was truly remarkable," says Blake Schwarzenbach. "There was an entire network of punk spaces in houses, lofts, studios, and then DBA, that seemed to run contrary to the whole indie triumphalism of NYC at that time. Lots of fun, scrappy bands, just doing it for their friends and with their friends . . . It was that unlikely. And then, on top of that, everyone working there and going there was cool—people seemed genuinely excited to be seeing affordable, handmade music in a scorched dive."

In the film's most affecting moment, Edan talks about his home of seven years: "It was some article in a business magazine that someone had reprinted. It was saying that the building wasn't living up to its 'economic potential.' Meaning, that we weren't generating money. We weren't generating X amount of dollars every year. But the memories I have here—just the amount of awesome shit I've been able to do— it's worth so much more than anything they're gonna get out of this building." His voice begins to crack. "I can't be upset, because I'm so full. I'm so rich with memories. I'm so much more wealthy in so many other ways than those people are ever going to be. And that's kind of enough, you know?"

Weyes Blood
(*The Outside Room*)

In 1999, the year the Mering family moved to Doylestown, Pennsylvania, the biggest albums in the world were by the Backstreet Boys, *NSYNC, Shania Twain, Ricky Martin, and Britney Spears. *American Beauty, The Matrix,* and *Fight Club* were in theaters. *Who Wants to Be a Millionaire?, The West Wing,* and *The Sopranos* first aired. On CNN's *Larry King Live*, Donald Trump considered a run for president. And in the *Harvard Business Review*, a pair of academics would ask: "Can Steve Jobs make Apple 'insanely great' again?"

For the eleven-year-old Natalie Mering—who had been raised on everything from Stevie Wonder, Joni Mitchell, and Nirvana *Unplugged* to XTC, Ween, and Dr. Dre—the culture seemed especially adrift. She said, "I noticed mainstream music was getting really bad. First it was Spice Girls and Hanson, and I was like, 'Something's not right.' And it got worse and worse with Britney Spears and *NSYNC . . . I asked my dad, because he was a musician: 'When are we going to have the next wave? When is someone going to reinvent music again?'"

* * *

In Flannery O'Connor's dark comedic novel *Wise Blood* (1952), a veteran named Hazel Motes resolves to live a life without belief, and starts the Church of Christ Without Christ. "Let me tell you what I and this church stand for!" he yells to a crowd from the hood of his car.

> "I preach there are all kinds of truth, your truth and somebody else's, but behind all of them, there's only one truth and that is that there's no truth," he called. "No truth behind all truths is what I and this church preach! Where you come from is gone, where you thought you were going to never was there, and where you are is no good unless you can get away from it. Where is there a place for you to be? No place.
>
> "Nothing outside you can give you any place," he said. "You needn't to look at the sky because it's not going to open up and show no place behind it. You needn't to search for any hole in the ground to look through into somewhere else. You can't go neither forwards nor backwards into your daddy's time nor your children's if you have them. In yourself right now is all the place you've got."

When Natalie first read the book, at age fifteen, the image stayed with her. "Just the title: *Wise Blood*. Like wisdom could exist separate from the body. I'd never looked at blood that way; it's like you could have the same blood as somebody from 300 years ago," she said. "I know it's supposed to be about, like, the characters have wisdom in their history, in their blood, but I really just like picturing that there's a bucket of blood somewhere that's wise."

Born in Santa Monica, to a family of "super born-again" Pentecostal Christians and seventh-generation Californians, she had an anarchist streak, a musical ancestry, and "a lot of extra emotional software that I didn't know what to do with," she said. Her older brother Zak makes music under multiple guises (Raw Thrills, Philippians, Greatest Hits); her mother is a singer; a grandmother was in vaudeville. Her father was the front man of a new-wave band that released an album on Elektra/Asylum in 1980, and worked with famed producer Jack Nitzsche; he also dated Anjelica Huston and Joni Mitchell. He only told the kids about his musical career long after, when he had found the church, and was working in medical publishing. "I remember the day that my brother and I found out," said Natalie. "I was probably five or six years old. He was playing Chuck Berry songs on his electric guitar and he started telling us stories about shows he used to play and bands he used to play with. I couldn't believe it because I had only known him as the church guy playing worship songs at church. I didn't know he had this secular rock-star background."

The Mering family was creative, loving, and pious. Her mom and dad were hippies who were swept up in the so-called Jesus movement that had started on the West Coast in the '70s. Her parents monitored her cultural consumption for indecent content, but looked the other way when it came to music. "There was some weird Christian reason why there weren't good cartoons for us to watch. Care Bears were too, like, hippie-communist, and Smurfs were homosexual because there is only one female Smurf," she said. "We weren't allowed to watch MTV, but we'd turn it on when my parents were out." Her mother told *The New Yorker*, "We were a Christian family . . . We came from an angle of, nothing was impossible. 'Look at God's creation—how intricate, how wild and bizarre. You can do anything you put your mind to. Don't limit yourself. There's freedom in Christ and God.' We weren't a religious household in the sense of having a lot of rules and regulations. We were kind of a different breed."

Her voice was noticed at an early age. "When I was a kid, I knew I had something going on. My mom would make me sing to Judy Garland . . . kind of doing fake Judy, and then I was really involved in choirs. My voice was good, but nobody ever gave me a big pat on the head, which I think is cool because I just kept growing and getting better." She started singing in madrigal and gospel choirs at her church. When she was eight years old, her father taught her how to play guitar. By the time she was in her teens, she had renounced her parents' faith. "We went to this creepy church in the middle of nowhere. Eventually we had 'home church,' which was basically our dad reading the Bible to me and my brother, and we'd both instantly fall asleep. We became allergic to church. We'd get there and just pass the fuck out.

"I was raised in a real spiritual, Bible Belt household. So I developed my own cynicism because there are always things in the Bible that really bum me out. I became really obsessed with *The Kids in the Hall*, and they had Scott Thompson, who's the one gay member. I remember having this feeling that, 'Scott Thompson isn't going to heaven? How could that be?' That was my first big tip-off that something wasn't quite right with dogmatic Christianity. And then I was just trying to undo it since the age of twelve."

She wasn't what you'd call the star student. "I was in detention a lot. There was a calendar in the principal's office and if I could be good a certain number of days, I'd get McDonald's. And I never got McDonald's. I was never good enough in a row. I had some kind of strange anti-authority thing that I think might have stemmed from something in my past life—if past lives exist—because I had no reason to be as troubled as I was. I was picked on a lot for being so extra . . . extra emotional, extra funny, extra weird. Just out there. Super hyper. So much energy. ADD to a T, but my parents didn't believe in putting me on speed—thankfully. So I was just unhinged. I did a project on the Nancy Spungen murder in seventh grade and I made a slideshow with all these graphic images. I was obsessed with Nancy because she's from Bensalem, which is the town over from Doylestown. I visited her grave and the high school she went to. I was fascinated by her story because it was all subversive dark energy. Like, nothing redeemable. Just the fringes of the culture."

* * *

"The first shows I ever went to were hardcore shows, and the hardcore circuit in America is something so special, because you could have these bands that every suburban kid knew about, but they're still playing these bunk-ass venues, with not even a real PA. That scene was so built to be DIY. There'd be these huge shows in an auditorium or a VFW hall with twenty hardcore bands, and all the bands would be hanging out in the parking lot with their busted-ass vans. It was for kids. Like, it was all middle school, high school kids. I think that was my first taste of, 'We can do whatever we want.' I didn't go to a show at a proper venue for a really long time. I just thought that was what music was supposed to be—this very communal, rebellious thing."

She started listening to classic rock, then college radio: Princeton's WPRB. "Things that were new, but sounded old," said Natalie. "I had a notebook, and I'd write down everything the college station played. They'd play ten songs and be like, "Okay . . . you . . . just . . . heard . . . ," and name twenty artists. So I would have to write it down and star the songs I liked." She heard the music of The Velvet Underground, Syd Barrett, and Alice Coltrane. She found a job at a mom-and-pop called Siren Records; it's still around. "I would comb the new arrivals. I started looking for weird music, because I was attracted to music that was different. I was like, 'We have to figure out what the next wave of music is going to sound like.' I really thought that the next wave was going to be noise, because I was like, 'This is the most new, the most angry, and the most weird, expressive thing. Of *course* everybody's gonna get into it.'" She read *Our Band Could Be Your Life*, by Michael Azerrad, and fantasized of being in a group like Sonic Youth. She took the train to Philadelphia for shows at the First Unitarian Church, where she saw the Yeah Yeah Yeahs, Sunn O))), and Lightning Bolt. She started frequenting the city's overlapping screamo, noise, and hardcore scenes, with all the zeal of a convert. "It was very Pentecostal in its own way," Natalie said.

"I would get there so early that they would sometimes just let me in for free. I'd come like four or five hours early, and they'd be like, 'There she is. Come on in.' I think they knew I was fourteen or fifteen, so they probably felt a collective responsibility for how precocious I was. There was a guy who had a record store—he would have a little stand inside the shows, and I would look through all the records. I was a little sponge. I was trying to soak everything up and see every band. And in some ways, being raised Christian kind of contributed to this religious fervor I had about DIY music, where going to a show—to me, that was like church. And moshing, and standing side-stage: these were all ways of transcendence."

She started making music of her own—initially, as Weyes Bluhd—and playing live at age fifteen. "The first Weyes Bluhd show was a house show in South Philly, where I probably played to a room of twelve people, sitting on the couch with an acoustic guitar. I drank the Kool-Aid. I was like, 'This is how we're gonna make an impact. It's not like how it used to be, where popular music is the most interesting of the day. The good music is underground. You have to seek it out—but then you get to have this very visceral, up-front, extremely close experience with it.'"

* * *

The year that Natalie first played as Weyes Bluhd, in 2003, the critic David Keenan wrote a story for *The Wire* magazine. Reporting from the Brattleboro Free Folk Festival in Vermont, Keenan saw the makings of "an alternative American narrative, irreconcilable with the prevailing neoconservative vision of the 'New American Century' . . . a vague movement, an attempt to muster the same recurrent, archetypal forms that archivist and mystic Harry Smith saw manifest in the American folk music of the early twentieth century and documented in his *Anthology of American Folk Music*." Around a baggy group of artists (Sunburned Hand of the Man, Matt Valentine, Erika Elder, Six Organs of Admittance), the writer coined a term that alluded to "the old, weird America" of Greil Marcus:

> Welcome to the New Weird America: a groundswell musical movement rising out of the U.S.A.'s backwoods, one that offers an alternative to the no-wave revivalism of the nation's urban centers. Loosely called free folk, the music draws on an intoxicating range

of avant-garde sounds, from acoustic roots to drone, ritualistic performance, Krautrock, ecstatic jazz, hillbilly mountain music, psychedelia, archival blues and folk sides, country funk and more.

The naming of "the New Weird America" would be prophetic. The years to come would bring significant LPs from Devendra Banhart, Joanna Newsom, Vetiver, Espers, CocoRosie, Animal Collective, and Anohni: the loose confederation known as freak folk, and Natalie's point of entry as a songwriter. "I started playing shows in high school, and it was usually just acoustic nylon-string guitar—like, in a room, with a couple saw players, or a tape player. It was very much of the freak-folk persuasion. Out of all the noise stuff at the time, I thought that freak folk was the thing. I loved Devendra Banhart, and Feathers, Diane Cluck, and Josephine Foster. That was kind of my zone."

Out of necessity—because nobody wanted to be in a band with her—she did it all alone. "There were bands I wanted to be in, but they wouldn't have me. I still mourn the loss of having a high school band. I never wanted to be a solo musician, but I just couldn't meet anybody as obsessed with music as I was. I always wanted to be like a Kim Gordon or a Tina Weymouth. I wanted to be the badass chick in a really amazing band. I thought I'd be a side note. It was always difficult to find people that were into what I was into, so I started hanging out with people in the city and just gave up on my town. Because everybody's music taste was stuck on Mars Volta and Radiohead. It's like nobody could get over that. I ditched the idea of being in a band and started recording with my four-track."

Her life was changed the night she saw a terrifying band from Michigan called Wolf Eyes in Philadelphia. She said, "I was fifteen. I had this crazy feeling that this was my generation's Stooges. I got infected by that energy. I started playing power electronics—harsh noise—because it was how I was feeling. But there also was a little bit of fear to really show my femininity. I was afraid I wouldn't gain the respect I really wanted from people who were becoming my friends. So there was a little bit of trying to quiet the beautiful side, in favor of the more violent. I was a little ashamed, because I had met a lot of men who didn't like female music to begin with. So I was like, 'When I play my girly folk songs or whatever, it doesn't incite as much of a reaction.'" Her music veered toward dissonance and aggression. "I had this instrument that I built in high school. It was a huge, six-foot-long stringed instrument, and I started playing with that amplified and singing through power electronics. I played these shows, and everybody would flip out. But before, I would play these folky shows and it was always like, 'This is so precious!'"

She graduated high school early and moved to Philadelphia for a year. She started going to New York. "There's a Chinatown bus from Philadelphia that's twenty bucks, and the first show I played in New York was opening for Dirty Projectors at the Cake Shop when I was seventeen. They kicked me out after I played, because I blurted out how old I was onstage, or something dumb." She studied music for a year in Portland, Oregon, at Lewis & Clark College. "I didn't really stay. But I got to see Grouper play six times in Portland. I got to see Yellow Swans." It was there that she met Tom Greenwood, from the band Jackie-O Motherfucker. "He invited me to go on tour with them, and that was my first tour, in 2007. Just playing guitar and improvising with them, and they would make jokes that I was the grunge Karen Dalton."

The music she had written on the East Coast was considered clichéd. "You could sense in the Pacific Northwest—they took that culture a bit more for granted, because it's so baked into the whole thing. I was really shocked. Coming from Philly and playing shows and feeling like I was this really special artist, I would get a little community of people to come out to each of my shows. And then I moved to Portland, and they're like, 'Look, we've got five other girls that do what you do, and a little bit better.' I went from a place where DIY culture was very sacred and special to a place where there's a vintage clothing store on every block. Everybody's a record collector. Everybody has a weird band . . .

I was one of a thousand people making that kind of music. No one was impressed with me at all."

She moved from Portland back to Philadelphia. She joined a band called Satanized, where she would use mashed fruit and exploding packets of blood to make it look as if her guts were oozing out. She toured in Europe as a member of the Brooklyn band Axolotl. She self-released a pair of challenging cassettes and CDRs: *Strange Chalices of Seeing* (2007) and *Evacuating Zombie Milk* (2008). The albums were almost punitive with ear-splitting discord and feedback. "A lot of my old fans were a little disappointed. Like, 'What are you doing? You were so good at singing and doing this other thing.'"

On April 27, 2008, she played the Philly stop of the nomadic International Noise Conference. "Which was this guy, Rat Bastard, from Miami. He had a band called the Laundry Room Squelchers. And it was just a notorious, fun, kind of traveling noise conference, and I was playing in a basement, and the amps caught on fire," she recalls. "I honestly felt like the devil had showed up to my gig and said, 'Don't do this anymore.' I mean, this was a basement full of people and the amps were on fire . . . And I was like, 'Oh, shit. There's no universal grace for me playing this heinously loud. I'm just not supposed to do it.' I think I realized I might be better at making beautiful music, even if nobody in my scene loves it. And that was when I made *The Outside Room*."

* * *

Around the time Natalie decided on a change of course, in 2008, Bear Stearns, the eighty-five-year-old investment bank, collapsed, and was bought by JPMorganChase in a fire sale. The shocking news sent markets plummeting around the world. In the fall, Lehman Brothers went bankrupt, and looked to take the rest of Wall Street down as well. By October 2009, ten percent of working-age Americans were unemployed—some fifteen million people. In just two years, at least four million lost their homes. It took until 2017 for unemployment rates to recover.

She bounced around the country for the next few years, beginning with a farm in rural Kentucky. She said, "I did some wildcrafting there. I helped some people build a sauna, made maple syrup by tapping maple trees. Just did all the back-to-the-land hippie stuff . . . I learned a lot about the culture of the South, which was very eye-opening. I got to eat a lot of wildcrafted food: wild meats, venison stew, hunter stew like beaver, groundhog." She studied herbal medicine in New Mexico, where she spent weeks camping in a tent. She moved to Baltimore, where she lived in a three-story dental-office-turned-residence named Tarantula Hill. It had a library, a sensory deprivation tank, a performance space, a sauna, a recording studio, and no central heating. "I was living off rice and beans and dumpster bread, and young enough that it wasn't a health problem yet," she said. The house was also where she recorded *The Outside Room* (2011): her first official record as Weyes Blood, and an album of the Great Recession.

Though it showed an artist shaking off her influences—Nico and The Velvet Underground, most of all—the qualities her later fans would come to know were already in place: otherworldly vocals, hypnotic harmonies, stirring ballads, exotic instrumentation, wordless interludes, and lush, romantic textures. It overflowed with sounds like church organ, industrial percussion, and acoustic guitar, all of which she played herself. "I was like, 'I'm gonna make this really psychedelic record. I'm going to play everything. And it's going to be cool because I'm finding all these private-press records that were made the same way.' It was like a soup. A weird, swampy pool of all my influences." The candlelit and melancholy ambience had much in common with contemporaries such as Julia Holter, EMA, and Beach House, but with an undercurrent of cacophony, reflective of the moment in which it was made.

"I was at the turning point of generations. People that were five or ten years older than me had a much easier time being an artist. Rents were cheaper, there weren't as many expenses, and there was a built-in safety net for Gen Xers—they were dumped into the most beautiful economy of anybody. Everything became a lot more expensive. I had this idea I was going to be an underground musician, playing shows, selling tapes, working a minimum-wage job, and somehow paying rent and health insurance. After two or three years, it became impossible. I saw which of my friends had connections or rich parents, and what that can do for you. It was a deep education in the fact that the world doesn't owe you anything." And then she packed up her belongings and came to New York.

* * *

When Natalie left Baltimore in 2011, the biggest-selling albums in the world were by Adele, Lady Gaga, and Michael Bublé. *The Hangover Part II, Bridesmaids,* and *The Artist* were in theaters. *Homeland, Portlandia,* and *Game of Thrones* first aired. At the White House, Times Square, and Ground Zero, Americans gathered to celebrate the death of Osama bin Laden. The president released his birth certificate. The 9/11 Memorial & Museum opened in lower Manhattan; *Girls* was being filmed in Greenpoint. In California, months before he died from cancer, Apple CEO Steve Jobs made his final public appearance—the unveiling of a three-million-square-foot, spaceship-style corporate campus. It was the year his company announced the iPhone 4S, the iPad 2, and a wealth of new features: iMessage, iCloud, and Siri. That year alone, they sold some 72 million iPhones, 42 million iPods, 32 million iPads, and 17 million Macs. That summer, Apple listed more cash on hand than the U.S. Treasury and surpassed ExxonMobil as the world's most valuable corporation. The stranglehold of the rectangular screen had begun—as was apparent early on to Natalie.

"Steve Jobs knew that this technology was going to be emotionally manipulative when he developed it. He knew that it was something people were going to take into their beds with them, and he was right," she said. In a matter of months, it seemed, the phone's corrupting impact was obvious (in terms of basic courtesy) as well as latent (in terms of our attention spans and culture as a whole).

"I was always so excited about going to little shows and being part of the community. But I did notice around the time of the smartphone that the scene really changed. It was cool to watch it all swell up. There was this moment where the noise scene was big. You'd go to a show, and it was *packed*. It felt like the place to be. And then it kinda waned a little bit in 2009, 2010. A lot of noise people were getting into techno and music that was more accessible, because noise was uncommodifiable. It didn't really make sense. And then the recession in America around 2008, you could feel the pendulum swinging toward more conservative music. When that stuff happened, you saw the pendulum swing toward, like, Grizzly Bear, and these really feel-good bands. Because they were like, 'This is safe.' I'm not saying that means it's bad. I'm just saying it's safe because people want to hear that. I think the music industry lost so much money, it was like, 'We're no longer interested in trying to take these risks.'"

* * *

She was a wandering minstrel for her first year in New York. "Anytime a place got weird I could very easily leave. My life was so small it fit in my car," she said. She lived at the Meat Wallet, which was a warehouse on Broadway, in Bushwick. It got its name because so many guys lived there: among them, Mac DeMarco and the band PC Worship. "I was just hopping around, subletting. I never signed a lease. I could never afford anything like that, so I was always kind of crashing with different people. I lived in all the neighborhoods: Lower East Side, Williamsburg, Greenpoint, Bushwick, Bed-Stuy, Crown Heights. I lived out of my car, basically. I ended up in Rockaway Beach because I befriended Andrew VanWyngarden from MGMT—we met through Ariel Pink—and he became a buddy. He took me surfing down there, and that was kind of my favorite place," says Natalie. "In the winter, it was desolate. I took some freezing walks on the beach. I remember that spring they were rebuilding the sidewalk that had been destroyed by Hurricane Sandy and I watched trucks off-load these vast amounts of sand on the site. It seemed so unnatural to bring in so much fake land that was going to be eaten away again. You find out about the history of that place and you realize it's been destroyed a couple of times by storms and a fire. Living there had a feeling of impermanence and transience."

Compared to Baltimore and Philadelphia, she found New York to be initially both underwhelming and unwelcoming. "In Baltimore, it's a little bit more Southern, so there's this warmth and these kind of culty small-town weirdos. Versus Philly, which has this hard Yankee vibe, and a little bit more of a rough-and-tumble thing. And then New York is so hip that, like: those are the people that have access to all the real culture, so there's a little bit more of a snobby quality."

She had a memorable encounter at Occupy Wall Street. "I'll never forget that day," said Natalie. "I was walking away from the protesters dressed as a zombie, carrying a weird sign. Lou Reed came up to me and said, 'How's the protest?' Then I held up my hand to shake his hand, but my hands were cold, so he started warming them. Which is crazy, because he wasn't known as a nice person. He was mean to a lot of people, but he was so nice to me. I happened to have [*The Outside Room*] in my car, and I gave him a copy. We just smiled at each other. I felt deeply connected to him. He's one of my favorite artists of all time. That was a huge moment for me."

The city that had birthed The Velvet Underground had all but disappeared. "I was like, 'That would be the New York that I would want, is the Laurie Anderson, Lou Reed New York.' I could sense in my heart: 'That time is over. Those artists got to experience this quality of New York that is no longer. The real cultural cachet is capital. It's money. And it's more about money than it's ever been.'" The haves and have-nots were as evident among the indie world as in American society at large. "My friends that were having cool bands, or living comfortably in New York: their parents definitely paid their rent. I knew very few people that were actually paying their own way. And if they were, they were *hustling*."

She strung together freelance work in bartending and catering. "I couldn't solidify a job. I remember trying to get a hostessing job, and it was like I wasn't good-looking enough. I didn't have enough rich-person vibes, or something, and I noticed that, without any kind of cachet, getting a job was really tough. I was catering an event at Soho House. I was just walking around picking up empties, and somebody came up to me like, 'Oh my God! I'm such a big fan of your music!' I was like, 'You've seen me play?' And they're like, 'Yeah, what are you doing here?' I was like, 'Oh, I'm working.' And they were like, 'Oh.' And then they stopped talking to me. They saw that I was working the event, and they were like, 'Oh, you're not a real musician.' I've never had luck with money and jobs. It's always been pretty fraught, and New York is a great place to get completely eaten alive by that stuff."

She signed with Mexican Summer, an indie label in Greenpoint. She spent the entirety of her advance getting her wisdom teeth pulled, and burst into tears when she found a ticket on her car, wondering how to pay for it. "I was trying to build a career. I was working with Mexican Summer. It was my first time on a label, and I was really struggling to make it all work. There wasn't a lot of faith in what I did. So I think at the times that I did play shows, where I had a really good set, people would be shocked. They'd be like, 'There's nobody here, and that was so good.' That was always a good feeling."

She played at Death by Audio, Glasslands, Union Pool, and Silent Barn in Bushwick. For some, the feeling was that Brooklyn's DIY community was on the wane. "It was a really fun time to be in New York, but it wasn't like a heyday," Natalie says. "It was sad to watch all those heydays and be a certain age in my mid-twenties in New York, and watching it just become so expensive that nobody could afford to do that kind of thing anymore. A lot of DIY venues closed, like Glasslands and 285 Kent. It was a period that felt like the culmination of the scene, but that very quickly fell apart.

"I think that I was late. I felt like I got there when that initial wave like the Cake Shop was dying down. That era of New York was really cool in terms of bands and shows. And it still felt like New York had this scene of bands. I think that by the time I was there, it was more like, 'Are you just doing techno music? Are you just doing house music? Are you just trying to, like, do yoga and smash?' It really shifted culturally at a certain point.

"I kind of hated it for a really long time. It took a while to get into the groove and really like the vibe . . . It makes close relationships and scenes kind of difficult. It's like a buffet of humanity at every level. I'm a peripheral person. I'm kind of a loner. But sometimes the city is a perfect place to be a loner." Her preferred neighborhoods were both on the water: Red Hook and Rockaway Beach. She said the latter was "like Venice [Beach] in the '70s. It's still kind of affordable. There's still some run-down zones where anything goes. There will be, like, a busted basketball court and then a beautiful beach. You can go surf, but then you go to the bodega and get a hoagie. And that's something that doesn't exist anywhere."

Her feelings toward bohemian Brooklyn were less affectionate. "Brooklyn is actually my least favorite [borough]. Just the homogenized hipster culture—the vibe isn't that inspiring sometimes . . . I lived on the Lower East Side during summertime, and that was actually my favorite. There were young people and really old people, and foreign people, and some hip people, and people that were just nu-metal—just all different kinds of people, without this oppressive Williamsburg skinny-fashion vibe, which is a little bit much."

The unexamined assumptions of the scene were a source of some ambivalence. "It was definitely predominantly white. It was *super* white. I'll say that much. I don't know if anybody talks about that. There were noise bands that toyed with some white-supremacist energy. I think that kind of stuff to me aged poorly, for sure. And when I think about the kind of diversity that exists in music now, and I think about that scene back then, I do get a little—like, 'This is really white.' But as far as the sexism and the chauvinism and rape culture—it was a different time.

I think there were a lot of problematic people in the mix. That energy is gonna be in any community or scene from that time. I think it was more politically informed than other scenes. And I didn't think that it was as damaging as some other things I've heard about. But I do think that—hipsters doing stupid shit, and people taking advantage of being cool—what else is new? The story's all the same."

Like so much else, the indie world was never quite the same again after the iPhone. "I really think the smartphone had the biggest impact on the death of it. Also exceedingly high rent, and strict landlords—things like that killed it, too. But a part of the charm of DIY, and a part of the charm of being at a weird house show in Toledo, was that you felt—because there was this continuous thread of the culture throughout the country and the world—it was the center of the universe, and everybody was fully engaged. Once the smartphone showed up, it was a bit like, 'We're at the show. Should we take a picture, or should we see what else is going on? Oh, looks like some other stuff is going on that looks aesthetically more pleasing.' If you look at pictures of the DIY scene before the smartphone, everybody didn't look great. The styles were kind of bad. Everybody's a little, like, dirty. Then, with the smartphone, things started getting glossy. Bands started getting a manager before they had even played a show. The culture shifted. It seemed like it was hard to get that naïveté back, and that naïveté played a large role in sustaining these scenes and making it feel special."

Her tenure in New York was mixed, to say the least. "New York was amazing. It was awful. It was, like, the worst, emotionally and physically. But I became who I am today because of New York. I think it taught me how to sing. Because, before that, I had just been doing my own thing in basements and playing these small towns where everybody likes to congratulate each other for being cool. And when I got to New York, people just could not give any less of a fuck about me. Every place I lived, I'd get kicked out of. I got fired from jobs. I couldn't get hired at places all the time. I really didn't have any luck, or any skeleton key.

I remember—I had a nanny job. And that's all a woman with no skills can hope for. When you're a musician, men can do construction work and art handling. They can do these unskilled jobs and make some cash. But if you're a woman, it's like, you want to waitress or nanny. And so I nannied and the little girl was like, 'You only have one pair of shoes?' She was disgusted by my poor situation. That I had one pair of pants and one pair of shoes, and I would wear them every day. And she started getting really upset. She fired me. The kid fired me. And the mom was like, 'Sorry?' I definitely didn't have the financial means to *present*. That was something I confronted in New York. David Byrne wrote about this. How all of a sudden you had to be a supermodel to get some job. You had to be really shiny fresh. You have to have this confidence that, unfortunately, being poor does not afford you. So entering that world and really struggling with the jobs, it pushed me so much deeper into making sure that my music was not just me in my head having a good time, but actually something that acknowledged the history of music before it.

"I think in general millennials are kind of burned out. We were positioned and set up to believe that the world was going to be a certain way and then it completely shifted. We haven't fully caught up to how our attention spans, our needs, biological things, have changed. The amount of expenses that we've accumulated in our technological society has made it increasingly difficult for anybody to lead a life of quality. Not just comfort. I mean peace of mind."

She wrote about communication, disappointment, and displacement on *The Innocents* (2014) and *Front Row Seat to Earth* (2016). She said, "I guess the one that's kind of about New York is 'Can't Go Home,' because I never lived in any one place for very long, but when I was in New York I was constantly moving, constantly dealing with people, and constantly living under the radar, not being able to afford anything. I was really struggling. Constantly moving to sketchy situations and looking for work, having a home, but not really having one. You can't go home."

She started playing "Everybody's Talkin'," which was recorded by Harry Nilsson for the film *Midnight Cowboy*. "It's one of my favorite songs to do," she said. "To me it sounds like he's talking about leaving New York, which is something I was trying to do ever since I moved here. And then I fell in love with it and gave up. 'I'm going where the sun keeps shining,' because the sun is not shining in New York; and 'Going where the weather suits my clothes,' which is true—I've always felt underdressed in the city. Being originally from California, it's just a beautiful, lost-soul, vagabond song. I could really relate to it."

* * *

She moved back to Los Angeles in 2016. By then, cacophony had been absorbed within the mainstream, much as Natalie had predicted, with noise-inflected albums by Madonna (*Rebel Heart*) and Kanye (*Yeezus*). Her breakthrough came that fall, with the release of *Front Row Seat to Earth*—the first of three consecutive albums to be awarded *Pitchfork*'s Best New Music. She signed with Kurt Cobain's first label, Sub Pop. She made a video that culminates with a homicidal cartoon iPhone. She went on tour with Father John Misty, Phoenix, and Beck; she worked with Tim Heidecker, Lana Del Rey, and The Killers; she performed at Coachella, Glastonbury, and the Sydney Opera House.

"I never had any kind of audience in New York until I moved to L.A. That's when my music career really took off. I was always a total underdog. I had a couple people that believed in me, but not really. By the time I was getting a little traction, I was working at a peanut brittle factory, and my boss was this girl in high school. I could not convince anybody I was cool enough to get a nice job."

Natalie came to love the city that she had eagerly fled. "It's funny, in hindsight. I've been back [in L.A.] about eight or nine years, and I go to the East Coast now, and I'm like, 'These are my people.' I think the intellectual stimulation of New York—there's a poetry to that city that's just completely—you can't create it anywhere else. I was excited to get

out of New York because I think that it had done what it needed to do
alchemically. I'd been extremely poor and destitute and depressed, and
all of that great stuff, and it made me ready to write some serious music,"
she says. "Soft rock with an apocalyptic edge was never my intent. But
it is what happened."

Adam Shore (III)

The story of the arts is a history of patronage. From the church of the Middle Ages to the nobles of the renaissance, from the eighteenth-century monarch to the modern corporation, art is indivisible from economics. The orchestra, the opera house, and the arrival of the leisure class all parallel the course of capital. In Austria, the Esterházy clan employed composer Joseph Haydn, inventor of the symphony and the string quartet. In the twentieth century, the Metropolitan Opera was supported by Texaco; Lincoln Center, Exxon; and the Brooklyn Academy of Music, Philip Morris.

From 1998 to 2019—an era when the record industry was foundering—the most important patron in the world of underground and independent music was a caffeinated beverage, invented in Thailand, and then mass-marketed from Austria: Red Bull. You can't exaggerate their role in nurturing a generation of emerging composers, producers, instrumentalists, bands, and DJs—as well as journalists, photographers, designers, promoters, and production staff. They were the Medicis of electronic music, noise, improvisation, and hip hop. The company wasn't alone, of course—by 2010, Intel, Converse, and Mountain Dew were funding similar initiatives—but they were easily the most esteemed, committed, and credible. It all originated with a pair of German club kids: Many Ameri and Torsten Schmidt.

* * *

In 1989, 150 people gathered in West Berlin for the inaugural Love Parade, a combination party and political rally for peace, grounded in dance music. The wall came down four months later. By 1999, an estimated 1.5 million were attending the event—now annual—and techno had become big business. "It was a time when brands didn't understand what was going on in the streets of Berlin—when people started dancing on these floats at the Love Parade," Many Ameri says. "A lot of things they thought would speak to youth were changing or not working. This was happening against a backdrop of intrusive brands that were exploiting these target groups. In Germany in the '90s, there was a strong link between Camel cigarettes and the techno movement, and you saw lots of money being poured into this scene . . . Creating shorter cigarettes that would be more attractive to ravers. Perfumes by Camel. It was gross. The same goes for mobile phone companies that would be at these parades. Candy companies doing raves. So it was madness and stupidity that was going on. I was always thinking about, 'What could be done for young people that would actually benefit them?'"

Born and raised in Munich to a family from Iran, Many started working at a communications agency in 1994, when he was still in college. "My job was looking at trends, and trying to do something beneficial for the audiences brands were trying to reach," he says. He pitched a concept to a client: a company in Austria named Red Bull, launched in 1987. "I had this idea to create an academy for musicians and DJs and producers. There weren't many [programs] at the time. The technology wasn't cheap enough for that to be an option in the mid-'90s. The academy would foster creativity and bring people together from different musical backgrounds. I tried to get the most cynical and critical minds that would look at this and say, 'Yet another brand is trying to sneak their way into an area that should be brand-free.'" He called the editor-in-chief of *Groove*, a German techno magazine. His name was Torsten Schmidt.

Torsten was from Thalfang, a tiny village in the west of Germany—a region that was home to multiple American air bases. "There were thousands of American troops stationed there with their families," says Torsten. "That also meant there were these infamous shops, the PX, where you could buy American things like Jordans, and tapes, and records. So in the absolute boonies—and some of them are still around—you would find clubs which had insanely good sound systems, and you would have either servicemen who would play there now and then, or the local DJs who would buy records off the servicemen that they brought from home. Also important was the radio, AFN, the Armed Forces Network, that would bring not only the American Top 40 countdown but, especially at night, dance music. You had a lot of really decent import-record shops, where you could get your records from Chicago and Detroit. In the end, that was all a benefit of the hypermilitarization of the area."

"We had a meeting," Many says. "Torsten and I, and four other editors of different music magazines. This is 1997, in Germany. So the musical background would be techno, house music, acid jazz, hip hop, turntablism. We tried to look at this and say, 'Is there a way to build something that would be around in five years, and what would that have to look like?' My role in this was to say, 'If we agree on a certain approach, I will make sure it happens this way.' Having Red Bull as a brand that had already stepped into sports in a similar fashion—the approach of actually stepping in there and not becoming a sponsor, but enabling the people in that scene to build projects. We had seen it in extreme sports. The hope was that they would be able to do that in music as well."

As a tastemaker and a veteran of the branding junket, Torsten was suspicious. "It was something I got invited to a fair amount, where some brand or institution wants to learn about subculture, and they wine and dine you," he says. "There were a bunch of people who, in Many's words, absolutely hate the idea of a brand like Red Bull being involved in underground music cultures. And I think his brief was, 'Let's assume this is about learning. And let's assume they were serious. What would it need to look like?'"

At best, the pitch to Red Bull was counterintuitive. The beverage had become a favorite of the nightlife world, but Many and Torsten weren't suggesting a party, or opportunities to sell vodka Red Bull; on the contrary. What they had in mind was a series of discussions and workshops—no more, no less. "The task was to explain how it can be equally exciting to sit on a couch and have a conversation about music as it is to drop into a half-pipe, and they got it," Many says. "It was a different company at the time. The people that were working there were all extreme-sports people—ex-skiers, downhill this and downhill that. It was a small company. They understood that this was something worth exploring with the right people. It could have been a sponsorship for three days—which is what other brands were doing—and they signed on for a bigger vision."

* * *

In 1998, the first installment of the Red Bull Music Academy was held in a repurposed warehouse in East Berlin. Two groups of thirty young musicians were selected by a jury made of industry professionals and journalists; the size was based on a traditional German classroom. The applicants were asked to fill out a twenty-page questionnaire, and offered access to recording studios, as well as full accommodation and ownership of anything they made, all at Red Bull's expense. "That's part of the opening speech: there is no catch," said Torsten. "We are going to offer you nothing in the end but inspiration and this chance of being here together." To kick things off, there was a conversation with the producer, DJ, and polymath Jeff Mills. "We were scared shitless," Many says. "This intellectual Detroiter. Pioneer. Sitting on the couch, and talking about life on tour, and washing his underwear in the sink. We saw there was a void that we could fill, where people we all listen to and experience as performers got a place to reflect. We opened it by saying, 'This is an experiment. We don't exactly know how this will work. We brought these people here because they have an interesting story to tell, and this is about the mutual respect we have, and listening to each other.'"

"When we did the first academy," says Many, "it was a bunch of Germans, Austrians, and Swiss. Pretty pale guys, mostly. For the next year, we had people from eight countries: Czech, Polish, Belgian, English, Dutch. And suddenly you saw, 'Here's people that know what it's like to sell records on a black market, that have been in a bunker, who are gathering through music.' And everything that happened afterward was built on that first year." They held the next edition in Berlin, the third in Dublin, and the fourth—beginning on September 1, 2001—in New York. And that was how they came to work with Adam Shore.

"My friend Todd Kasten was asked to help out with the academy," Adam says. "He hired me to listen to submissions so they could select the participants, and to book lectures. We had ten amazing days. It was only lectures. No events at night. And in the afternoon, they would have workshops. I had booked David Mancuso and Nicky Siano. I was taking care of the participants—these thirty kids from all over the world who had never been to America before. And then September 11 happened. We watched it from the roof of a building the academy was in, on the Lower East Side, and they were freaked out, and we were freaked out. That was a pretty intense time."

They went to São Paulo in 2002, Cape Town in 2003, Rome in 2004, Seattle in 2005. "Year by year we came to a new city, got to meet the people who made up the very foundations of the local scene," Many recalled. With the help of past participants, they started hosting workshops that were open to the public: five, then ten, and then 300 in some sixty countries every year. They launched a twenty-four-hour station, RBMA Radio; they sponsored mixers, lounges, and festival stages at Sónar, Movement, and Montreux Jazz. The list of lecturers ranged widely: Hugh Masekela, Gilberto Gil, Bob Moog, Carl Craig. They went to Melbourne in 2006; Toronto, 2007; Barcelona, 2008. They started a series of so-called Bass Camps and Weekenders in cities like Beirut, Johannesburg, Beijing, and Moscow. The pool of applicants swelled to 5,000 a year; eventually, alumni included Fred Again . . . , Black Coffee, Nina Kraviz, Aloe Blacc, Lucrecia Dalt, Hudson Mohawke, and Flying Lotus. London, 2010; Madrid, 2011. They planned a special celebration for their fifteenth anniversary in 2013: a five-week, city-wide blowout, with thirty-four events and 200 artists. The only place to do it was New York.

"Before we started contemplating what the live series would look like," Adam says, "we'd have these conversations: 'Every music event already happens in New York. What do we contribute?' What we didn't want to do was take away from what promoters already do—which is what a lot of brands do when they do events. If an artist is playing your event, you've taken them out of the touring cycle, and they can't come back to New York for a while. If your event is free, then you're distorting the pricing. If we're taking away artists and messing with ticket sales, that hurts promoters. That hurts venues. These are the people that Red Bull actually relies on all the other months that we're not doing the festival. So it was like, 'How can we be a positive benefit to the music ecosystem, and find a way where we can help artists and venues, and complement what they normally do?'"

They gave themselves parameters. "We determined we should never do a show that would happen otherwise," Adam says. "We tried to use nontraditional venues. We would bring in original sound design. We'd give artists the ability to expand their live show. To connect them with choreographers or set designers. Let them do things they could only do with an organization like RBMA. We also did a lot of shows around a sound, or a label, or a moment in New York City history. We wanted to do shows that nobody else was doing, that couldn't exist if it weren't for us." The offerings included talks by Erykah Badu, Brian Eno, and James Murphy; shows devoted to dub, drums, and drone; "United States of Bass"; "Twelve Years of DFA"; Ryuichi Sakamoto and Alva Noto at the Met Museum; and Giorgio Moroder's first-ever DJ set.

The festival was the subject of a profile and a podcast from *The New York Times*. "For music fans, it is a cornucopia," wrote Ben Sisario, and "perhaps the most elaborate example of the reach of corporate brands into popular culture." He interviewed musician Steven Ellison, better known as Flying Lotus. "The people behind the academy, they're not just suits; they are really special people who are passionate about artists," said Ellison. "Above them they have some suits to deal with, but I've never dealt with any of them." The *Times*'s Ben Ratliff admitted, "There's something about this that feels different, and it has to do with the details . . . I'm troubled by my wholeheartedly positive reaction to a festival underwritten by a drink that I've never had in my life, and hope I never do . . . I still feel wary and skeptical about corporate sponsorship of the arts." The lone dissenting voice was the artist Matthew Herbert, a past participant. "My overriding impression of any music industry Red Bull tie-in is that the brand is always louder than the art," he said. "I don't think one would come away from any interaction with them thinking that they were interested in anything else other than selling caffeinated sugary drinks." As time went on, it was a minority view.

"If you compare the Red Bull Music Academy festival in New York to, say, Budweiser's Made in America festival," wrote a critic in *Forbes*, "you will see few similarities . . . there are no merch tables or Red Bull drinking gardens, and artists like Brian Eno are not drinking Red Bull onstage at events. In fact, aside from the festival's name, the brand's product is largely absent from events."

They picked a class of sixty-two participants from thirty-five countries. They hired the architect Jeffrey Inaba to build a lecture hall, an office, and a set of studios on four floors in Chelsea. They blanketed the city with a black-and-white event calendar—in the subway, on the street. They printed twenty-two editions of *The Daily Note*, a bespoke newspaper made for the festival, edited by Piotr Orlov, with contributions by the likes of Jami Attenberg, Geeta Dayal, Hua Hsu, and Simon Reynolds, in a daily run of 75,000 that was distributed at over twenty subway stations. "We were hiring New York editors, photographers, video directors, production crews, people distributing the newspapers," Adam says. "I think by virtue of the amount the *Times* wrote about it—that was the turning point, where the people inside the company understood, like, 'This is bigger than us.'"

The first RBMA festival was a resounding triumph with the public and the press—so much so that it would be reprised in New York City every spring for the next half-decade. There was a block party and tribute to Larry Levan near the old Paradise Garage; a site-specific work for sixty-plus performers at the Guggenheim by Solange Knowles; a dance commission at a hangar in Industry City with FKA twigs; premieres by Oneohtrix Point Never and Anohni at the Park Avenue Armory; and lectures from Harry Belafonte, Robyn, D'Angelo, Werner Herzog, La Monte Young, and A$AP Rocky. They added festivals in Paris and Montreal (2016), São Paulo and Los Angeles (2017), Chicago (2018), and Atlanta (2019)—twenty-two in total. They hosted conversations with Iggy Pop, Ice-T, and Björk. They commemorated Arthur Russell, Eddie Palmieri, and Alice Coltrane. They commissioned a symphony for an ensemble of fifty violins and fifty speakers (by composer Tristan Perich), and another for a hundred cars (by Ryoji Ikeda). And then—on April 3, 2019, only weeks before the seventh annual festival in New York—the company announced that it would no longer be funding the academy.

"After twenty years of supporting artists worldwide with its music program in a rapidly changing world, Red Bull will maintain its purpose of providing a global platform to promote creativity—but it is changing the means of delivery," a statement read. The Austrian corporation would "gradually phase out the existing structure and will implement a new setup which empowers existing Red Bull country teams and utilizes local expertise." Torsten and Many wrote a statement of their own: "We have had the privilege to work with some of the brightest and most talented people in the world. So, we want to use this opportunity to thank all of the people who have made this journey possible . . . We met more fascinating minds and characters than we could have ever imagined. For that we are grateful." A festival was planned and then postponed for 2020, with confirmed appearances by Charli XCX, 100 gecs, Pop Smoke, Rema, and Megan Thee Stallion. It never got rescheduled.

Most would have given themselves a pat on the back for two decades of support for the arts. In all the years that Red Bull underwrote the annual academies, the workshops, the lectures, the festivals, the studios, the Bass Camps, the Weekenders, and a thousand alums of RBMA, they never once revealed the sum. (A source disclosed it was "very very low eight digits.") "This was about dedication and people, not numbers," says Torsten. Nevertheless, the company reported sales of over twelve billion cans in 2024 alone, an upsurge of three hundred percent since 2011.

"I think this should be proof that it's possible to do something that is actually meaningful to many, many people, whatever criticism you might have, and that it can be beneficial for a brand to do this," Many says. "But it lives from sticking with it, and making it something that you want to stand for . . . There should be more companies that do this. There should be more means that are poured into culture, and I don't understand why that is not the case . . . I don't think it's a question of money. In the context of the money brands are spending, there has to be a way that something like this can exist. I thought that this was what the world was like. That there were many organizations that should be doing this. I think it's both a matter of how the times have changed in the world of brands, and what guides them, and, I don't know—maybe less courage. There's no reason why there shouldn't be ten academies, or whatever they are. Something where you say, 'Okay, these people are in this for the next five years. And they mean it.'"

Buscabulla (*EP I*)

On his final day as New York City's mayor, Michael Bloomberg thanked a cheering crowd of staffers for their work. He tweeted, "Best of luck to the de Blasio administration. May the best days for our city be ahead of us." Surrounded by family, friends, and flashing cameras, he headed to the subway stop at city hall. He swiped his MetroCard and rode the express train to a private party uptown. His policies (the smoking ban, the waterfront, and the High Line) had earned him praise around the globe. Despite his faults, the *Times* conceded, "New York is in better shape than when he became mayor." The media reported that the city ended the year with its lowest murder rate in half a century. But for all the glow of Bloomberg's big finale, the swearing-in of his successor eighteen hours later was a kind of exorcism—a public stoning.

The temperature was twenty-six degrees as Bill de Blasio was sworn into office on New Year's Day, 2014, the sun extending little warmth while thousands braved an arctic freeze. De Blasio had campaigned as the anti-Bloomberg, describing New York under his predecessor as a tale of two cities: the wealthy and the rest of us. The ceremony was remembered for an unusually explicit airing of the city's racial and economic fault lines: a pastor's words about "the plantation called New York"; a poem about "brownstones and brown skin playing tug-of-war"; and fierce denunciations of police abuse, developers, and million-dollar condos. "We are called to put an end to economic and social inequalities that threaten to unravel the city we love," said de Blasio. "And so today, we commit to a new progressive direction in New York."

He chose for his police commissioner Bill Bratton, who had promised long-overdue changes to the policy of stop-and-frisk. "We will not break the law to enforce the law," Bratton said. "That's my solemn promise to every New Yorker, regardless of where they were born, where they live, or what they look like." And for the first six months, both homicides and police stops were less frequent. But on July 17, on Bay Street, on Staten Island, twenty-nine-year-old police officer Daniel Pantaleo was caught on video asphyxiating Eric Garner, aged forty-three and a father of six. Eleven different times, Garner cried, "I can't breathe." His body lay exposed among the dust and grime on Bay Street for eight long minutes. An autopsy found that he died from a choke hold. His crime was selling untaxed cigarettes from out of state. On August 9, in Ferguson, Missouri, Officer Darren Wilson fired a dozen shots at Michael Brown—unarmed and eighteen years old—hitting him six times. His body would remain out in the baking heat for at least four hours. Police released a video of Brown shoplifting some cigars; TV anchors said he was "no angel."

In November, a Ferguson grand jury decided not to indict Darren Wilson. Long-simmering resentment boiled over in a series of enraged protests, attended by tens of thousands. Police in riot gear and military-grade equipment ordered demonstrators to disperse by firing rubber bullets and canisters of tear gas. Residents pelted police with rocks and water bottles. There were reports of heavy gunfire in some neighborhoods as the authorities diverted flights from local airspace. In cities large and small, demonstrations sprang up against police brutality and the unending murders of black lives. In Chicago, protesters organized a sit-in at the mayor's office. In Los Angeles, they stopped traffic in both directions of the 101. And in New York, thousands converged on Times Square, the

FDR, the West Side Highway, and the Brooklyn Bridge. They were chanting, "I can't breathe," or "Mike Brown! Mike Brown!" They carried signs that read "Stop racist terror," "Hands up, don't shoot," and "Black Lives Matter." They hoisted pictures of Tamir Rice, John Crawford, Renisha McBride, Laquan McDonald, and Trayvon Martin. They represented young and old; queer and straight; white, black, and brown. Less than two weeks later, a Staten Island grand jury chose not to indict Pantaleo, and the protests started right back up again: in Boston, San Francisco, Minneapolis, Baltimore, Washington, D.C., London, and New York. That Eric Garner had been choked to death on video by the police made no difference whatsoever.

It was the year protesters would sing Kendrick Lamar's "Alright" in Ferguson, and the year that Roberto Lange composed a song entitled "Young, Latin and Proud" under his moniker, Helado Negro ("black ice cream" in Spanish). "I read stories about Mike Brown's mother and the education system in his district," said Roberto. "Black Lives Matter marches were happening outside my door in Brooklyn." A nod to Nina Simone's "To Be Young, Gifted and Black," the single was released in June of 2015—the month that Donald Trump descended from the golden escalator and launched a campaign for the presidency. The song would soon become an anthem for an age of xenophobia, and represent a turning point for Spanish-speaking artists from the indie world— among them, Xenia Rubinos, Empress Of, Nick Hakim, Hurray for the Riff Raff, and Buscabulla, the married duo of Raquel Berrios and Luis Alfredo Del Valle.

* * *

Raquel was twenty-six when she arrived in Brooklyn. A native of Trujillo Alto, Puerto Rico, near San Juan, she studied textiles at the Rhode Island School of Design. "I hated it there," says Raquel. "I hated Rhode Island, but I loved going to RISD. I always knew that I was gonna move to New York. I graduated in 2007. And when I moved to the city I was really broke. I was trying to get a job, and slept on friends' couches, and kind of struggled for the first year." She found a job doing textiles in the East Village. "So, you know, there were cats, and I could work barefoot. It was kind of hippie. There was a loom. It was really fun to be in the East Village. CBGB was still open—I think it was the final year. Mars Bar was still open. It was an interesting time, because it felt like old New York was dying, and the condos were coming up."

She started frequenting the Caribbean Social Club, a lively bar in Williamsburg. "At the beginning, all you really saw were these old-timers—Puerto Rican people from the Williamsburg projects hanging out," she says. "But then slowly, a lot of young people, primarily Latino, started hanging out at this bar." Around the end of 2008, she stepped into a record store called Tropicalia in Furs, on East Fifth Street. "I met the owner, Joel [Oliveira], with this huge Afro—proud, black Brazilian from São Paulo—who dealt all these Brazilian gems. So for the next few years, when I would get out of work, I would go there and hang out with all these producers and DJs. I got really good with Portuguese. That moment in my life revealed something deep—that I needed to make music.

"I would always get seasonal depression in the wintertime, and there was one winter where I started downloading music off of blogs. I didn't have enough money to buy Brazilian records, but I would listen at my friend's store, then download the records I found, and I would sample them, then loop them using Serato, which is a DJ interface. And I would have this very artisanal way of making my own beats, and I would play guitar on top of them. I had the most primitive setup, but I felt like those experiments were fun, and then my friends would come over and we would make this music. It wasn't about playing live or anything serious. It was liberating. And that's how I started making music."

At Tropicalia in Furs, she met Edan Portnoy, a rapper and DJ. They collaborated on some recordings. "He was one of the first people I started making music with—a lot of stuff that he never put out—like, experimental, weird rock," says Raquel. "And it was really great. It wasn't at all what my thing was—this sort of '60s and '70s Latin thing. But I really appreciated that world around Edan. He played a lot at Southpaw. I remember doing a couple of shows on East Village Radio with Joel and this show called Chances with Wolves. But then, at the same time, there was this whole Brooklyn scene, and all these kids that had graduated from Berklee School of Music in Boston. There were a lot of either Hispanic or Latino, or people that had some kind of roots—we gravitated toward each other. I particularly remember seeing Lorely [Rodriguez] from Empress Of, and her whole crew . . . To me, those moments were between the East Village, and then the shows in Williamsburg, and then our own Latino scene. That's what those years meant to me."

Mostly for laughs, she started performing publicly with a group of girlfriends. They called themselves N'Teta (Spanish for "tits out"). "It was mostly to pass the time and have fun," she said. "We were all single, and we were writing about being single in the city. It was a silly project. But we were playing our own songs, and we used to do weird Spanish covers of pop songs." They played a party on Thanksgiving of 2011. "We were doing a cover of 'Bad Romance' by Lady Gaga in Spanish. I didn't know the chords. And Luis comes in. He's like, 'I know the rest of the chords.' And then we finished the song, and just like that . . . we started making music and we fell in love."

* * *

Luis Del Valle came to New York in 2010, at the height of the Bloomberg era. Born and raised in Ponce, on Puerto Rico's southern coast, he learned guitar from studying Oasis and the New York rock bands of the early aughts. "As a Puerto Rican, you're always hearing about New York," says Luis. "A lot of Puerto Ricans have a deep connection to New York. There's even a kind of Puerto Rican that's born there—the Nuyorican— so everybody has an extended Nuyorican family. It's a big part of the culture. Growing up, I was a fan of The Strokes and the stuff that was happening in New York when I was a kid. Being from a small island in the Caribbean—you're looking for a place to expand your horizons. I moved in 2010. Manhattan felt like Disney World. Everything was very sanitized and well-maintained. I remember thinking, 'Did I get punked?' Like, 'Did I get fooled into thinking New York is this place where your dreams will come true?' But there is also some truth to that. That did happen to us in New York. I went there looking for a songwriting partner—somebody to make music with—and I found that."

Luis remembers, "Raquel had an unorthodox rig. She would put two turntables into GarageBand, then back into the turntables, and then into some other thing. I still don't get it. It was really weird, but really cool. The way she was building these tracks was sort of punk rock and very free. She was using DIY tools and DIY methods to come up with sonic landscapes—using sound as sculpture—which was very different from what I was used to. It didn't come from orthodoxy. It was a Stevie Nicks, Lindsey Buckingham thing. It was somebody looking at music from a fresh point of view."

"I like to take these male Latin genres—Latin culture is known to be very male and chauvinistic—and I like to turn it around and put it in a new context," said Raquel. "When I started making the first songs for Buscabulla, I had all of this amazing music in Spanish. I always wanted to integrate samples from that world. People would always sample old R&B, funk records, and hip hop. I felt Latin music wasn't being referenced."

They started crafting songs out of Raquel's early demos. The music was synthetic by design: the words were sung in Spanish over lounge-y beats and textures, which helped to cloak a certain sadness; the vocals were at once seductive and withdrawn. They called the project Buscabulla—slang for "troublemaker." "Luis was actually impressed," Raquel says. "He had studied production. He had been in bands on the island since he was twelve, and he was like, 'Yo, these are great.' He saw a lot of potential in these really early demos."

They went to shows at 285 Kent, Glasslands, and Silent Barn in Bushwick. "When I first encountered that scene, I kind of felt like an outsider," Raquel says. "I was just starting to work on music, so I never felt like I belonged there. It's like, I wanted to belong—and, in a way, those feelings of wanting to belong to that scene were really what propelled me and Luis to start making music." As Helado Negro made his third LP, *Invisible Life* (2013), the artists Xenia Rubinos, Empress Of, Balún, and Nick Hakim made their debut. A Latin indie scene was being born.

Luis was working at an electronics store in Williamsburg. One morning, the musician and producer Dev Hynes (a.k.a. Blood Orange) walked in the door. "We had already done two or three songs," Raquel says. "Dev came in one day, talking about music. Luis was like, 'I make music with my girlfriend.' And Dev was like, 'You should participate in this contest that I'm working for. You should send me your music.' We sent him one of our songs, and Dev was blown away. He was like, 'You should apply to this contest.'"

* * *

The record industry had its worst-ever year in 2013—and again the year after that. In the U.S., revenues from recorded music fell to \$7 billion in 2014, down by more than half from 1999. The Sony corporation sold its U.S. headquarters; the Warner Music Group moved to smaller offices in midtown. "We're no longer in the music business—it doesn't exist anymore," said mogul Scooter Braun. "We're in the multimedia business." It was the year that the producer Nigel Godrich said, "Making new recorded music needs funding . . . If people had been listening to Spotify instead of buying records in 1973 I doubt very much if *Dark Side of the Moon* would have been made." In *The Guardian*, David Byrne observed, "What's at stake is not so much the survival of artists like me, but that of emerging artists and those who have only a few records under their belts . . . Without new artists coming up, our future as a musical culture looks grim. A culture of blockbusters is sad, and ultimately it's bad for business."

Raquel was dubious about the contest—officially, "Get Out of the Garage," presented by Converse and Guitar Center. "I've always been really wary of corporate collaborations. I remember Luis coming home and telling me about it, and me thinking immediately that it was total bullshit. I was telling Luis, 'I don't know. This is in Spanish. It's kind of experimental.' I'm a pessimist. Luis just said, 'Let's see what happens.'" The winning band got to record an EP with Dev Hynes at Converse Rubber Tracks—a state-of-the-art recording studio in Williamsburg—as well as equipment from Shure, Martin, Vox, and Fender; an invitation to South by Southwest; a digital distribution deal; and a check for $25,000. The competition was announced in August of 2013. More than 5,000 bands applied. Buscabulla learned that they were one of five finalists. Then they found out they were pregnant. Then they were declared the winners. They recorded *EP I* with Dev in 2014. Then they had a daughter, Charly.

"It wasn't that weird to me," says Luis. "Why wasn't it weird? Because I wanted to make it in music, and there was almost nothing I wouldn't do. It seemed like too good of a package to say, 'I'm above that.' Raquel felt a bit different. I think she felt like it compromises the art a bit, and I get it." It was a moment when a century-old industry appeared to be on its last legs. "I looked at it like, 'The record labels are changing,'" says Luis. "Now these companies are here. They're offering you a record deal without any of the negatives. That's how I looked at it. If all they want is a brand association, and they're giving me the opportunity of a lifetime, it seems like a fair trade. I don't have any record labels offering free equipment, studio hours, producers, EPs, connections, music videos—nobody's doing that for me. This brand is doing it. I'm gonna give it a shot. What is there to lose?" As it turned out, there was something the duo lost: "To an extent, it's been a thing that's followed us. Like, we release an album ten years later and it's, you know, 'This band that came up through this contest.' It put the Converse stamp on the project in a way that maybe wasn't foreseen."

"I kind of cringe at the videos," Raquel says. "And I kind of cringe that when we did interviews, people kept mentioning it. You know, it's

like: 'You guys won a contest.'" Especially for a young band, the prize
was invaluable. "I mean, come on. We used the hell out of those studios.
Like, we rehearsed there. We recorded additional music there. We got free
shoes. Independent of how corporate it could be, I actually wore Converse
shoes. We honestly benefited from that kind of initiative, which doesn't
seem to exist right now. There was an aspect of it that was super cheesy,
and it kind of sucked, but at the same time, I don't know where we would
be. I mean, we got to work with an artist that we really admired. They
gave us all these instruments. They ended up paying for a music video.
They connected us with our first label. I don't know where we would
have been if we had said, 'No, we're too cool for this.'"

They toured the country with Helado Negro, and self-released *EP
II* in 2017. It was the year of Hurricane Maria—the deadliest for Puerto
Rico in a century—where nearly 3,000 perished. They started PRIMA,
a fund that offered micro-grants to Puerto Rican musicians. They signed
with Ribbon Music, a Domino subsidiary, and used their advance to
move back home. "Our lives were just the hustle," says Raquel. "It was
pretty much—work, come back home, work on music, go to bed, get
up early, and go to work. When we had our little girl, it was our friends
who helped with babysitting. There was a point where, between being
musicians, and working to pay rent, and having a baby was wild. When
you're younger, you're fine living in—you know—a shithole. As you get
older, everybody's priorities change, and eventually we felt the call to
come back to the island." They moved back home in 2018, and also
played Coachella that April. *Regresa*—"return," in Spanish, and their first
full-length—was released in 2020. They soon contributed to "Andrea," a
song with their compatriot Bad Bunny. The following year, they opened
at the Hollywood Bowl. They still get back to New York—most recently,
to perform at Prospect Park and Lincoln Center.

The city that they moved to in their twenties is a different place,
but inextricable from their music-making. "It was a cool moment, and
one that I attribute to the creation of our band," Raquel says. "Then we

came to Puerto Rico and went on to explore other things. But the way I started making music—and the whole project—is due to that amazing moment that I lived through. Those whole ten years." She wonders if there's anything analogous today. "Sometimes I ask Luis, 'Is it just me, or has music in the past few years really sucked?' Every time I go back to New York, it feels like—I don't think there's a scene like that happening now. Maybe there is, and somebody else will write a book about it. But right now, I haven't heard or read about any type of scene. It's almost like there's no counterculture. It's like streaming just decimated these little communities."

"Right when we were leaving," says Luis, "it really felt like, 'Man. We're starting to be part of something cool.' Then we left, because the rent got really insane. When we got to New York, you could afford to live with three people and work at a store, and still pay rent. By the time we got out, we had to be paying almost $2,000 for two people, and we had a child. We were basically on the outskirts of the city. So it got a little tough for us. But I do remember that feeling of, 'At least we got to be a part of something.' I feel like I got in and out. I did what I wanted to do."

Amen Dunes (*Love*)

You didn't ask, and ordinarily, I'd keep it to myself. But in the interest of transparency, I should tell you I spent the better part of 2014 completely heartbroken, disconsolate, bereft.

As people do in middle age, I had made the mistake of reconnecting with an ex. We were together off and on when we were in our early twenties, and essentially still kids; we hadn't been in touch for years. We started hanging out again. She was a resident in neuroscience at a hospital on the Upper East Side—literally, a brain surgeon. She hadn't aged a day. She was brilliant, beautiful, and utterly uninterested in me. It would take me years to understand this.

I told myself that we were supposed to be together. I wrote her long, impassioned letters with an inky hand. I sent her music that reminded me of her: the soundtrack to *Under the Skin*, by Mica Levi; *You & Me*, by The Walkmen. I started meeting some of her colleagues and friends. I waited by the phone and gave myself an ulcer from anxiety. On the occasional night when she would text me, I ran to be with her. More often, though, my letters, calls, and invitations went unacknowledged.

I didn't take it well. I spent my days and nights in bed, reading sad books, listening to sad songs, and staring into space. I was a physical and emotional wreck; my heart was in a thousand shards. I thought about her first thing in the morning, when it was still dark outside, and in the middle of the night, when I would lay awake. I filled entire notebooks with entreaties that I never mailed. I couldn't seem to get away from her; I heard her name being called everywhere I went. I didn't think I would ever love anyone again. The only thing that made it hurt a little less was a record, ironically, named *Love*; that year alone, I must have played it a hundred times from start to finish.

For reasons that seem foolish now, I'd quit my job at LPR the year before, and was fully freelance. We didn't know it then, but in a few short months, the scene in Williamsburg would look much different. Artistically, the indie world was standing still, it seemed: aside from ambient releases by Eluvium (*Nightmare Ending*), Laurel Halo (*Chance of Rain*), James Holden (*The Inheritors*), and Donato Dozzy (*Plays Bee Mask*), I'd lost most interest in the music of my peers. The War on Drugs, Mac DeMarco, Cloud Nothings, Parquet Courts: I kept forgetting which nostalgic indie act was which. To judge from the indifference that would greet Dirty Projectors' *Swing Lo Magellan*, Animal Collective's *Centipede Hz*, Grizzly Bear's *Shields* (all 2012), and TV on the Radio's *Seeds* (2014), it wasn't only me. That was when a totally unknown and unsuccessful folk singer in Brooklyn made a perfect album: a summing-up and epilogue to the age of indie.

You didn't ask, and ordinarily, I'd keep it to myself. But in the interest of transparency, what got me out of my heartbreak—what gave me comfort, hope, and fortitude—was *Love* (2014), by Amen Dunes.

* * *

In the fall of 2006—when bombings killed and wounded hundreds of civilians in Iraq, and voters gave the Democrats control of the House and Senate, and CBGB closed, and Tower Records went bankrupt—a man retreated to the woods with a guitar, intent on making music in isolation. Unconsciously or not, he was enacting a much-mythologized American archetype: one dating back to Dylan and *The Basement Tapes* (1967), or to Thoreau's *Walden* (1854), which said, "I went to the woods because I wished to live deliberately . . . and see if I could not learn what it had to teach, and not, when I came to die, discover that I had not lived."

It took him several weeks to acclimate. Eventually, the songs poured out of him like oil from the ground. He sang about regret, and shame, and fear of mediocrity. He worked for up to fourteen hours at a time; the days began to bleed together in his mind. The songs that he recorded in the woods were both soliloquies and singalongs, confessional and communal. Through word of mouth, the music found its way to a label in the Midwest, who offered to release it the following year.

The paragraphs above could refer to the musician Justin Vernon—a.k.a. Bon Iver—who legendarily recorded most of the LP *For Emma, Forever Ago* (2007) in a secluded Wisconsin cabin. They also could describe his underrecognized and exact contemporary, the songwriter Damon McMahon—a.k.a. Amen Dunes—who unbeknownst to anyone would spend November 2006 in a trailer in Shandaken, New York, in the Catskills, where he recorded the material that would comprise the album *DIA* (released in 2009). But where the songs of Bon Iver would win an instant global audience—especially in coffee shops and farm-to-table gastropubs—it took at least a dozen years before the world acknowledged Amen Dunes.

* * *

He was the product of an isolated upbringing, born in 1980, raised in rural Connecticut. His mother was an atheistic New York Jew, descended from Holocaust survivors. His father was from Philadelphia, Irish Catholic, working-class, with roots in West Virginia, and a mother who sang traditional and gospel music in a church trio. "I was a curious child," Damon said. "I was obsessed with dinosaurs and fish. I would have encyclopedias of aquatic life and I would memorize the statistics." He was inseparable in childhood from his younger brother, Alexander, himself a musician.

His music education came in fits and starts. In the fourth grade, he randomly found a cassette on the sidewalk one day: it was a mixtape of selections from *The Geto Boys* LP, which sparked a long fixation with hip hop. His uncle introduced him to *Exile on Main Street*; the father of a friend played him Brian Eno's *Another Green World* and Love's *Forever Changes*. It was the mid-'90s: he learned about The Velvet Underground and David Bowie in a book about "alternative music." He pestered clerks behind the counter at a mom-and-pop in New Haven. He started listening to electronic producers like The Future Sound of London, Orbital, and Aphex Twin when he was fourteen, and going to raves in New York.

When Damon was fifteen, his mother found him a guitar teacher and bought him lessons for a year—the only training that he ever had. His teacher made him a cassette of country and acoustic blues from Texas and the South; the songs would percolate into his DNA. His father disapproved of music as a vocation; at the same time, he introduced his two sons to Bob Dylan and The Band. "I think somewhere deep inside he probably wanted to be a musician and he resented that I was doing it," said Damon. "He came from a hard-knocks background so, for him, if you were doing anything that could be considered impractical or frivolous, it was no good . . . He didn't think it was what a grown man should be doing. My whole life."

He barely graduated from Swarthmore College, near Philadelphia. He spent his junior year in China and Taiwan. He moved to New York in the summer of 2001.

Along with his brother, he was a member of a short-lived, self-destructive buzz band named Inouk, which benefited from a major-label bidding war amid the hype around The Strokes, amid an industry with capital to spend. "It was still the old era of the music business," Damon says. "So that means money, opportunity, prestige, importance, self-importance, etc." The band recorded one EP, *Search for the Bees*, and one full-length, *No Danger* (both released 2004); they wined and dined on corporate credit cards with A&R executives; they shared a stage with

Modest Mouse, Phoenix, and The Walkmen. Then they disintegrated in a blaze of youthful hubris, jealousy, and narcotics.

He was a major-label singer-songwriter signed to Astralwerks at the age of twenty-four. To celebrate the release of *Mansions* (2006), he played the thirty-fourth-floor penthouse of the Capitol-EMI building in midtown; champagne was served in plastic flutes. The label carpet-bombed the city in promotional posters. The album was acoustic, hushed, and largely unaccompanied—guitar, harmonium, and voice, with bass and piano overdubs. The songs were almost painfully sincere and unadorned. In the liner notes, Damon wrote, "This record was recorded in the two days before Christmas Eve 2004." It sounded like an album made in Laurel Canyon in the '70s, across the street from Jackson Browne. It sounded like a person singing from the heart.

Reviews were uniformly withering. In language that recalled a college seminar, *Pitchfork* gave it a 3.2: "The images, standing alone, neither communicate directly nor open the songs to interpretation and internalization." (It ran a month after the site gave Jet's *Shine On* a 0.0, and illustrated it with a video of a chimp urinating into its mouth.) "To call Damon McMahon a wimp wouldn't be entirely fair or entirely accurate," Rick Anderson wrote for *AllMusic*. "But on the evidence presented by his debut . . . it doesn't seem like it would be entirely unfair or inaccurate, either."

He took it on the chin. "I had this naïve expectation that it would be welcomed, like Inouk was, and it was not," Damon says. "They were like, 'This sucks. This guy sucks.' It was so humiliating. I just crashed and burned, and I retreated." He'd fallen flat in front of everybody: his former band, his father, and the entire record industry. He told himself he had to flee New York. "I was burnt out on music and the music scene. I'd been pursuing music in New York for four, five years, and I just wanted out. Before I left, I decided to go upstate and record something that was totally for me. I wasn't, like, the man going to the woods just for kicks. I went because I was destroyed. And I was like, 'If my band members and the public don't like what I'm doing, I'll just do this for myself.'"

The isolation and encroaching darkness of the Catskills in November were reflected on the album *DIA*, his first as Amen Dunes. "I was in this trailer, and it was hunting season, and I'm up in the mountains. There's nobody around except my landlord down the hill. The sun goes down at 4:15. And it was *really* dark. It was so scary to be there alone at night that I resorted to playing. I would play until I was so tired I had to go to sleep. Incredibly loud. Just to keep the spirits out. And that's where I kind of learned to be free."

The songs were improvised, and all recorded in one take, with over-dubbed percussion and keyboard. A few were pastoral, romantic, and drenched in reverb; a few were confrontational, cacophonous, and enshrouded in rust. Inspired by psychedelia from Japan (Les Rallizes Dénudés), sludge metal (Eyehategod), '70s folk (Judee Sill), and New Zealand noise (The Dead C), they borrowed from the blues, garage, rockabilly, surf, and freak folk. It was an album that rewarded repeat listening; it sounded like a person making music for himself. He handed off some copies of the songs to a few friends. And then he packed up his guitar and bought a ticket to the other end of the planet.

* * *

Damon moved to Beijing in the summer of 2007. The Dow was at an all-time high; the iPhone was released in stores; *The Sopranos* concluded and *Mad Men* debuted. His second week in town, he got an offer from Chicago's Locust Records to release the songs he had recorded in the woods, which had developed a cult following thanks largely to Amanda Colbenson, a buyer at the store Other Music. (Because he was abroad, it took another eighteen months for *DIA* to come out.) He had a label job that didn't last for long. He found a cheap apartment in municipal housing, taught English, and wrote freelance. He traveled every opportunity he got, and visited almost every province in the country. He tried to sneak across the border into Pakistan. He nearly died during an earthquake in Chengdu. He found himself among a wave of riots in Xinjiang. But mostly, he recorded music by himself.

"I was living in China as an expat and I started to feel connected to my roots as an American, being over there, thinking about what it meant to be an American," said Damon. "I didn't have a studio. I was just in my apartment with a guitar and a laptop. That's all I had. And so I started playing a lot of old American traditional songs. And out of that process came the songs I wrote for *Murder Dull Mind*. That record is a lot more about nostalgia—for home, and for America, and for things past. It was about distance."

Around the time that Damon landed in Beijing, Caleb Braaten, a record-store employee at Academy, in Williamsburg, would start the label Sacred Bones. It rapidly became identified with dark, mysterious, and esoteric sounds. A label in the lineage of Factory, Blue Note, and ECM, its cover art was uniform in its design: the logo, upper-left; a tracklist, upper-right. You always knew when you were looking at a Sacred Bones release, and what you would encounter: a self-contained universe. Along with indie labels such as Woodsist, Captured Tracks, and Mexican Summer, it helped to bring the DIY community in Williamsburg to international esteem. By decade's end—with a roster that included Zola Jesus, Blank Dogs, and Gary War—it was among the most distinctive independents in America.

"Caleb is a real iconoclast," Damon says. "Sacred Bones was one of those real art labels. It was the opposite of The Strokes and big business. It was a time of anonymity. When Burial put out his first EP, it was anonymous. It was a time of mystery, and Caleb did it perfectly with Sacred Bones. He wrote me on Myspace and said, 'I love *DIA*. Do you want to do an EP?' I'll never forget it. I know exactly where I was when I read it." The label would release the songs that he amassed in China on the *Murder Dull Mind* EP (2010) and *Through Donkey Jaw* (2011), extensions of the sound world on *DIA*; ironically, the latter was recorded in the very room where The Strokes had made *Is This It*.

He came back to New York in the spring of 2009, in the maw of the recession, with a new first family in the White House. He worked in delis, bars, and restaurants, construction jobs, and as a courier. With musician Sarah Shaw, he started playing shows again at Monster Island, Death by Audio, and Glasslands. He recorded pop songs from Ethiopia on a seven-inch, *Ethio Covers* (2012). He self-released an instrumental album entitled *Spoiler* (2013) that was too eccentric even for Sacred Bones. He went on tour in Europe and the States; there were a lot of empty rooms. For all the Internet's utility to independent musicians, it didn't quite encourage the attention demanded by an album like *Through Donkey Jaw*, which a reviewer pointed out: "As download culture brings small labels and obscure artists unheralded levels of exposure, often it amounts to just a cursory appraisal, a moment's distracted scrutiny that sends plenty of substance slipping through the cracks, waiting to be rediscovered," wrote Cian Traynor for *The Quietus*. "*Through Donkey Jaw* warrants bedding-in time; it's the kind of album that needs to be taken outdoors, to be absorbed and engaged with, before you can be pulled in by its hypnotic undercurrent."

It wasn't clear that he was getting anywhere. Damon recalls, "I was playing music that was meant for people, and it just wasn't reaching them. It's very demoralizing. I guess it's not so much about money. There's just a great indignity to it—in being asked to drive seven hours, and to play to twenty-seven people, and get paid, like, fifty dollars in ones. Many times, five people. And this is five albums in."

* * *

It might have been because he'd gone as far as he could go with the improvisational approach. It might have been because, at last, he had the time, the resources, the studios and mix facilities. It might have been because of a relationship that was about to end. It might have been because he saw his friends becoming successful: Mac DeMarco, Sharon Van Etten, Kurt Vile. It might have been because he'd reached the age where he was thinking of the past—his mother's alcohol abuse, and his father's disapproval. It might have been because the news was full of misery: the mass shootings in Connecticut and Colorado, Trayvon Martin, and

Hurricane Sandy. It might have been because by then he had a decade's worth of songs; it might have been that he was ready for a masterpiece.

"It took a long time," says Caleb. "I believe he scrapped a whole version of that record that he did, that he just didn't like, and then started over again from scratch. He toiled over it. I heard a lot of early versions of those songs. And it was like, 'He's really onto something here. This is the one.'"

Recorded and mixed over a year and a half in Montreal and Williamsburg, with the core of Jordi Wheeler (keyboards, guitar) and Parker Kindred (percussion), in five studios, with eleven different musicians—among them, Colin Stetson, Sophie Trudeau (A Silver Mt. Zion), Stephen Tanner (Harvey Milk), Elias Bender Rønnenfelt (Iceage), Efrim Menuck (Godspeed You! Black Emperor), and Damon's brother Alexander, who performs as Xander Duell—*Love* was an old-fashioned record, obsessively crafted, intended to be heard from front to back: ideally, with the lyric sheet in front of you. Where the persona found on *DIA* and its successors was reclusive and opaque, the Amen Dunes on *Love* was meant to be of service to others, accessible, and self-exposed.

"I wanted to make a record that was more open emotionally," he said. "Not necessarily a record that would sell more. But something more outward as opposed to inward. Generous." *Love* saw itself as having more to do with cosmic and devotional music (Pharoah Sanders's *Karma* and Marvin Gaye's *What's Going On*) over anything contemporary. Its themes were nothing less than life and death, and knowledge of the self, and letting go of one's regrets, and finding comfort in an unforgiving world, and overcoming your environment and upbringing. In forty-nine unfaltering minutes, it offers everything: anthems ("Lonely Richard"), ballads ("White Child"), love songs ("Splits Are Parted"), drug songs ("Lilac in Hand"), sweetness ("Sixteen"), self-help ("I Know Myself"), freak-outs ("I Can't Dig It"), and symphonies to God ("Love"). It's superficially a breakup album, much like *Rumours* or *Blood on the Tracks*, recorded in the aftermath of a relationship. I think of it as punk rock from a folk singer.

"Those recordings are so cared for," says the drummer Parker Kindred. "There's so much intention behind them. Like, microscopic moves. There's an innocence to *Love* . . . That was a tricky time for Damon. He had tinnitus and a paralyzed vocal cord. He was dealing with a lot of crap. It was super emotional for him . . . I knew we made a great record. It was the best thing out there at the time. There was nothing else as good when that record hit; there was nothing else going on. In that moment, it was the band that we all wanted to be in."

The centerpiece was the eight-and-a-half-minute title track, "Love," a piano-driven hymn that he took weeks to write the lyrics for, repeatedly reworked, and recorded in one transcendent take. (Parker and Jordi devised the arrangement on the spot; their contributions to the album were significant.) It's less a song about romantic love than learning to let go, and discovering your purpose. "I think people can hear it and identify with it as a breakup record," he told *Interview* magazine. "But what do you learn when you go through a breakup? You never had that person to begin with. All you ever have is you, and you better get right with that, because at the end of the day, that's all you're ever going to have. Love is not about crushing out on a really hot girl with brown hair. That's not love. Love is something far more severe and beautiful and stern . . . That's why Pharoah Sanders and Elvis Presley and Marvin Gaye come to mind. They weren't writing about some relationship that went bad. They're writing about God. They're writing about the life sentence and the lifelong gift of being a musician. You're connecting to the universe and to other people and to yourself." He told Natasha Young, an interviewer: "This album is about not self-destructing. The other albums are sort of about self-destructing."

* * *

It's not exactly fair or accurate to say that nobody heard *Love*. The musician Carey Mercer wrote a long and glorious appreciation for *The Talkhouse*. It made the year-end critics' list in *Newsweek*; profiles ran in *BOMB* and *The Believer*; *Pitchfork* gave it a 7.8. But on the evidence presented by its sales, its plays on Spotify, and its reception on the road, it doesn't seem like it would be entirely inaccurate, either. It didn't even crack the top one hundred of the annual *Village Voice* critics' poll. He went on tours with Mac DeMarco and The War on Drugs; he kept his job in landscape construction. He played to bigger venues in New York and crowds in double digits out of town.

"I expected it to be a big deal, immediately," says Caleb. "But it wasn't. And I know that felt frustrating for me, and I'm sure for Damon, because, sometimes—there are these records that—there's an amazing record, and you're like, 'How come people aren't freaking out about this?'"

Damon took it in stride. "I don't make pop music, and it's hard to make a living making music," he told an alt-weekly in Montreal. "I've been doing this a long time. I've been making records actively since I was twenty-one. So it's been about thirteen years now. It hasn't been an easy road. That's sort of what this record is about, and I hope people can hear that. The song 'Love' is about exactly this. It's about failure, perseverance, and making music. There have been times I've been tired of slogging along and playing to nobody, playing for no money. Paying to play, as they say. I'm a lifer, and I haven't given up yet, and I don't plan on it, either."

*   *   *

It only took him fifteen years. Depending how you counted, it was either his fifth, sixth, or seventh official release. With *Freedom* (2018), he had his long-awaited critical and commercial triumph. "The fifth album from Damon McMahon is his euphoric breakthrough," wrote Sam Sodomsky in a *Pitchfork* Best New Music review (8.6). "It's the scale of *Freedom*'s sound that cements it as an instantaneous classic," said the *NME*. It ended up on year-end lists in *Pitchfork*, *Spin*, *Esquire*, and *Uproxx*, as well as two dozen others. Compared to *Love*, it was an even more elaborate affair, recorded with a litany of instruments and guest musicians at Electric Lady Studios. Where *Love* had been inspired by the world of cosmic jazz, *Freedom*'s influences were thoroughly more populist: Tom Petty, Michael Jackson, INXS. In part, the songs were the result of time that Damon spent the past few years caring for his mother, who had been diagnosed with terminal cancer. He sang about her in the song "Believe," which soon became a cult favorite; he sang about his father in the song "Blue Rose." He talked about her cancer in his interviews. He spent her final hours by her side. He started getting letters in the mail from survivors. He quit his day job; he signed with Sub Pop; he played around the world to full houses. He started getting recognized by strangers on the street. He had a wedding and, eventually, two daughters. He even got his first and only compliment from his father: apparently, the next-door neighbor was a fan.

Perhaps predictably to anyone who'd followed his career, the follow-up to *Freedom* was a hard left turn: the claustrophobic and largely electronic *Death Jokes* (2024). And then he would surprise even his oldest fans at the end of the year with *Death Jokes II*—or rather, its accompanying press release. Amen Dunes had come to a conclusion. "This is the last chapter of the final volume," he wrote. "Goodbye, I've barely said a word to you, but it's always like that at parties—we never really see each other, we never say the things we should like to; in fact it's the same everywhere in this life." Then Damon went off on his own and started making music for himself again.

Vagabon (*Persian Garden*)

Laetitia Tamko saw her first concert at the age of twenty-one, when she was in her junior year at City College of New York. It was not for lack of trying. The venue was the Silent Barn. The year was 2014. The artists were Told Slant, The Flies?, and Vagabon—the nom de plume of one Laetitia Tamko.

Born in Yaoundé, the capital of Cameroon, she was a Scorpio, the oldest of three, and grew up speaking French, in a household of over-achievers. "People who are doctors, and have their MBAs, and have their law degrees, all in one person," said Laetitia. "That was always the expectation." Her mother had a law degree in Cameroon, but wanted to attend an Ivy League law school; to bring her family to the U.S., she moved by herself to New York, worked in Harlem, and later graduated from Penn Law. The family emigrated in waves, initially in 2001. Laetitia was eight years old and learning English from *The Fresh Prince of Bel-Air*. "We were living in the Bronx. I was going to a public school. That time is kind of immortalized by 9/11, and being taken out of school. Our family was concerned back home, so we were back and forth a bit."

She battled feelings of depression and ingratitude. "As a child, I was always—sad. Of course there was a time when I was innocent enough to only have been happy. But getting into those double digits of age, I always remember having something that felt somber, and I didn't feel like I could talk about it, or that I could be that way, or that it wasn't weakness. I remember being really young—at, like, fifteen—having the feeling of, 'There has to be more to life than this. There just has to be.'"

She liked to watch musicians on TV. "I was really into awards shows. To see live music. Now, I know it's not live, but it would be the only way I could see people performing." She listened to Mariah Carey, Destiny's Child, and 3LW; West African pop, jazz, and funk; and her brother's MP3s of Slipknot and System of a Down. "I was fourteen years old, looking up studios on the Internet. I had no idea what I was doing. I would call these studios and I'd pretend like I was my mom and ask to come in. Just a clueless fourteen-year-old. I had no idea what I was going to do with it. I just knew there was this thing I wanted to do, but didn't know how." She begged her parents for guitar and piano lessons, but got "a hard no. My parents always said, 'There is no room for starving artists here. After you finish your degree, do whatever you want.' I don't believe they knew how seriously I would take that."

The family settled in Westchester County. Her parents made it known that academics were the sole priority, and sent her to an all-girls' Catholic high school. "I had a better time in high school, but I couldn't really find my crowd. In Dobbs Ferry, New York, there weren't a lot of people who were like me. My graduating class was sixty-five people. So there wasn't a lot of opportunity to meet the people who fit you. I couldn't wait for high school to be over." Attempts at waywardness were well-intentioned and unfortunate: "In my desperate claw at rebellion, I threw a couple house parties. I later learned that when you throw a party in your parents' house, you do it in the basement, or one specific area."

Her parents bought her a guitar from Costco as a graduation present. "I screamed," says Laetitia. "It came with this disclaimer: 'You have the summer before college. Once college starts, no more horsing around.' I

went through the instructional DVD and studied like I know how to do."
She taught herself to play from songs by Taylor Swift. And then she put
the instrument away at the end of August, as she'd been told. She lived
at home and double-majored in electrical and computer engineering, all
while working as a software-engineering intern.

Her junior year, she met a person in an engineering class who had
a band and a recording studio in his basement in Sunset Park. Inspired
by her classmate's songs, she recommitted to composing music of her
own. She found her old guitar and started sneaking into practice rooms
on campus. In January of 2014, she uploaded a demo of "Vermont,"
her first recorded song, an open letter to a former flame. She sang, "I
see your face in every crowd." Because her name (le-TEA-see-uh) was
always mispronounced, she called the project Vagabon. "I was toying
with the idea of constantly feeling displaced or trying to find my footing. Not only in music, but in general."

The lyrics were intensely personal. "It was about a relationship I
had where he had moved to Vermont, and I really wanted to be that girl
that would, you know, follow him there, and be his girlfriend, and we'd
live happily and work on the farm. It ended up—'Vermont' is about not
being that girl, and wishing I could be, and being pissed at myself that
I wasn't. That whole first EP—what brought me to write it was a boy
that I loved, who was really infatuated with another girl who was an
artist, and he kept talking about how she's an artist, and I was just an
engineering student, and I was just learning quantum mechanics and
calculus. And I kind of had this moment of, 'I can be an artist. How hard
can it be?' And when I got my heart broken, it was this thing of, 'See?
I wrote all these songs.'"

She made her live debut that March. "My classmate talked about the
Silent Barn. 'That's where the cool kids play.' He and his band couldn't get
a show there, and they wouldn't reply to his emails. I did some digging
and found a musician who was playing there. I emailed him. 'Can I open
the show?' And he said, 'Yeah.' The world had opened up a little bit . . .

My grandmother's a choir director, so I was always going to church and around gospel music. But no one ever called it anything. No one called it music, no one called it art, no one called it singing or dancing . . . I remember feeling really welcomed. I remember being awed that everyone was doing it themselves. The people who worked the door were my age. The people who worked the bar were my age. I was only familiar with pop culture, served to the masses."

* * *

The Silent Barn had spent eighteen months in exile after the M.A.R.C.H. raid and robbery. The tenants found alternate arrangements while they scouted new properties. "The longest year and a half of my life," says Joe Ahearn. The crowdfunding effort had drawn over $80,000—and a new set of stakeholders. "It was not appropriate for us to be unserious, because we had asked for money. Suddenly, we had a lot of people who felt very passionately invested in the space, and what it was, and what it meant to them. And it meant a lot of things to a lot of different people," says Joe.

They found ideas in a timely source. "That was right when Occupy was starting. There were a lot of people learning from these working-group structures. We were inspired by that, and we decided to pursue this nonhierarchical structure. We realized we were going to need a much bigger building than we had ever imagined, and then we ended up getting a building even bigger than that. And we operated with a lot of the same structures we had observed from Occupy Wall Street."

They had left the old location in Ridgewood without a plan. "This was very contentious," says Joe. "The time of comments on *Brooklyn Vegan*. There were people who wanted their money back. There were people who were like, 'You guys are scammers who are just trying to profit off this,' which was of course ridiculous." They combed the neighborhoods of Long Island City, Bushwick, and Ridgewood, in search of "For Rent" signs. Eventually, they found a mixed-use, three-story warehouse at

603 Bushwick Avenue. They talked to lawyers, hired architects, and applied for permits. "In the first iteration, there was a lot of calculated ignorance," said Lucas Crane. "In this iteration, we're actually trying to figure out the details." They signed a lease in late October 2012—the week of Hurricane Sandy—and had their first show on December 30. In May, the *Times* would write that Silent Barn "attract[s] the weird and the surprising: noise bands, 'zine librarians, urban agriculturists, piñata sculptors, jellyfish experts, makers of digital art . . . The list of bands can often read like a dystopian tone poem ('Weed Hounds / Psychic Blood / Softspot / Bueno')." It also noted that they had a bill of $20,000 from their contractor, "and no clear way to meet the payment."

"Silent Barn felt like the feelings venue," says Laetitia. "Everyone was emotional about everything having to do with Silent Barn. And there was almost like a lack-of-business thing that kind of made it frustrating for people who couldn't play a show there, but made it special for people who were in it. It's kind of run in a way that you're not sure *how* it's running, and you have all these young kids who are getting to do whatever they want—and sometimes have too much power to do whatever they want—and also some of the, like, cool kids' stuff, which had always been my critique of Silent Barn. And it's important to know the barrier of entry felt pronounced, because it was the 'cool' venue. But I think what stood it apart for me is that it's where I feel like people really had their heart in it. I don't know if it's because there's this extra layer of people living in it and taking care of it in a home setting or providing housing for artists who are passing through and wanting to have a kind of home feeling to it. But for some reason it feels like a lot of people had a lot of stakes in that venue. You felt it when you went to a show. You felt it with the people who played. You felt it with the hang outside in the courtyard. You felt the stakes were higher than, like, 'That's seven dollars. Have fun.'"

At its best, this iteration of the Silent Barn was an experiment in radical democracy, inclusiveness, and horizontal governance. An early resident was Neon Mashurov, a writer and curator. "I grew up going to Brooklyn DIY spaces and the old Silent Barn," says Neon. "When I got there, it started out like all the other DIY spaces, but it evolved. The core group [in Ridgewood] started with a bunch of dudes. By the time the second space opened, it included more women, and, as the years went on, more queer people and people of color."

They offered studios at a rate of $3.50 a square foot, and a dozen artist residencies. They hosted screenings, theater, classes, and, in time, grassroots arts organizations like Educated Little Monsters, for kids from the neighborhood. The booking team, which would include Neon, Lani Combier-Kapel, and Liz Pelly, prioritized programming that centered women, queer, trans, and BIPOC artists. There was a concert space, a gallery, a record store, a barbershop, a bar and a café, a zine library, and an inviting backyard. But at its worst, it could be insular, impractical, and juvenile, a parody of the bohemian bourgeois, exemplified in its pecking order, or lack thereof. The Barn's consensus-based, collectivist philosophy was founded on the metaphor of cooking. In place of committee heads, there were some fifty "chefs": a calendar chef, who booked events; a press chef, who did publicity; an art chef, who oversaw installations, and so on. There was a lexicon (The Ghost Hunter, Octopus Garden) and an imaginary form of currency called the barnacle, a kind of donation. "The feeling is co-ed fraternity on an IV drip of neo-dada," wrote the *Voice*. The rent was $14,000 a month.

* * *

Among the people in the crowd for Vagabon's debut was a musician named Mitski, who remembered: "You could tell she cared, she took it seriously, this wasn't just a thing she was doing as an excuse to hang out and party, or to boost her ego. This mattered." Mitski helped arrange Laetitia's second show, at the irreverently named Shea Stadium in Bushwick. It was a moment of transition for the DIY community of Brooklyn. 285 Kent closed in January 2014; Death by Audio, in November; and Glasslands, on New Year's Eve. By then, construction work had started to convert the building into offices for Vice.

Laetitia told her parents she was spending evenings at the library; they approved. She started playing at Market Hotel, Palisades, and Todd P's new venture, Trans-Pecos, in the former Silent Barn. She soon befriended Emily Sprague, of the group Florist; Greta Kline, who plays as Frankie Cosmos; and Michelle Zauner, who performs as Japanese Breakfast. "I made genuine friendships," says Laetitia. "Silent Barn would have twenty-four-hour shows, and I would play all of them. I wanted to get good, because every night I was leaving these shows and wanting to write a song. I felt like something really special was happening, and I wanted the respect of my peers, the way that I respected them. So I wanted to play as much as possible, and I made it known that I was always available. I never said no to a show—anywhere, at any point, with any notice—and it ended up being sort of every weekend I was playing at Silent Barn. And wanting to be as good as the people I was seeing, and also having a deep insecurity, because I had spent all this time learning a whole different skill, and a lot of these people had been on an art track their whole lives, and feeling like I had to catch up."

She kept her musical ambitions a secret from her family. She hid her instrument in the trunk of her car. "My parents didn't bring me here for me to say, 'I want to make art.'" By day, she was the dependable daughter, attending classes, earning As; by night, she was finding her way as an artist. "I did feel very misunderstood. And I say I did, because I guess now it matters less if I'm understood by my family. But I did feel so weird and bizarre—like the things that I wanted were so unreasonable. I think the early stuff that landed me at Silent Barn, the music I was writing: I wrote that in my parents' house. I wrote those as I was clawing to be a person on my own. I felt this strong sense at one point that it would never be enough unless I just took over my own life. And making music, writing songs—but specifically making music in the way I ended up doing it—it sort of saved my life, because my mental health was so low, and feeling like I couldn't get help, and didn't know how to be helped, or how to be taken seriously. That scary feeling of, 'If I want to find what this is really about, I'm gonna have to disappoint and potentially damage forever the relationship with my family.' I lost a lot to play to even twenty-five people at Silent Barn. It felt like fighting for my life, which might sound dramatic, but it really felt that way. Because of how much I was willing to sacrifice for it."

She channeled her despondency and doubt in six heartrending songs released as the *Persian Garden* EP (2014). "There was this feeling of, 'Do I get to?' A lot of the songs on my first album are, like, 'Do I get to? Can I? Or is this just my fate? Is this how it's supposed to be?' I'm not a parent, so I don't know what I would have done differently, given the material they had, but my experience was that I didn't feel—I felt equipped for the world in so many practical ways, in the skills I have, and being responsible, knowing how to cook, and being very smart academically on paper. Getting a good job at some point. I was built up in those ways. But in the other ways of, like, emotional care, I felt bankrupt."

She made the EP mostly for herself; she saw it as a stepping stone. "To me, it was never intended to be listened to. I just told myself I had to get it out, and then I will record a real album, and all those songs can still be on it, but I had to go through that initial sharing process." Her voice was human and heroic, tentative and bold. The songs were in the second person ("I see you happy," "I thought you'd wait"), lending a palpable intimacy. "The songs feel deliberate, like she wants to enter the world at her own pace," Hua Hsu observed in *The New Yorker*. "She is the protagonist of her own story." The final song was "Sharks." She sang ecstatically, "Run and tell everybody that Lactitia is a small fish . . . and you're a shark that hates everything." It instantly became a fan favorite and singalong: a song that put a lump in your throat.

"You packed your bags and took a flight," she wrote in "Vermont." "You're leaving your mom's house." The song was about an ex, but also had the feel of destiny. "I got into a car accident," said Laetitia. "My first and last car accident. Where my car flipped over on its side on I-87 as I was driving to school. And I had a moment of, 'Holy shit. What am I doing? I can't keep wasting all this time, hoping I'll eventually get to real life. Why can't I just do it now?' Through the guilt, and through that—I moved out of my parents' house the day of my accident."

She self-released *Persian Garden* through Bandcamp on November 7, 2014, the week the new World Trade Center opened. It came to the attention of NPR's Lars Gotrich, who gushed about it on Twitter. She graduated in the spring, and went on tour in the summer. She told her family she was driving cross-country, and that her friends were playing music now and then. "Those shows I played and saw, the tours where I played basements and people's kitchens and apartments—those motivated me. You leave feeling inspired. You think, 'How is it possible that only ten people saw that amazing musician play?' I had that thought so many times. Like, 'How did I get so lucky?'" She shared the stage with Mal Devisa, Waxahatchee, Girlpool, and Mitski, to name a few. The word was slowly getting out, but at some cost. "I started making a name locally for myself. It really rattled this classmate of mine who'd been doing music his whole life." He told Laetitia she was bad at the guitar, and that people only cared because she was a black woman.

* * *

Her parents finally heard her music on November 13, 2016, at Webster Hall, supporting Frankie Cosmos and Big Thief before a crowd of 1,500. "They were kind of like, 'What is happening? Who are all these people? Where did they come from?'" she said. "I wanted to present it when I felt like I had something to show . . . I wanted to be like, 'Look: this is something meaningful.'" Four months later, her first LP, *Infinite*

Worlds (2017), received *Pitchfork's* Best New Music (8.5). She quit her job and spent the next two years on tour with Allison Crutchfield, Tegan and Sara, Courtney Barnett, and Angel Olsen.

The Silent Barn was damaged by a fire in the fall of 2015, a little less than three years after moving in. They raised $30,000 to rebuild. But the fire raised the cost of their insurance and, by 2017, they were staring at a deficit of $70,000. It was the year that Michael Bloomberg and Ronald Perelman gave $75 million apiece for new performance venues in New York, where theater, dance, and opera would grace the stage. There didn't seem to be a dollar for the small and the scrappy.

The Barn would close for good in April of 2018, after almost thirteen years in Ridgewood and Bushwick. "It was always in this weird in-between space where it wasn't anarchic enough to be edgy-cool but also not sleek enough to be professional," said Neon. "We did everything by the rules, to a fault—got all the permits, did all the paperwork, put in all the fire extinguishers, filed workers' comp." The final weeks included an "ABC No Rio in Exile Matinee"; a "Last Rites" party; and a sold-out show with L'Rain, Zenizen, and Vagabon. Laetitia told Jenn Pelly in *Pitchfork*, "To headline a bill with all black women at the Silent Barn made me feel like the norms in punk communities are shifting with each woman of color and person of color who enters the space and is able to thrive."

In many ways, Laetitia had outgrown Silent Barn. "It's especially important for me to reach beyond the community I started playing music in. I love that community, but a lot of people who look like me aren't in that community. I can't reach them if they can't see me, and that's what I want to do." She signed to Nonesuch for her second album, *Vagabon* (2019), and worked with producer Rostam Batmanglij for a dance record, *Sorry I Haven't Called* (2023). All the same, she still keeps a saying of her late best friend, Eric Littmann—"forever underground"—in her Instagram bio. "Being in the underground scene in New York . . . We couldn't hear ourselves, the monitors never worked—so we played louder and we screamed into the microphone. All our friends, we were all self-taught, figuring out how to play these instruments," said Laetitia. "We were babies together, and that's what makes it pure."

Epilogue: 2025

The experts all agreed: New York was in a slump. The crowded, restive, ornery world capital that long drew millions had been hobbled by a perfect storm of COVID, crime, migration, and morale. By 2023, at least a half a million people had left the city since the start of the pandemic, which itself had claimed the lives of 50,000 New Yorkers. A terrifying spree of stabbings, shootings, and violence fed a steep decline in subway ridership. Manhattan's office vacancies stood at almost twenty-two percent—the highest rate recorded—or forty skyscrapers the size of the Chrysler Building. Over 200,000 migrants had arrived in the city since 2022, at a cost projected to run $12 billion over three years. The governors of Texas and Florida had been sending refugees to so-called sanctuary cities, weaponizing the weakest for political gain. The mayor—Eric Adams, a Democrat—had called it a humanitarian crisis, and one that would "destroy New York." Exactly twelve months later, Adams and his aides were charged with bribery and fraud. He took a page from Trump and said he had been targeted in a witch hunt; the charges would be dropped for his cooperation with the president-elect. A professor at Columbia was writing of an "urban doom loop," in which remote work and vacant offices led to dwindling taxes, revenue, storefronts, and foot traffic, which in turn accelerated crime, grime, and cuts to public services.

* * *

The invitation came by email, on a Friday, at 3:34 P.M. The sender was John Atkinson, an artist friend whom I had met a decade back, from the band Aa. The date was August 7, 2020. The subject line was "Sunday in Red Hook." It read as follows:

> hey friends, hope y'all are staying safe, sane, and finding ways to enjoy NYC summer energy in new ways!
>
> along those lines, I'm playing a show on bells, chimes, electronics, and field recordings of weird Australian birdsong at an outdoor, socially-distanced, extremely vibey spot in Red Hook this Sunday:
>
> Sunday, August 9 at 7 P.M. sharp
> John Atkinson and Julian Bennett Holmes
> corner of Richards Street and Commerce Street in Red Hook
> BYOB and obviously please mask up and distance
>
> the zone is outside the studio of my good pal and former Aa drummer Julian. it's isolated, there's a ton of room, and basically no foot or car traffic . . . he'll also do a set this Sunday before or after mine, it'll all start prompt at 7 and be over by 8.
>
> ALSO - if you music makers or anyone you know might want to play this 'venue' at some point let me know, we're gonna try and 'book' one or two 'acts' in the classical/ambient/jazz realm weekly so long as it makes sense.
>
> luv
> John

The signs went up around the neighborhood in late July. The shows took place on Sunday evenings, at magic hour—eight in all—along a quiet stretch of Red Hook just a block from the expressway. At the intersection of two secluded streets, on the sidewalk, there was a series of performances: some ambient, some improvised, all technically "unauthorized." The week that I first went, John and Julian played percussion and synthesizers. The second time, it was for Parts & Labor's Dan Friel, who had his Yamaha toy keyboard; I brought my younger brother and his four-year-old. We bought a six-pack from the bodega and left it in the shade. There were about a dozen people there when we arrived, and maybe forty when the show started. We sat on the cement, cross-legged, masked, or stood and listened from the corners of the street. There was an upright speaker powered by a long extension cord. The sound was resonating off the surrounding red-brick buildings and once-full warehouses. The sky was lit with lavender and burgundy. At one point, a car alarm went off, unseen; Dan improvised a motif in the same key. On Commerce Street, a passing vehicle slowed to a crawl, clearly confused. On Richards Street, a group of firefighters stood and watched, applauding at the end. For most of us, it was our first experience of live music in the past five months, and easily among the most inspiring, all-time. We said hello to people that we hadn't seen in months; we gave our extra beers to perfect strangers; we passed the hat around and piled bills for the musicians. On the walk home, I told my brother it reminded me of something from the past, though it was hard to say exactly what.

* * *

I started writing what became this book in the spring of 2020, when it appeared as if the simple act of going out to see a show was now a luxury, which I suppose it always was. Aside from the unbroken keening of emergency sirens, the only sounds you heard outside was when we cheered and honked and banged our pots with wooden spoons to thank the thousands of essential workers every night at seven, on the dot. Along with the entire concert industry—musicians, bartenders and service staff, security, stagehands, tour managers, T-shirt sellers, sound engineers, and lighting designers—I would be out of work and climbing up the walls for the foreseeable future. I started writing just to give myself a task while everything was upside down, when I had reached the end of *The Sopranos, Boardwalk*

Empire, and all the other shows on HBO. I didn't have a purpose or a plan, which would have saved a lot of time: I wrote about whatever came to mind—my memories—which usually involved music.

I wrote about the afternoon I saw the Boredoms on the Brooklyn waterfront, accompanied by seventy-seven drummers; the night that Parts & Labor played their final show (with bagpipes, two drum kits, and brass section) at 285 Kent; the time I got to see Jeff Mangum play in someone's loft; the first few years at LPR; working at Nonesuch and Lincoln Center. I did this once a day for several months. I wasn't overly concerned about chronology or dates. I think I was reminding myself that it had happened, and that it mattered—at a time when it was clear how readily the world could live without the concert industry.

I started putting the exercises in sequence at a certain point. I started looking up precise dates and put them all into a timeline. It was only then that I realized how most of the events fell between 2004 and 2014—the Bloomberg years, which weren't exactly understood to be a golden age for art—and not by chance, my first ten years of living here. I had my doubts that anyone would find it of interest; I'm well aware that everybody thinks the city they experienced was New York in its prime, and what came after, something less. I just assumed that everyone went out to see a band four nights a week when they were twenty-eight years old—that every decade in New York was more or less the same.

Around this time, I came across an interview with the musician Taja Cheek, who performs as L'Rain, conducted by the newsletter *Tone Glow*. She talked about the early aughts, and her experience growing up in Brooklyn:

> Q: Going from one venue to another, what are some of the earliest memories you have of performance spaces or cultural institutions in the city?

> A: I really started coming into my musical sensibilities in high school, as most people do. I didn't have a fake ID, so all-ages venues were

really crucial for me to be able to see music. There was also a lot more free music available to all New Yorkers. There were a lot of festivals that would happen around the city and literally all you had to do was just show up—those were really formative moments for me. I remember going to Coney Island—I think it was called the Siren Festival? And then there were the McCarren Park pool parties . . .

Q: Damn, so you were basically around for the peak of Brooklyn DIY.

A: I was very much around (*laughs*). It was a wild time. Or the shows at the pier . . . there was so much free music. I really miss that because I don't know what else I would have done as a kid. I wouldn't have seen any music!

Q: Other than the lack of free shows now, what else has changed about the city's live-music landscape?

A: That's a good question. I have to think about that one, honestly. (*Pauses.*) It's the freeness, but there was also such an interconnected culture of DIY spaces that was also a really important part of my life and the way I was able to access music and culture. That doesn't really exist now in the same ways. It probably exists in different ways and I'm just too old to know (*laughs*). But it doesn't exist in the same ways it did when I was a kid.

I'm cautious when I see a phrase such as "the peak of Brooklyn DIY." By definition, it implies a scene whose time has come and gone, which only erases the work of those still here. Nevertheless, it was my first indication that the subject wasn't academic—that there were others who had gotten something from those years as well.

* * *

As most of us regained a sense of normalcy post-pandemic, it was a time of insecurity and dread for working musicians. In March of 2022, Epic

Games acquired Bandcamp—the cherished independent retail site—only to flip it eighteen months later to Songtradr, a music-marketing platform, who promptly fired half the company. In the fall, Animal Collective announced the cancellation of their European tour the following month. They wrote: "Preparing for this tour we were looking at an economic reality that simply does not work and is not sustainable . . . From inflation, to currency devaluation, to bloated shipping and transportation costs, and much much more, we simply could not make a budget for this tour that did not lose money even if everything went as well as it could."

That same week, the singer-songwriter Will Sheff told *Stereogum* he expected to lose between five and seven thousand dollars on his coming U.S. tour, and double that amount abroad. "These tours feel like you have to charge in with the bayonets and cannons," he said. "You already know from the manager telling you and every other band telling you, 'It's a tough climate, there's no money—go out and fail!'" His fatalism echoed a statement made by Santigold in late September, when she was forced to cancel a North American tour: "I have tried and tried, looked at what it would take from every angle, and I simply don't have it . . . I will not continue to sacrifice myself for an industry that has become unsustainable for, and uninterested in the welfare of the artists it is built upon." (The tour would be rescheduled in 2024.) Meanwhile, fattened on a feeding tube of poverty-level payouts and "convenience" charges, Spotify and Live Nation reported record earnings in 2025.

The world of media had been similarly transformed by the pandemic and the shift to work-from-home. In mid-2022, the Greenpoint offices of Kickstarter were listed for some $29.5 million; they sold three years later for $17 million. In May of 2023, Vice filed for bankruptcy protection; once valued at nearly $6 billion, it was sold to a group of lenders for $350 million. In August, the company disclosed that it was vacating its offices on South Second Street in Williamsburg—almost nine years to the day of Death by Audio's eviction. (According to employees, the building was reportedly haunted, and infamous for having nonexistent phone reception.) Also that month, *The New Yorker* said that, after ninety-eight years, it was cutting its arts listings ("Goings On About Town") from six pages to two. Almost a year later, *The New York Times* announced that it was reassigning five expert writers on its culture desk. Among them were Jon Pareles (chief pop critic since 1988), Javier Hernández (classical, opera, and dance reporter), and Zachary Woolfe (classical critic and former editor). Appropriately, perhaps, Woolfe was offered the option of joining the obituary department.

* * *

I can't pretend to know about the state of underground and DIY venues in New York the way I did when I was young, or where a person in their twenties spends their time today; it would be suspect if I did.

It's easy to be cynical about the Brooklyn of the present day. To walk along the stretch of Kent where Glasslands, Paris London New York West Nile, Death by Audio, and 285 Kent once stood, you find a foreign country: luxury apartments, high-end stores, Prada ads, and bottomless brunch. On any given weekend in Bushwick, East Williamsburg, the Navy Yard, and Industry City, you can find thousands of people out and about—at vast, impersonal venues such as Brooklyn Mirage, Brooklyn Steel, and Brooklyn Storehouse. It's not that shows don't happen anymore in lofts and warehouses. It's more that when they do, they tend to be promoted—understandably, and out of caution—as a "secret location." But then again, I'm probably the wrong person to ask. When I go out these days, it's usually to see a string quartet; if I go see a band, it's one I know I just can't miss, like Deerhoof, Lightning Bolt, or Oneida.

Despite my usual propensity for fretfulness and gloom, I find a lot of reason to have hope.

Every Thursday afternoon—sometimes Wednesday, sometimes Friday—the longtime Brooklyn writer, editor, and event producer Piotr Orlov sends out his newsletter, *Dada Strain:* an all-embracing roundup of performances and parties in New York that fall within the rubric of "Rhythm + Improvisation + Community." Week in, week out, you will find some twelve to twenty-five concerts, DJ sets, dance parties, block parties, jam sessions, residencies, and recitals. In Sunset Park, Clinton Hill, Greenpoint, Ridgewood, Bushwick, Red Hook, Bed-Stuy, and Gowanus, you will find hip hop, jazz, funk, R&B, disco, techno, noise music, chamber music, and the occasional indie band. At independent venues such as Roulette (which is now in downtown Brooklyn, and where Matt Mehlan is the artistic director), Union Pool, Baby's All Right, Elsewhere, Public Records, Pioneer Works, Issue Project Room, and Mama Tried, you will find artists from Arooj Aftab and L'Rain to Ravi Coltrane and the Sun Ra Arkestra. At dance clubs such as Nowadays, Earthly Delights, Jupiter Disco, H0L0, Good Room, and Bossa Nova Civic Club, you can hear the world's foremost producers and DJs. At Property is Theft, Blank Forms, Trans-Pecos, Light & Sound Design, Market Hotel, Striped Light, FourOneOne, Barbés, The Owl, and Cassette, the principles of DIY are more than flourishing, and in the hands of those who aren't pale and male, as it was in my time. A part of me suspects I'm tempting fate merely by mentioning these names in print; a part of me believes that they will always exist in some form.

The New York of today faces a situation very much analogous to the 1970s. A city built around a way of doing work that dated to another time confronts a crisis and an opportunity. In lower Manhattan, midtown, and Long Island City, buildings zoned for office space sit undercapitalized or empty. While landlords and developers petition to convert their properties for residential use, seventy-seven million square feet go unused in Manhattan alone. Why can't an enterprising landlord rent a vacant floor or two to someone like Noémie Lafrance, Brooke Baxter, Rachel Nelson, Zeljko McMullen, or Edan Wilber? Why can't a space that otherwise would sit unoccupied be used instead to reinvigorate a block? Why can't another neighborhood become a synonym for DIY activity? Why can't another Silent Barn or Death by Audio emerge out of the Bronx, Jersey City, Rockaway Beach, or Manhattan for that matter? It might be hard for us to picture the emergence of a youth movement in midtown or the financial district; but then, the same was true of Brooklyn in the not-so-distant past.

Acknowledgments
and Sources

This book is based on over one hundred interviews with sixty-plus musicians, impresarios, label owners, writers, booking agents, and civilians. For their trust, time, candor, and willingness to be interviewed, my thanks to Joe Ahearn, Many Ameri, John Atkinson, Anna Barie, Brooke Baxter, Raquel Berrios, Caleb Braaten, Anne Brewster, Colin Brooks, Michelle Cable, Jonathan Cargill, John Chavez, Taja Cheek, John Colpitts, Lani Combier-Kapel, Luis Alfredo Del Valle, John Fitzgerald, Larry Fitzmaurice, Emilie Friedlander, Dan Friel, Delia Gonzalez, Rami Haykal-Manning, Julian Bennett Holmes, Jordan Michael Iannucci, Michael Kaufmann, Parker Kindred, Thimali Kodikara, Allan Kozinn, Noémie Lafrance, Roberto Carlos Lange, Ric Leichtung, Zachary Lipez, Barry London, Jason Lucas, Neon Mashurov, Damon McMahon, Jason McMahon, Zeljko McMullen, Matt Mehlan, Natalie Mering, David Moore, Rachel Nelson, Chris Newmyer, Aku Orraca-Tetteh, Akwetey Orraca-Tetteh, Todd Patrick, Jake Rosenthal, Gavilán Rayna Russom, Torsten Schmidt, Devang Shah, Jeff Sheinkopf, Adam Shore, Victoria Sobel, Laetitia Tamko, Robertson Thacher, Sam Valenti, Darius Van Arman, Jordan Warner, BJ Warshaw, Christopher Weingarten, Frank Wells, Matt Werth, Edan Wilber, Jeri Yoshizu, Erik Zajaceskowski, and Greg Zinman.

I only have a life in music thanks to those who gave me a chance well before I was remotely deserving. I'm in your debt, Norma Hurlburt, Jeanne Lunin, Valerie

Guy, John Gingrich, Megan Dunn, Ryan Zumsen, Caleb Burhans, Drew Flaherty, Enrique Marquez, Limor Tomer, Joe Melillo, Bill Bragin, Melissa Smey, George Steel, Rachel Chanoff, Jack Walsh, Jessi Rinehart, Jimmy Lane, Jay Mahoney, the Ramsden family, Cathal Moore, Sarah Frankel, Conor Brown, Ken Waagner, Ben Levin, Glenn Kotche, Nels Cline, Jenny Lin, Jay Ryan, Andrea Troolin, Ben Goldberg, Kris Chen, Jeremy DeVine, Ian Ilavsky, Don Wilkie, Brian Foote, Bonnie Wright, Amanda Ameer, Alex Ross, Steve Smith, Allan Kozinn, Michael Azerrad, Bob Hurwitz, David Bither, Karina Beznicki, Ian Noble, John Scher, Bob Liebeskind, Jim Romeo, Jane Moss, John Znidarsic, Kate Nordstrum, Terra Reneau, Minna Choi, Jad Abumrad, Bryce Edge, Erica Frauman, Josh Penn, Dan Janvey, Dean O'Connor, John Best, Liz Hart, Hlynur Guðjónsson, David Handler, Justin Kantor, Piotr Orlov, Zan Emerson, and Richie Clarke.

I owe a special word of thanks to Leah Petrakis at Europa Content, who believed in this book when no one else did; to Emilie Friedlander, whose conscientious editing made it worlds better; to Soyolmaa Lkhagvadorj, Janet Rosenberg, Eli Mock, Amy Vinchesi, Sarah Masterson Hally, and Chris Peterson at Abrams; and especially to Natalie Elliot, for her endless delight, encouragement, love, and enthusiasm for the city of New York.

Books and Films

Jill Abramson, *Merchants of Truth: The Business of News and the Fight for Facts* (Simon & Schuster, 2019).

Spencer Ackerman, *Reign of Terror: How the 9/11 Era Destabilized America and Produced Trump* (Viking, 2021).

Suroosh Alvi, Gavin McInnes, and Shane Smith, *The VICE Guide to Sex and Drugs and Rock and Roll* (Warner Books, 2003).

Michael Azerrad, *Our Band Could Be Your Life: Scenes from the American Indie Underground 1981—1991* (Back Bay, 2002).

Marshall Berman and Brian Berger, eds., *New York Calling: From Blackout to Bloomberg* (Reaktion, 2007).

Joe Boyd, *White Bicycles: Making Music in the 1960s* (Serpent's Tail, 2006).

Cisco Bradley, *The Williamsburg Avant-Garde: Experimental Music and Sound on the Brooklyn Waterfront* (Duke University Press, 2023).

Winifred Bryher, *The Days of Mars: A Memoir, 1940—1946* (Harcourt, 1972).

Joe Carducci, *Enter Naomi: SST, L.A., and All That . . .* (Redoubt Press, 2007).

Geoffrey Cobb, *The Rise and Fall of the Sugar King: A History of Williamsburg, Brooklyn, 1844–1909* (North Brooklyn Neighborhood History, 2017).

Matt Conboy, *Goodnight Brooklyn: The Story of Death by Audio* (Dishwasher Safe Films, 2016).

Robert Draper, *Dead Certain: The Presidency of George W. Bush* (Free Press, 2007).

Robert Draper, *When the Tea Party Came to Town* (Simon & Schuster, 2013).

Thomas Dyja, *New York, New York, New York: Four Decades of Success, Excess, and Transformation* (Simon & Schuster, 2021).

Ralph Ellison, *Shadow and Act* (Random House, 1964).

Thomas Friedman, *From Beirut to Jerusalem* (Picador, 1989).

Fred Goodman, *Fortune's Fool: Edgar Bronfman Jr., Warner Music, and an Industry in Crisis* (Simon & Schuster, 2010).

Lizzy Goodman, *Meet Me in the Bathroom: Rebirth and Rock and Roll in New York City 2001—2011* (Dey Street, 2017).

Dave Haslam, *Life After Dark: A History of British Nightclubs & Music Venues* (Simon & Schuster UK, 2016).

John Heilemann and Mark Halperin, *Double Down: Game Change 2012* (Penguin, 2014).

John Heilemann and Mark Halperin, *Game Change: Obama and the Clintons, McCain and Palin, and the Race of a Lifetime* (HarperCollins, 2010).

Will Hermes, *Love Goes to Buildings on Fire: Five Years in New York That Changed Music Forever* (Farrar, Straus and Giroux, 2012).

Clinton Heylin, *From the Velvets to the Voidoids: The Birth of American Punk Rock* (Chicago Review Press, 2005).

Gary Indiana, *I Can Give You Anything But Love* (Rizzoli Ex Libris, 2015).

Lenny Kaye, *Lightning Striking: Ten Transformative Moments in Rock and Roll* (Ecco, 2022).

Steve Knopper, *Appetite for Self-Destruction: The Spectacular Crash of the Record Industry in the Digital Age* (Free Press, 2009).

Richard Matson, *Towncraft: Notes from a Local Scene* (Matson Films, 2007).

Jane Mayer, *The Dark Side: The Inside Story of How the War on Terror Turned Into a War on American Ideals* (Doubleday, 2008).

Brian McCullough, *How the Internet Happened: From Netscape to the iPhone* (Liveright, 2018).

Gavin McInnes, *How to Piss in Public: From Teenage Rebellion to the Hangover of Adulthood* (Scribner, 2012).

Jeremiah Moss, *Vanishing New York: How a Great City Lost Its Soul* (Dey Street, 2018).

Flannery O'Connor, *Wise Blood* (Farrar, Straus and Giroux, 1952).

Evan Osnos, *Wildland: A Journey Through a Divided Country* (Farrar, Straus and Giroux, 2021).

George Packer, *The Unwinding: An Inner History of the New America* (Farrar, Straus and Giroux, 2013).

Garrett Peck, *A Decade of Disruption: America in the New Millennium* (Pegasus Books, 2020).

Eleanor Randolph, *The Many Lives of Michael Bloomberg* (Simon & Schuster, 2019).

Paul Raphaelson, *Brooklyn's Sweet Ruin: Relics and Stories of the Domino Sugar Refinery* (Schiffer, 2017).

Red Bull Music Academy, *For the Record: Conversations with People Who Have Shaped the Way We Listen to Music* (Gestalten, 2013).

David Remnick, *The Bridge: The Life and Rise of Barack Obama* (Vintage, 2010).

Simon Reynolds, *Rip It Up and Start Again: Postpunk 1978–1984* (Penguin, 2006).

Jesse Rifkin, *This Must Be the Place: Music, Community and Vanished Spaces in New York City* (Hanover Square Press, 2023).

Lucy Sante, *Low Life: Lures and Snares of Old New York* (Farrar, Straus and Giroux, 1991).

Lucy Sante, *The Other Paris* (Farrar, Straus and Giroux, 2015).

Jean Edward Smith, *Bush* (Simon & Schuster, 2017).

Matt Taibbi, *I Can't Breathe: A Killing on Bay Street* (Random House, 2018).

Marvin J. Taylor, ed., *The Downtown Book: The New York Art Scene 1974–1984* (Princeton, 2006).

Scott Timberg, *Boom Times for the End of the World* (Heyday, 2023).

Anna Wiener, *Uncanny Valley: A Memoir* (MCD/Farrar, Straus and Giroux, 2020).

Sean Wilentz, *The Age of Reagan: A History, 1974–2008* (Harper, 2008).

Stephen Witt, *How Music Got Free: A Story of Obsession and Invention* (Viking Penguin, 2015).

Lamia Ziade, *Bye Bye Babylon: Beirut 1975–1979* (Interlink Books, 2012).

Articles and Reviews

Steve Albini, "The Problem with Music," *The Baffler* 5, December 1993.

Ken Auletta, "After Bloomberg," *The New Yorker*, August 19, 2013.

Saul Austerlitz, "The Pernicious Rise of Poptimism," *The New York Times Magazine*, April 4, 2014.

Amos Barshad, "When Critics Could Kill," *Slate*, May 1, 2018.

Robert A. Bennett, "Whoever Dreamed That Up?," *The New York Times*, December 29, 1985.

Stuart Berman, "Dragons of Zynth: *Coronation Thieves*," *Pitchfork*, October 16, 2007.

Andy Beta, "Interview: Black Dice," *Pitchfork*, May 31, 2002.

J. Iddhis Bing, "I Was at the 2004 GOP Convention Protest. It Was the Worst of US Policing," *The Guardian*, January 15, 2014.

Julie Bosman, "Hey, Kid, You Want to Buy a Scion?," *The New York Times*, June 14, 2006.

Ethan Brown, "New Rock City," *New York*, September 19, 2003.

Nadine Brozan, "A Crumbling Pool Divides a Neighborhood," *The New York Times*, July 30, 1990.

David Byrne, "Will Work for Inspiration," *Creative Time Reports*, October 7, 2013.

Ada Calhoun, "Where All the Neighborhood is a Stage," *The New York Times*, February 6, 2005.

Maureen Callahan, "Rebel with a 401(k)," *New York Post*, May 19, 2005.

Truman Capote, "A House on the Heights," *Holiday*, February 1959.

Jon Caramanica, "Upstart Music Site Becomes Establishment," *The New York Times*, July 14, 2010.

Diane Cardwell, "City Is Backing Makeover for Decaying Brooklyn Waterfront," *The New York Times*, May 3, 2005.

Diane Cardwell and Marc Santora, "At Least 900 Arrested in City as Protesters Clash With Police," *The New York Times*, September 1, 2004.

Tobias Carroll, "Interview: Weyes Blood," *BOMB*, January 13, 2015.

Stevie Chick, "After the Crash: Oneida's John Colpitts Interviewed," *The Quietus*, March 1, 2022.

Ian Cohen, "Blog Rock Revisited," *Pitchfork*, June 23, 2015.

Byron Coley, "Parts & Labor: *Groundswell*," *The Wire* 269, July 2006.

John Colpitts, "Death by Audio's Doc Inspires Us to Move Forward as We Look Back," *The Talkhouse*, October 12, 2016.

Aly Comingore, "Amen Dunes' Higher Power," *Interview*, May 12, 2014.

Chris Dahlen, "Travis Morrison: *Travistan*," *Pitchfork*, September 27, 2004.

Trinie Dalton, "Inner Space Odyssey: How Delia & Gavin Are Making Earth Cooler," *Arthur* 21, March 2006.

Justin Davidson, "Shiny, Alluring, Ugly, Visionary, Inspiring, Incomplete," *New York*, September 6, 2013.

Loren DiBlasi, "An Oral History of 285 Kent," *Bedford + Bowery*, January 8, 2014.

Brent DiCrescenzo, "Radiohead: *Kid A*," *Pitchfork*, October 2, 2000.

Josh Freedom du Lac, "Giving Indie Acts a Plug, or Pulling It," *The Washington Post*, April 30, 2006.

David W. Dunlap, "Old Bathhouse Defended as Brooklyn Landmark," *The New York Times*, March 6, 1989.

David W. Dunlap, "Relics of the Domino Sugar Refinery, Frozen in Time and Syrup," *The New York Times*, October 23, 2013.

Stuart Elliott, "Advertising: Toyota Turns to Smaller Agencies to Set the Stage for Its New Scion Line," *The New York Times*, July 15, 2002.

Sean Feinstein, "Interview with Amen Dunes," *Montreal Rampage*, June 2014.

Alan Feuer, "Joyful Noise in Silent Barn, an Alt-Arts Mecca," *The New York Times*, May 25, 2013.

Larry Fitzmaurice, "An Attempt at Defining Indie Music in the 2010s," *Vulture*, January 10, 2019.

Larry Fitzmaurice, "Grizzly Bear's Daniel Rossen on His New Solo Album, the Late 2000s, the Grateful Dead, and the Future of Grizzly Bear," *Last Donut of the Night*, March 9, 2022.

Larry Fitzmaurice, "How Indie Rock's Class of 2008 Changed the Music Industry," *Vulture*, October 23, 2018.

Hillary Frey, "Pitchforkmedia.com Music Dudes Dictate Culture from Chicago," *New York Observer*, November 29, 2004.

Andrew Friedman, "Red Hot Car: How a Japanese Auto Maker Fueled the Rise of EDM," *Fact*, April 12, 2016.

Sasha Frere-Jones, "A Paler Shade of White," *The New Yorker*, October 15, 2007.

Emilie Friedlander, "A Walking Tour of Manhattan's Rock 'n' Roll Past: the 2000s," *The New York Times*, November 20, 2018.

Emilie Friedlander, "Chillwave: A Momentary Microgenre That Ushered in the Age of Nostalgia," *The Guardian*, August 21, 2019.

Emilie Friedlander and Patrick McDermott, "Ten NYC DIY Venues That Closed This Year and Why We'll Miss Them," *The Fader*, December 17, 2014.

Hannah Frishberg, "An Oral History of Silent Barn," *Gothamist*, May 1, 2018.

Jenny Gathright, "'There Will Be No Darkness': Laetitia Tamko on the Making of *Vagabon*," NPR, October 15, 2019.

Kim Ghattas, "How Lebanon Transformed Anthony Bourdain," *The Atlantic*, June 9, 2018.

Jael Goldfine, "In Conversation: Gavilán Rayna Russom and Cosey Fanni Tutti," *Paper*, January 7, 2020.

Jessica Goodman, "Art in Every Crevice: The Silent Barn Is Back," *The Village Voice*, January 9, 2013.

Adam Gopnik, "Times Regained," *The New Yorker*, March 14, 2004.

Steven Greenhouse, "Bitter Strike at Domino Finally Ends," *The New York Times*, February 27, 2001.

Mark Greif, "What Was the Hipster?," *New York*, October 22, 2010.

Vanessa Grigoriadis, "The Edge of Hip: Vice, the Brand," *The New York Times*, September 28, 2003.

Pete Hamill, "Brooklyn: The Sane Alternative," *New York*, July 14, 1969.

Cortney Harding, "Scion A/V, Toyota's Record Label, Says It's 'Signing Off,'" *Billboard*, October 25, 2016.

Rob Harvilla, "On the Exhausting Exhilaration of Oneida," *The Village Voice*, July 28, 2009.

Hendrik Hertzberg, "Blues," *The New Yorker*, November 7, 2004.

Brian Hiatt and Evan Serpick, "Music Biz Laments 'Worst Year Ever,'" *Rolling Stone*, January 13, 2006.

"The History of the *Pitchfork* Reviews Section in 38 Reviews," *Pitchfork*, May 25, 2021.

Olivia Horn, "The Relentless Determination of Vagabon," *Pitchfork*, July 17, 2019.

Hua Hsu, "Who Sings Along?," *The New Yorker*, October 21, 2019.

"Interview: Oneida," *Pitchfork*, September 6, 2006.

Dave Itzkoff, "The *Pitchfork* Effect," *Wired*, September 1, 2006.

Jesse Jarnow, "Monster Island's Last Hurrah," *The Village Voice*, September 7, 2011.

Jesse Jarnow, "New York's Crackdown on Brooklyn DIY Spaces," *The Village Voice*, December 28, 2011.

Jesse Jarnow, "Silent Barn Burglarized; Ridgewood Venue Organizes Fundraising Campaign," *The Village Voice*, July 20, 2011.

David Johnston and William Rashbaum, "Vast Force Is Deployed for Security at Convention," *The New York Times*, August 25, 2004.

Britt Julius, "LCD Soundsystem's [Gavilán Rayna Russom] Comes Out as Transgender," *Pitchfork*, July 6, 2017.

Dan Kois, Nitish Pahwa, and Luke Winkie, "The Oral History of *Pitchfork*," *Slate*, March 19, 2024.

Greg Kot, "The New Tastemakers," *Chicago Tribune*, April 3, 2005.

Greg Kot, "Parts & Labor Finds a Steady Groove," *Chicago Tribune*, November 9, 2008.

Gia Kourlas, "Car Hop," *Time Out New York*, April 29, 2004.

Katie Kurtz, "Oneida's Factory-Sized Experiments," *Bandcamp Daily*, June 12, 2023.

Steven Kurutz, "Williamsburg. What Happened?," *The New York Times*, January 29, 2024.

Jeff Leeds, "After a Judgment, Music Label Files for Chapter 11 Bankruptcy," *The New York Times*, February 20, 2008.

John Leland, "Advertisements for Themselves," *The New York Times Magazine*, March 11, 2001.

Robert Levine, "Stage Rage," *New York*, May 4, 2007.

Hugo Lindgren, "Brooklyn Calling," *New York*, November 16, 2009.

Jed Lipinski, "The Bad Old Days at McCarren Park Pool," *Politico*, July 13, 2012.

Christian Lorentzen, "Why the Hipster Must Die," *Time Out New York*, May 31, 2007.

Madelaine Lucas, "An Interview with Amen Dunes," *The Believer*, April 17, 2018.

Madelaine Lucas, "An Interview with Weyes Blood," *The Believer*, July 9, 2019.

Joe Lynch, "Red Bull Music Academy Turns 20," *Billboard*, September 26, 2018.

Scott Lynch, "The Boredoms: 77Boadrum Under the Brooklyn Bridge," *Scoboco*, July 9, 2007.

Dorian Lynskey, "Indie Rock's Slow and Painful Death," *The Guardian*, January 16, 2012.

Devon Maloney, "Indestructible Room: The Story of 285 Kent," *Pitchfork*, January 17, 2014.

Leo Maymind, "Zeljko McMullen, On Deck," *Interview*, March 31, 2014.

Robert D. McFadden, "Vast Anti-Bush Rally Greets Republicans in New York," *The New York Times*, August 30, 2004.

James McKinley, Jr., "Underground Musicians Lose a Haven," *The New York Times*, September 11, 2011.

Carey Mercer, "Amen Dunes' *Love*," *The Talkhouse*, December 24, 2014.

M. H. Miller, "That Feeling When You Miss the Early 2000s," *T: The New York Times Style Magazine*, May 8, 2018.

Brian Montopoli, "Little-Known Bands Get Lift Through Word-of-Blog," *The New York Times*, June 6, 2005.

Jake Mooney, "Polishing the Grunge," *The New York Times*, November 5, 2006.

David Moore, "Arcade Fire: *Funeral*," *Pitchfork*, September 12, 2004.

Colin Moynihan, "The Death of Death by Audio," *The New Yorker*, March 14, 2016.

Nick Neyland, "An Oral History of Oneida's *Each One Teach One*," *Drowned in Sound*, October 29, 2010.

"Oneida: *The Wedding*," *PopMatters*, May 10, 2005.

Chris Opfer, "The Downward Spiral of TVT Records," *The Village Voice*, October 20, 2010.

Piotr Orlov, "'There Is No Done': Gavilán Rayna Russom on the Dialogue Between Creation and Identity," NPR, October 26, 2017.

Jon Pareles, "CMJ Music Marathon: Dragons of Zynth," *The New York Times*, October 17, 2007.

Jon Pareles, "Play Well, and May the Blog Buzz Be With You," *The New York Times*, October 22, 2007.

Phil Patton, "Like the Song, Love the Car," *The New York Times*, September 15, 2002.

Bill Pearis, "Death by Audio Closing in November," *Brooklyn Vegan*, September 8, 2014.

Jenn Pelly, "Lessons from the Closing of NYC's Silent Barn, a DIY Institution," *Pitchfork*, May 24, 2018.

Liz Pelly, "Cut the Music: Inside M.A.R.C.H., the NYPD's Secret, Venue-Closing Task Force," *The Baffler*, February 12, 2018.

Amy Phillips, "*Pitchfork* Unites Blog Collective for New Music Site Altered Zones," *Pitchfork*, June 29, 2010.

Buzz Poole, "Zebulon Rising," *The Village Voice*, November 19, 2008.

"Popcast: Red Bull, Highly Caffeinated Tastemaker," *The New York Times*, May 3, 2013.

Ben Ratliff, "Helping a Stage Expand Beyond the Living Room," *The New York Times*, December 16, 1996.

Ben Ratliff, "Metal Variety: Death, Doom, Black and Cars," *The New York Times*, March 14, 2010.

Ben Ratliff, "Metalheads of All Alloys, Swirling Into the Night," *The New York Times*, June 3, 2012.

Mark Rechtin, "Toyota Works on New Image for Scion," *The Atlanta Constitution*, August 16, 2008.

Jesse Rifkin, "After 9/11, We Wanted the Old NYC. Instead We Got The Strokes," vice.com, September 10, 2021.

John Rockwell, "Going for a Waterless Dip with Roller Skaters, Bikers and Superstars," *The New York Times*, September 15, 2006.

Andrew Romano, "The Rise of the 'Yupster,'" *Newsweek*, January 9, 2006.

Melena Ryzik, "Off the Beaten Beat," *The New York Times*, May 11, 2007.

Kelefa Sanneh, "Indie Bands That Made the Grade in Webland," *The New York Times*, July 19, 2005.

Kelefa Sanneh, "The Rap Against Rockism," *The New York Times*, October 31, 2004.

Patrick Sauer, "The McCarren Park Pool Parties: An Oral History," *We'll Have to Pass*, November 9, 2020.

Ryan Schreiber, "The Amps: *Pacer*," *Pitchfork*, 1996.

Ryan Schreiber, "Broken Social Scene: *You Forgot It in People*," *Pitchfork*, February 2, 2003.

Ryan Schreiber, "Pitchfork's Top 100 Favorite Albums of the '90s," *Pitchfork*, 1999.

Audra Schroeder, "The Cult of *Pitchfork*," *The Austin Chronicle*, August 4, 2006.

David Shapiro, "The End," *The New Yorker*, January 21, 2014.

Aaron Short, "The Politics of McCarren Park Pool," *The Awl*, July 9, 2012.

Russell Shorto, "The Industry Standard," *The New York Times Magazine*, October 3, 2004.

Ben Sisario, "All Hail Brooklyn: Alt-Rock Thrives in Alt-Borough," *The New York Times*, March 9, 2008.

Ben Sisario, "Backing Indie Bands to Sell Cars," *The New York Times*, September 27, 2011.

Ben Sisario, "Live Music and a Canned Patron," *The New York Times*, April 25, 2013.

Michael Slackman and Al Baker, "With Restraint and New Tactics, March Is Kept Orderly," *The New York Times*, August 30, 2004.

Michael Slackman and Diane Cardwell, "Police Tactics Mute Protesters and Messages," *The New York Times*, September 2, 2004.

Dirk Smillie, "As Music Mags Fall, *Pitchfork* Is Booming," *Forbes*, July 7, 2009.

Andy P. Smith, "Ten Years of Music in Williamsburg 2002–2012: An Oral History," *Medium*, March 4, 2015.

Laura Snapes, "*Pitchfork*'s Absorption into *GQ* Is a Travesty for Music Media— and Musicians," *The Guardian*, January 18, 2024.

Sally R. Sommer, "Everybody Into the Pool (and Dance)," *The New York Times*, September 4, 2005.

Jesse Sposato, "An Oral History of Zebulon," *Politico*, January 10, 2013.

Jennifer Steinhauer, "City Cracks Down on Nightclubs and May Revise Its Policies," *The New York Times*, November 10, 2002.

Tim Stelloh, "Seeking to Recapture the Glory of the Past. Or Maybe Not," *The New York Times*, April 9, 2006.

Michael Sugarman, "A Scene Grows in Brooklyn: The Genesis of Mas Ysa," *VICE*, October 3, 2013.

Ron Suskind, "Faith, Certainty and the Presidency of George W. Bush," *The New York Times*, October 17, 2004.

Margaret Talbot, "California Dreamer," *The New Yorker*, November 7, 2022.

Joe Tangari, "Parts & Labor: *Groundswell*," *Pitchfork*, March 7, 2004.

Tarra Thiessen, "60 NYC Showspaces That Closed in the 2010s," *Audiofemme*, December 18, 2019.

Anthony Tommasini, "Teresa Sterne, 73, Pioneer in Making Classical Records," *The New York Times*, December 12, 2000.

"Track by Track: Amen Dunes—Love," *DIY*, May 12, 2014.

Alex Vadukul, "A Brooklyn D.I.Y. Landmark Changes with the Times," *The New York Times*, February 21, 2024.

BJ Warshaw, "Ten Years of Parts & Labor," *Impose*, February 24, 2012.

Christopher Weingarten, "The Decade in Music Genre Hype," *The Village Voice*, December 22, 2009.

Christopher Weingarten, "Grow Up Like a Rock Star," *The Village Voice*, January 15, 2008.

Christopher Weingarten, "R.I.P., Brooklyn: How Grizzly Bear, Animal Collective, and Dirty Projectors Changed Pop," *Spin*, September 20, 2012.

Bill Werde, "The Music Blog Boom," *Rolling Stone*, September 8, 2004.

Carl Wilson, "The Trouble with Indie Rock," *Slate*, October 18, 2007.

Michael Wilson, "The Nonesuch Story," nonesuch.com.

William Yardley, "The Last Grain Falls at a Sugar Factory," *The New York Times*, January 31, 2004.

Natasha Young, "Interview: Amen Dunes," *No Clue*, 2014.

Further Listening

In addition to the albums in the text, some personal favorites are included below (one per artist), any one of which would merit their own chapter.

2004
The Concretes, *The Concretes*
Devendra Banhart, *Rejoicing in the Hands*
The Fiery Furnaces, *Blueberry Boat*
Grizzly Bear, *Horn of Plenty*
Jolie Holland, *Escondida*

2005
The Books, *Lost and Safe*
Broadcast, *Tender Buttons*
The Mountain Goats, *The Sunset Tree*
Why?, *Elephant Eyelash*
Wolf Parade, *Apologies to the Queen Mary*

2006
Belong, *October Language*
Brightblack Morning Light, *Brightblack Morning Light*
Casiotone for the Painfully Alone, *Etiquette*
Nathan Fake, *Drowning in a Sea of Love*
Oxford Collapse, *Remember the Night Parties*

2007
Arthur & Yu, *In Camera*
Besnard Lakes, *Are the Dark Horse*
Papercuts, *Can't Go Back*
Sandro Perri, *Tiny Mirrors*
Woods, *At Rear House*

2008

Frightened Rabbit, *The Midnight Organ Fight*

Grouper, *Dragging a Dead Deer Up a Hill*

Juana Molina, *Un Día*

Thee Oh Sees, *Thee Hounds of Foggy Notion*

The Walkmen, *You & Me*

2009

Animal Collective, *Merriweather Post Pavilion*

Dirty Projectors, *Bitte Orca*

Jónsi & Alex, *Riceboy Sleeps*

Real Estate, *Real Estate*

Sharon Van Etten, *Because I Was in Love*

2010

Beach House, *Teen Dream*

Deerhunter, *Halcyon Digest*

Emeralds, *Does It Look Like I'm Here?*

Mountain Man, *Made the Harbor*

Oneohtrix Point Never, *Returnal*

2011

The Caretaker, *An Empty Bliss Beyond This World*

EMA, *Past Life Martyred Saints*

Pure X, *Pleasure*

Craig Taborn, *Avenging Angel*

Youth Lagoon, *The Year of Hibernation*

2012

Hangedup & Tony Conrad, *Transit of Venus*

Julia Holter, *Ekstasis*

Peaking Lights, *Lucifer*

Perfume Genius, *Put Your Back N 2 It*

Max Richter, *Vivaldi Recomposed*

2013

Donato Dozzy, *Plays Bee Mask*

Eluvium, *Nightmare Ending*

Laurel Halo, *Chance of Rain*

Helado Negro, *Invisible Life*

James Holden, *The Inheritors*

2014

Flying Lotus, *You're Dead!*

Steve Gunn, *Way Out Weather*

Mica Levi, *Under the Skin*

Angel Olsen, *Burn Your Fire For No Witness*

Sylvan Esso, *Sylvan Esso*

Index